Nicholson

Holiday Guide
THE LAKE DISTRICT
& CUMBRIA

Robin Neillands

English
Tourist Board

Robert Nicholson Publications

Also available in this series:
Nicholson/ETB Holiday Map of the Lake District & Cumbria
Nicholson/ETB Holiday Guide to Devon
Nicholson/ETB Holiday Map of Devon

A Nicholson Guide

First published in 1986 by **Robert Nicholson Publications Limited**
62–65 Chandos Place, London WC2N 4NW and the **English Tourist Board**
Thames Tower, Black's Road, London W6 9EL

© Text, Robert Nicholson Publications Limited 1986
© Maps and town plans, Robert Nicholson Publications Limited 1986
Based upon the Ordnance Survey with the sanction of
Her Majesty's Stationery Office. Crown copyright reserved.

Line drawings by **Towler Cox**
Design by **Bob Vickers**
Edited by **Jacqueline Krendel**

The publishers and the author gratefully acknowledge the assistance
of the Cumbria Tourist Board and the local Cumbrian Tourist Information
Centres during the compilation of this guide.
The author would also like to thank Estelle Huxley for additional research.

Great care has been taken throughout this book to be accurate,
but neither the publishers nor the English Tourist Board can
accept responsibility for any misinterpretation of the contents
or for any errors which may appear or their consequences.
The author and Robert Nicholson Publications are responsible for
the final selection of entries in the guide. In the six
gazetteer sections, the lists of eating and drinking establishments,
and camping and caravanning sites do not represent a recommendation
by the English Tourist Board.

Phototypeset by Input Typesetting Limited, London
Printed in Great Britain by Chorley & Pickersgill Ltd,
Leeds and London
ISBN 0 905522 98 2

Contents

Key to Area Maps

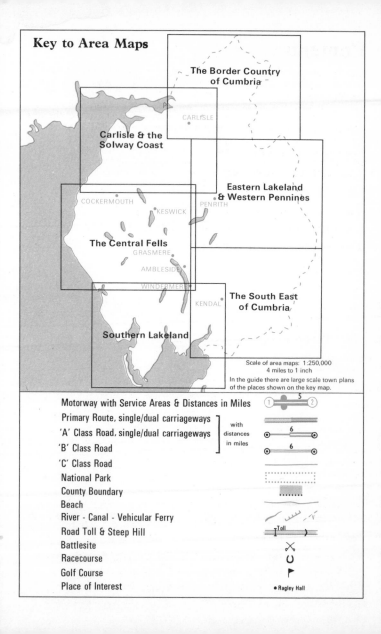

The Border Country of Cumbria

CARLISLE

Carlisle & the Solway Coast

Eastern Lakeland & Western Pennines

COCKERMOUTH

KESWICK   PENRITH

The Central Fells

GRASMERE

AMBLESIDE

WINDERMERE

The South East of Cumbria

KENDAL

Southern Lakeland

Scale of area maps: 1:250,000
4 miles to 1 inch
In the guide there are large scale town plans
of the places shown on the key map.

Motorway with Service Areas & Distances in Miles	
Primary Route, single/dual carriageways	with distances in miles
'A' Class Road, single/dual carriageways	
'B' Class Road	
'C' Class Road	
National Park	
County Boundary	
Beach	
River - Canal - Vehicular Ferry	
Road Toll & Steep Hill	Toll
Battlesite	
Racecourse	
Golf Course	
Place of Interest	● Ragley Hall

Using this guide

For the purposes of this guide, Cumbria has been divided into six areas –
Southern Lakeland, The Central Fells, Carlisle & The Solway Coast, The
Border Country of Cumbria, Eastern Lakeland & The Western Pennines,
The South East of Cumbria. Each one has a gazetteer section, with its own
detailed contents page. At the beginning of each section is a map of the area
covered. The text is separated into a wide range of topics and all entries are
listed alphabetically, usually appearing under a town or village name. Postal
addresses and phone numbers are also given. Wherever possible, text entries
are grid referenced to the area maps at the beginning of each section. Specific
directions and distances to and from main towns or villages are supplied
when a particular place is very small or out-of-the-way. Town plans of several
of Cumbria's major urban areas and holiday centres have also been included.

The publishers, in association with the English Tourist Board, have also
produced a detailed 'Holiday Map of the Lake District & Cumbria' which
is designed to be used in conjunction with this guide.

The following symbols and abbreviations have been used through the text:

Pop	Population	m	Miles
EC	Early closing day	*L*	Lunch
MD	Market day	*D*	Dinner

Credit cards:

A	Access (also Master Card, Eurocard)	Dc	Diners Club
		V	Visa (including Barclaycard)
Ax	American Express		

The word **Charge** denotes an entry fee.

Eating & drinking

The price symbols are predominantly used to indicate the cost of a three-
course meal for one, including service and VAT, but not wine, beer or spirits.
The lowest price symbol also applies to simple meals and snacks in cafes,
pubs, tea shops and fast food places.

£	£5 and under	£££	£10-£15
££	£10 and under	£££+	£15 and over

Camping & caravanning

Prices at camping and caravanning sites reflect the range of facilities and
services available.
Cost per person per night:

£	around £2 (modest)	££	around £3 (improved)

NB These prices were accurate when this guide went to press. But, as prices
can change at short notice, these symbols should be used as a guideline only.

Symbols used on town plans

Castles	Historic houses	Cathedrals/abbeys/churches
Museums	Features of interest	Mountain rescue stations
Picnic sites	Youth hostels	Ancient monuments
Cinemas	Pleasure steamers	Tourist information centres

An introduction to the Lake District

This is a guide to a part of Britain that is, without doubt, one of the best known, most explored and most popular tourist regions in the entire kingdom – the Lake District. To produce a new slant on such a small area of country is a challenging task, but there is one considerable compensation: the Lake District and the much larger county of Cumbria, which enfolds the Lake District National Park as the setting does the central jewel, is not one place but many, encapsulating a whole variety of views and viewpoints. There is the Lake District of Wordsworth and the Lake poets, the Lake District beloved of walkers and climbers, the Lakes of literature and history, the Lakes of today, inundated by modern tourism. In addition, since the mid 1970s there have been certain accretions to historic Lakeland in the larger county of Cumbria which now includes all or part of Westmorland, Cumberland and Lancashire. Administrative boundary changes have altered the geographical shape of traditional Cumberland, which makes for a certain confusion, so let it be clear that this is a guide to the Lake District *and* Cumbria, encompassing all the land now enclosed by the modern county of Cumbria. Within that boundary and this book there is something for everyone, a vast sweep and variety of town and village, fell, forest, lake and mountain chain. Although the holiday centres get very crowded in high season, it is still an area well-endowed with those high remote places which are the true Lakeland, at least in the mind's eye and in popular imagination.

Lakeland, however, has changed, and such change is probably inevitable. It plays host every year to millions of visitors and the effects of this annual visitation are not easy to ignore. Inevitably, the results of mass tourism present a rather unexpected picture to those who travel to Cumbria anticipating scenes of lake and fell discreetly veiled behind a host of golden daffodils. Lakeland has suffered the fate foretold by Wordsworth when he and his friends contested the advance of the railway into Windermere – it has become popular. However, it takes a short time to see, appreciate and enjoy the fact that not a lot has really changed beyond the touristic trappings. The lakes are as beautiful as ever, the fells as distant, the Cumbrian people, those farmers and shepherds, or those who live in the towns and hamlets, as dour and clannish as ever. To enjoy the Lake District and Cumbria requires a little patience, a little knowledge of the past – and this guide with its companion map.

Time has provided Lakeland with manifold attractions so that, whatever interests the visitor, Lakeland can probably provide it. This is an old, old land, rugged, and, as already noted, not much altered away from the tourist centres. Prehistoric man survived rather well here, chipping stone axes from the local flint, building curious stone circles which still stand as at Castlerigg near Keswick. Then the Romans came to drive roads across the fells from Ravenglass and to build the great Hadrian's Wall which straddles the county from Bowness on the Solway to Newcastle in the east. When they passed away the Vikings came and their memorial is more enduring in words like *fell* and *beck* and *thwaite*. The Normans built fine churches, their descendants erected imposing castles down the Eden Valley. All history is here if you look for it.

Those who like literature have come here on pilgrimage for over a hundred years to see Dove Cottage, the Wordsworths' home at Grasmere, or Beatrix Potter's little farm at Hill Top, Sawrey, Arthur Ransome's Wildcat Island on Windermere – or is that now really Peel Island on Coniston? Writers and poets have flocked to Lakeland and the list is almost endless; Southey, Coleridge, Ruskin, Hugh Walpole, Matthew Arnold, Walter Scott, Tennyson among them. Those who want a literary theme for their visit will have a vast choice of subject.

The fells of Lakeland form another enduring attraction, drawing climbers and fell walkers by the thousand every summer. Wildlife and outdoor life lovers of a less energetic kind will also not be disappointed. There are nature trails and bird sanctuaries, and many interesting species of birds and mammals – the roe deer and the red deer, pine martins, ravens, buzzards, even golden eagles. If you come to Lakeland, don't forget your binoculars. In the lakes and streams, fish are plentiful, some common like the trout, other local varieties like the Windermere char and the Ullswater schelly.

On another front, Lakeland is a holiday playground *par excellence*. There are hotels of all kinds, camp sites and caravan parks, and a host of things for visitors to do, all against the mighty natural backdrop of the fells.

There are as many reasons to visit Lakeland as there are visitors – and most of them return year after year and still find something new to delight in.

HISTORY & GEOLOGY

To begin at the end, the modern county of Cumbria is England's second largest county, embracing all of pre-1974 Westmorland and Cumberland, plus parts of Lancashire. Within this whole lies the Lake District, and within this again lies the Lake District National Park. The Lake District National

Park, where the bulk of this book is set, encompasses some 880 square miles of mountain, fell and lake. It is a region unsurpassed in beauty, a magnet to visitors from all over the world. The park was set up in 1951 and is still the largest National Park in Britain. Cumbria is almost exactly three times as big at 2682 square miles, and has about ten times the population of the National Park; about 500,000 people live in Cumbria, of whom around 45,000 reside in the National Park.

Geologically, Cumbria is a mixture of plain and mountain, and as always, the geology has influenced the area's history. The Lake District has often been described geologically as a wheel, with the spokes represented by the lakes spinning out from the central peak of Scafell, split on a north-west to south-east axis by the Cumbrian Mountains. This a county of grit and sandstone, of limestone, coal and iron ore, smoothed into round tops, ridges and deep, steep valleys by the grinding floes of the last Ice Age. It has never supported a large population, and yet most of those different peoples who have made their mark in Britain found time to settle here. There are prehistoric henges, Roman roads and forts, Saxon and Norman churches, medieval pele towers built as defences against the Scots, handsome Georgian houses, once-prosperous 19th century industrial ports and evidence in plenty of Victorian enthusiasm and enterprise throughout the region. Nor has Cumbria escaped the uncertainties of the atomic age and the nuclear power station at Sellafield, Seascale (formerly Windscale) is a testament to a new presence on the landscape. The history of Britain lies all about you in Cumbria if you only take the time to take it in.

This is not a land to rush, which perhaps explains its long-standing attraction for walkers who have made this county very much their own and continue to possess those high windy parts that lie along and above the tourist-crowded valleys. Popular it may be, but well worth getting to know, a place where wise travellers will try to get off the too-well-beaten track, and under the skin of the people and the places.

HOW TO GET THERE

Good communications to Cumbria, and the Lake District in particular, have certainly increased tourist pressure on the environment.

By road

The ever-expanding motorway network has placed Windermere within five hours steady driving of London, up the M1 and M6 motorways, the latter being the main Lake District artery which slices through Cumbria from north to south. The mileage from central London to Penrith is 280 miles, and from Birmingham, Bristol, Manchester or Leeds, the motorway distances and times are even shorter.

East to west, the A69 from Newcastle passes through Brampton and joins the A6 at Carlisle. From Workington in western Cumbria, the A66 cuts across the heart of the Lake District through Cockermouth, Keswick, Penrith, Brough and on to Scotch Corner in North Yorkshire, where it meets the A1.

Access from both Edinburgh (on the A7) and from Glasgow (on the M74 and A74 continuation) is direct, with both routes ending in Carlisle.

By rail

The main junction for all trains into Lakeland is at Oxenholme, where most visitors alight or change for Windermere, but there are also mainline stations at Penrith and Carlisle. The eastern edge of Cumbria is served by the marvellous Settle to Carlisle route. Oxenholme is on the main Inter-City line via Preston, Lancaster and Carlisle, and getting there by train is quicker than by road, and a good deal less fatiguing. From London (Euston) the journey time is around 3hrs 30mins; from Glasgow 2hrs 15mins; from Manchester 2hrs. Full details on train travel and excursions to Oxenholme from all parts of Britain can be obtained from local travel agents, tourist information centres (TICs), or any British Rail information office at a mainline station.

By coach

The Lake District has always been a popular target for coach excursions and with the expansion of the motorway network, more and more coach operators offer trips and tours into Cumbria from all the main provincial centres, Leeds, Birmingham, Bristol, York, as well as such capital cities as London, Edinburgh and Cardiff. These services tend to be almost as quick as the rail journey and are considerably cheaper. Full details of trips to Cumbria are available from local bus and coach companies, the various provincial bus and coach stations or local tourist information centres (TICs). Victoria Coach Station is the principal departure point from the south.

GETTING AROUND

Getting about in Lakeland is as easy as getting there and often far more fun, especially if the visitor is prepared to be flexible and take full advantage of the many special local facilities and services. Full details are given in the appropriate sections of this book, but travellers within the Lake District should particularly note the following.

By bus or coach

Apart from a host of small coach companies, the two major bus companies in Cumbria are the Ribble and the Cumberland, both of which offer regular coach trips from main centres such as Carlisle, Kendal, Keswick, Penrith and Windermere, as well as a variety of special tickets and concessions. Two unique Lakeland companies are Mountain Goat Minibuses, which operate from Windermere, and Fellrunner, which operates in the Western Pennines and from Penrith. Another most useful local service is the Post Bus which, as the name implies, uses GPO-operated minibuses to provide a regional bus service as part of the mail collection and delivery service. Full details on all these services from the local bus stations or TICs. There are also a number of local coach companies, and their addresses are given in the gazetteer sections of this guide.

By train

Rail services within Lakeland and Cumbria are limited but highly scenic. Two notable tourist runs are on the Ravenglass & Eskdale Railway and the little Lakeside & Haverthwaite Railway. But visitors should also consider three routes which skirt the Lake District central fells; the Lakes Line from Preston to Carlisle; the West Cumbrian Line from Barrow-in-Furness, round the Solway to Carlisle; and most of all, in Eastern Cumbria, the Settle to Carlisle Line, one of the most spectacular railway journeys in Britain. There are a wide number of excursion fares and rail-rover tickets available.

By steamer

No visit to Lakeland would be complete without a cruise on a Lake 'steamer', though the word 'steamer' often encompasses a large launch. These craft ply on the major lakes, Windermere, Coniston, Ullswater, Derwent Water, and often organise their timetables to tie in with coach or train excursions.

By car

Car travel within Cumbria and the Lake District is always possible but bear in mind that the roads are narrow and often crowded, the passes steep, and the car parks infrequent and frequently full. Allow plenty of time for any journey, particularly during the tourist season. Car hire is available in all the main towns.

By cycle

Cumbria is perfect cycling country and a bicycle with good low gears is probably the best way to get about and see the sights of Lakeland. Wise cyclists will take care in the narrow, steep-sided lanes.

The Cumbria Cycle Way is a designated cycle route which runs for 280 miles (450km) around the county, taking in all the most attractive parts of Cumbria, although it avoids the high passes of the Central Fells. It is well worth following.

Those who arrive in Cumbria without a bicycle can always hire one locally, and lists of cycle hire shops are given in the relevant gazetteer sections.

Walking

Cumbria in general, and the fells of the Lake District National Park in particular, is walking country *par excellence*. However, it should be noted that this is mostly hill-walking country, not ideal for gentle suburban rambling, so anyone contemplating a walking holiday in Cumbria should be well shod, well clothed, and above all, experienced in the many aspects of outdoor lore.

One of the most common sights in the Lake District and the Western Pennines is of groups of plastic-draped walkers trudging down from the fells, or sitting around in the cafes waiting for the mist and rain to clear on the hills above. It is therefore necessary to stress in any guidebook to the Lakes, that hill-walking in this part of Britain cannot be undertaken lightly, *especially by those who choose to lead groups of children*. The hills empty of people within a mile of the road, the distances are often long, the paths steep, and the weather very variable. Cumbria is a rugged, remote part of Britain, and the weather can make it very dangerous indeed at very short notice. Included in each of the six gazetteer sections of the guide is a selection of walks taking in many of Cumbria's most memorable views and beauty spots. The walks are planned to be within the reach of any reasonably fit person and are without undue difficulty. The approximate time to be allowed and the total distance for each walk is given at the end of the relevant description.

Precautions for walkers

Walkers must be prepared and equipped for a rapid change of weather, with low cloud, mist and rain as constant possibilities. No one should set out to walk on the high fells without checking first on the weather, a rule that applies as much in high summer as during the months of spring or autumn. Sensible equipment should include: boots, gaiters, warm clothing, a waterproof cagoule and over-trousers, and a hat or some suitably secure head covering. Carry relevant OS maps, scale 1:25 000 in the 'Outdoor Leisure' series, a compass, first-aid kit and some spare dry clothing and food in a rucksack. Always let someone know where you are going and when you expect to be back. Outside high summer, carry and use an ice axe and crampons. Again, check the weather before leaving and turn back at once if the weather becomes unpleasant. This point must be stressed. These may sound extreme precautions but if they were followed more often the Lake District Mountain Rescue teams would not be so busy.

CLIMATE

One of the best kept secrets of Cumbria is the fact that it rains up there. The tourist brochures are strangely reticent on this point, but it is a fact and one which all visitors should take into account. Seathwaite in Borrowdale is actually the wettest place in England with up to 130 inches in a year. Having said that, it is only fair to add that in the course of several visits to Cumbria for the purpose of writing this book, the author experienced a week's continuous sunshine, a week of continuous rain, and a week of alternating weather with low cloud and snow showers.

It is possible to enjoy fine weather in May and June, but summer rain is not infrequent even in the high summer months of July and August. Visitors are advised to come prepared and pack a raincoat and umbrella with their shorts and should check the weather forecasts daily. Prevailing winds from the west bring rain in from the Atlantic, although the extent of the rainfall in Cumbria depends on locality and along the coast, in the Solway estuary or along the wider valleys, the rainfall drops dramatically. Fluctuations in the weather, even within the hour, can be striking – especially in the Lake District proper. And for holidaymakers, it is the unpredictability coupled with the sudden variability of the weather that can give cause for concern.

Weather forecasts

A recorded forecast and a fell-top conditions report (the latter updated twice daily) can be obtained from the Lake District Weather Service, Tel Windermere (09662) 5151. Weather forecasts can also be consulted at Visitor Centres, TICs and in the local daily papers.

INFORMATION

Tourist information centres

Given that Cumbria is a very popular tourist region, good up-to-date information is always worth having and the main means of acquiring it is either through the numerous tourist information centres (TICs) operated by the English Tourist Board throughout Britain, or at the British Tourist Authority offices abroad. TICs are always marked with the blue tourist information sign with its red rose. They vary in size and in the range of services they provide. Within the county of Cumbria, the visitor is served by a generous number of TICs, some of them offering assistance with accommodation, either on a local basis only for a small charge, or further afield in towns which have centres with a reciprocal service. All can advise on places of interest, tours, attractions and activities in the immediate area and supply leaflets, which are free, and maps and guides for sale. The larger TICs offer information on a wider basis, both regional and national, and they may be able to provide an official guide for groups.

Not all TICs are open all year. Some open seasonally (Easter-October), some open for limited hours on limited days if demand is light – a telephone call is recommended before a special trip is made. The TICs in the Lake District and Cumbria are listed, complete with addresses and phone numbers, at the beginning of their relevant area sections in this guide.

In Cumbria, the principal centre for information is: The Cumbria Tourist Board, Ashleigh, Holly Road, Windermere, Cumbria LA23 2AQ. Please note that this office handles written enquiries only.

In addition to the officially recognised TICs, there are also many display boards in car parks, town centres and picnic areas, which carry useful tips about what to see and do, where to eat and drink.

Other Visitor Centres and National Park information centres throughout Lakeland can provide detailed localised information and their services are well worth using. These centres are also included in the guide under the area sections which they serve.

National Park information centres

One essential stop for all visitors to Lakeland has to be at The National Park Information Centre at Brockhole near Windermere. The full address is: The Lake District National Park Centre, Brockhole, Windermere, Cumbria OA23 1LJ. Tel Windermere (09662) 2231. Set in superb grounds, this centre is the place to acquire that special, general understanding of the county, its inhabitants and the wildlife. There are other National Park centres at Seatoller and Sedbergh, details of which are given in the gazetteer.

Radio

BBC Radio Cumbria is a local station which broadcasts tourist information during the summer months on 206, 358 and 397m medium wave; 755, 145kHz; 95.6 and 96.1 VHF.

Telephone

What's On: Telephone Tourist Information – dial Windermere (09662) 6363.

Local press

Apart from the services provided by the Cumbria Tourist Board and the sources listed above, visitors will also find it useful to consult the following publications: 'The Westmorland Gazette' (weekly); 'Whitehaven News' (weekly); 'Cumbria (Lake District) Life' (monthly); 'Cumbria Life' (monthly); 'Lakeland Life' (monthly). All these papers and the occasional free sheets can be obtained from any local newsagent.

ACCOMMODATION

One thing the visitor to Cumbria will not lack is a wide choice of accommodation of all kinds and all standards – from luxury country house hotels to farmhouses and self-catering cottages. The largest concentration and variety of accommodation is in and around the tourist centres of the National Park. On the fringes of Cumbria, hotels become much harder to find, although bed and breakfast accommodation is plentiful.

It usually pays to book ahead, certainly in the high season summer months, at weekends at any time, and around Easter. Youth hostels tend to fill up very quickly, as do caravan sites, so it is always advisable to ascertain in advance of arrival whether there is room available.

There are a number of guidebooks listing accommodation addresses, the most comprehensive of which is 'Where to Stay', published annually by the

English Tourist Board, and which includes hotels, motels, guesthouses, hostels and inns registered with the English Tourist Board. The official guide 'Cumbria: English Lake District' (free), published by the Cumbria Tourist Board, has an accommodation section, as well as detailing things to do and places to go. A more selective choice of modestly priced inns, small hotels, farms and country houses in Cumbria is included in Elizabeth Gundrey's fifth edition of 'Staying Off The Beaten Track', published by Arrow Books.

Those wanting an unplanned holiday will find that most TICs in Cumbria will advise on accommodation in their own locality, and some will make bookings elsewhere in the county for the following night. (See the sections on **Tourist information centres** in this guide.) Caravan travellers and campers can get help in finding a site/pitch by consulting the booklet 'Sites for Touring Caravans and Tents', which is published by The National Park Information Service in conjunction with the Cumbria Tourist Board, and which is on sale at most information centres in Cumbria.

Prospective youth hostellers should obtain a copy of the 1986 edition of the official guide published by the Youth Hostels Association.

A wide range of camping and caravanning sites, with full descriptions of facilities provided, has been included in all six area sections of this book. Youth hostels throughout the region are covered as well.

EATING AND DRINKING

Popular though it is, the Lake District cannot really be regarded as a gastronomic region of Britain, with a truly identifiable local cuisine. There are local dishes, but the majority of the restaurants in the main holiday centres aim at satisfying a transient tourist population with fast, filling meals. There are, however, some excellent restaurants in unexpected places and a rather surprising number of vegetarian ones.

Many Cumbrian restaurants are, in fact, cafes or hotel-restaurants. Outside the tourist centres, establishments which are purely restaurants, open at set hours for lunch and dinner, are rather thin on the ground. This can mean snatching a snack or booking a table in a hotel dining room which is normally full of residents. Most hotel-restaurants allow for non-residents and also offer children's portions.

The local pubs make a great effort to serve good, home-cooked food and many cater especially for families with children, as well as providing sustenance (often much-needed) for walkers.

A number of the better hotels, pubs and restaurants offer regional specialities, such as Eden salmon or trout, char from Lake Windermere, Cumberland sausages, or Lancashire hot-pot. By and large the standard of local cooking is quite high, with an increasing number of places using fresh produce only. So, where a pub or restaurant features local food as a speciality, it is worth trying. All in all, the visitor will eat as well in Cumbria as anywhere else in Britain, and generally at no great cost.

It is also worth pointing out that Cumbria lies in the North of England and therefore the evening begins early. Quite a few of the less expensive establishments serve a substantial high tea in place of a proper evening meal and may close around *19.00* or earlier. Even in some of the more sophisticated places, it is not unusual to find 'dinner' being served from *17.30* and stopping sharp at *20.30*. The best attitude for visitors to adopt is that of the residents: flexibility and check first. Regard any published times with a degree of caution.

The **Eating & drinking** sections in this guide offer a wide range of restaurants, hotel-restaurants, pubs, cafes, tea shops, snack bars and fast food places to suit all tastes and pockets. The top family holiday centres, such as Windermere, Ambleside and Keswick, are so rich in places serving holiday food (grills, fish and chips, hamburgers) that no attempt has been made to list them all. On the other hand, a few really good, expensive, out-of-the-way places for a special treat have been included since those are harder to find without some information. Places which welcome children have also been clearly indicated.

NIGHTLIFE

Cumbria has theatres, cinemas and summer shows, and where they are reasonably permanent fixtures the venues for these events are given in the **Leisure & entertainment** sections. There is, in addition, a vast amount of ad-hoc entertainment of the folk music, poetry and a pint variety, held in pubs and little halls. Details are given in the local papers or found on local notices. Lakeland certainly isn't dull and the alert visitor will find plenty to do after dark, particularly between Easter and October.

FISHING

If hill-walking is the great outdoor pursuit in Cumbria, fishing is also available in great variety. Along the long coast, in the moorland streams and becks, from the banks, or in boats on the lakes, the fishing in Cumbria is superb. Salmon, trout, perch, char are plentiful. The local tourist board produces a leaflet 'Fishing in Cumbria', which is full of information, and the best place to look for good fishing is in the pages of this leaflet, obtained at any TIC. A licence is needed to fish the local waters and a list of licence suppliers is included in the **Fishing** sections of this guide. Many of these suppliers are owners of tackle shops, whose staff are full of useful information.

TIPS

Any writer on the Lake District or Cumbria inherits a great burden from the past – or a great legacy. It depends on your point of view. This part of Britain has been the recipient of much literary attention and according to one excellent recent survey, no less than 50,000 titles have been published on the Lake District since the late 18th century, of which some 300 are currently in print! Add to this the prolific output of the tourist authorities in leaflets and brochures and it must be clear that visitors to Lakeland will never be short of information. However, there are still gaps, not least in the coverage of those little local tips or bits of information which can either make a visit enjoyable, or spoil it with a string of irritations or disappointments.

Indeed, it is in this area that the professional travel writer finds the Lake District hard to pin down. The local people tend to part with information reluctantly and hedge about with 'ifs' and 'buts', so it is dangerous to become dogmatic. If spring comes early, shops and services open before their appointed season. If the day is wet or the crowds absent, the reverse happens, and the late arrival may find the shop closed or the bus gone. Other than such fairly certain fixtures as at a main town museum, be prepared to take all timings with a pinch of salt. However, in the hope that this book will help the visitor to avoid too many minor upsets, herewith a few hints and tips on how to travel happily in Lakeland.

Preparation

Do try and read up on the Lake District and Cumbria extensively before setting out, particularly if the area is not at all familiar. The publishers, in association with the English Tourist Board, have also produced a fully comprehensive 'Holiday Map of the Lake District & Cumbria' which should be used in conjunction with this guide and which is recommended to readers who are planning to travel around. It is usually worthwhile plotting the various points and centres of interest on the map and then working out a route which covers them, where possible on minor roads. For those with specific interests – walking or fishing perhaps – it is also worth writing off for information leaflets in advance. See **Tourist information centres** at the beginning of each area section of this guide for addresses.

Walkers and climbers, especially, are recommended to purchase the detailed OS 1:25 000 maps in the 'Outdoor Leisure' series. The relevant maps covering the Lake District are:

English Lakes North East   English Lakes South East
English Lakes North West   English Lakes South West

Other useful OS maps in the 1:50 000 'Landranger' series are sheets 85, 86, 89, 90, 91, 92, 96, 97 and 98.

When to go

One rule that holds good for any tourist anywhere is, travel out of high season whenever possible, although the timing of school holidays tends to make families less flexible. Even out of season, however, there are still snags. The main benefit is that the roads are empty and the car parks have lots of space.

The main disadvantage is that many of the attractions, museums and services are not open or only operate on restricted hours. The weather is less of a problem, for Cumbrian weather is always uncertain.

Local papers

Apart from the wealth of places and suggestions included in the various sections of this guide, visitors will also find the local newspapers a useful source of information on events, cinemas, one-day festivals and other more immediate activities. See the section on **Local press** on p.13 for a list of publications which can be obtained from local newsagents.

Addresses

One essential tip, given the looseness of Cumbrian addresses is: *always ask for directions* to your hotel, camp site, or restaurant when pre-booking. To help you pinpoint your destination, the gazetteer entries are grid referenced to the touring maps at the front of each area section of this guide. Directions and distances from (or to) main towns and villages are given in the text when a particular place is very small or likely to be hard to find. Restaurants, pubs, camping and caravan sites, places of interest, leisure and entertainment venues, and special local events or craft centres are listed with their postal addresses under the nearest town or village to their actual location.

Opening hours

Tradespeople in Cumbria tend to be quite vague about opening and closing times. Much depends on the weather, the crowds and the season, the mood of the moment. If October is sunny, then most places which normally close on 30 September will stay open. If it is raining, a shop usually closing at *20.00* may close at *17.00*. If the crowds arrive, the tills will continue to ring – so be prepared for this and err on the early side. It is also worth noting that shops and places of interest (eg museums) in villages and some towns often close up for an hour at lunchtime, even in high season.

Specific opening and closing times have been given in this guide wherever possible. These were accurate at the time this book went to press, but all published times should be treated with caution as they are frequently subject to change at short notice. Telephone numbers are also supplied with individual entries, so it is always advisable to check first before making a special journey.

SOUTHERN LAKELAND

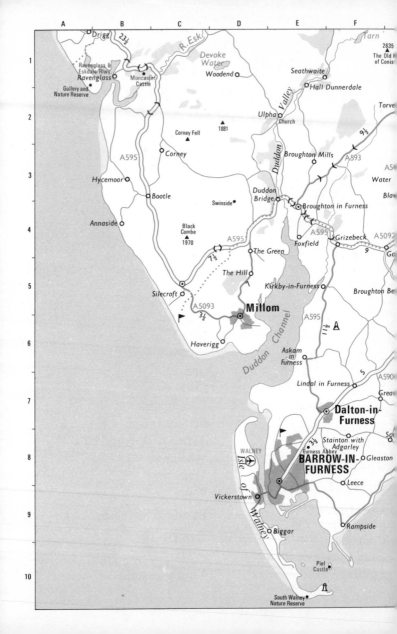

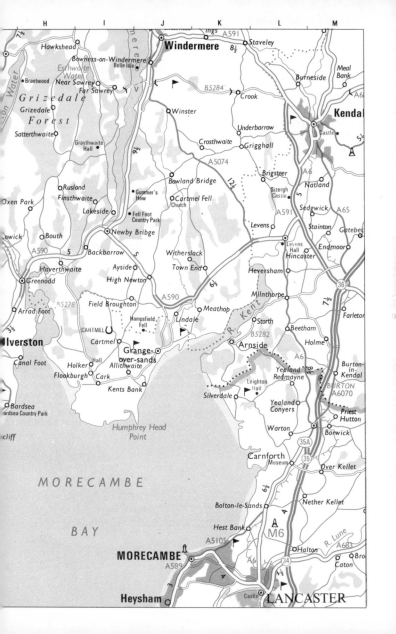

Tourist information centres

Barrow-in-Furness **E8**
Civic Hall, 28 Duke St. Tel Barrow-in-
Furness (0229) 25795. Access for
disabled. *Open all year.*

Coniston **G1**
1 Yewdale Rd. Tel Coniston (0966) 41533.
Operates local bed-booking service.
Access for disabled. *Open Easter–Oct.*

Grange-over-Sands **J6**
Victoria Hall, Main St. Tel Grange-over-
Sands (04484) 4026. Operates local bed-
booking service and 'Book-a-bed-ahead'
accommodation service. *Open Easter–Oct.*

Hawkshead **I1**
Brown Cow Laithe. Tel Hawkshead
(09666) 525. Operates local bed-booking
service. Access for disabled. *Open
Easter–Oct.*

Kendal **M2**
Town Hall, Highgate. Tel Kendal (0539)
25758. Operates local bed-booking service
and 'Book-a-bed-ahead' accommodation
service. Access for disabled. *Open all
year.*

Millom **D6**
Millom Folk Museum, St Georges Rd. Tel
Millom (0657) 2555. Access for disabled.
Open Easter–Oct.

Ravenglass **B1**
Ravenglass & Eskdale Railway Car Pk. Tel
Ravenglass (06577) 278. Operates local
bed-booking service and 'Book-a-bed-
ahead' accommodation service. Access for
disabled. *Open Easter–Oct.*

Ulverston **G6**
Coronation Hall, County Square.
Tel Ulverston (0229) 57120. Access for
disabled. *Open all year.*

Windermere **J1**
Victoria St. Tel Windermere (09662) 6499.
Operates local bed-booking service and
'Book-a-bed-ahead' accommodation
service. Access for disabled. *Open all year.*

The Countryside

The southern part of the Lake District is
really a microcosm of the whole. Though
set at a slightly lower height than the
Central fells, the south offers an agreeable
mixture of coast and countryside, of open
fells and close, and forested country. This
part is not overburdened with lakes, but it
has two of the most famous, in
Windermere, which is also the largest, and
Coniston Water of waterspeed fame. It
also has one of the prettiest at Tarn Hows.
Most visitors to Lakeland will enter the
region through this southern district,
either by turning off the M6 motorway by
Kendal, or leaving their train at
Oxenholme or Windermere. This eastern,
inland part is farming country, a region of
cow-filled fields, with small copses on the
crest of the ridges, stone walls and a litter
of whitewashed houses gathered together
into small villages, all linked by a network
of narrow, high-banked country roads in
which it is all too easy to get lost.
Here, south and east of Kendal, the
countryside is pleasant rather than
dramatic and if the fields look lush and the
cows contented, this may have something
to do with the fact that this eastern section
of the region lies in the rain shadow of
the fells which rear up west of Coniston
and is therefore perceptibly wetter than
parts to the south, or along the coastal strip
that runs from Millom up to Ravenglass.

Skirting Kendal and climbing up and over the rolling country to Windermere, this countryside opens out, offering the first of these marvellous Lakeland views, although an alternative route is to avoid the crowded road that runs to the south along the eastern shore of Windermere from Bowness to Newby Bridge, opting instead for a wandering route through Cartmel Fell and Witherslack and down to the coast at Grange-over-Sands. This route, or routes, for there are many minor roads to follow, runs through a green, dense and jumbled country, beside the little River Winster and past Helton Tarn, the views opening out as the southern parts grow nearer. West of this route, between Windermere and Coniston, lies the vast expanse of Grizedale Forest, now largely controlled by the Forestry Commission but a popular centre for walkers and wildlife lovers, who fan out into the woods from the Visitor and Wildlife Centre at Grizedale or up into the higher country hereabouts which, while still a mixture of fields and forests, is nudging now towards the 1000ft mark, or even exceeding it on Bethecar Moor, where Top O' Setside by little Arnsbarrow Tarn stands at 1091ft. Moving west again, on the far side of Coniston stands one of the famous peaks of Lakeland, the Old Man of Coniston (2635ft), overlooking the village and the lake itself far below. Here, the main fells run south and west from the Old Man to open-topped moors, thick with bracken and heather, tousled by the wind. To be quite accurate, these southern fells fall into two broad groups and are divided by the deep valley of the River Duddon which runs up to Seathwaite, before pressing on to the Hardknott Pass.
East of the Duddon Valley lies Broughton Moor, Dow Crag at 2555ft and Caw Fell (1735ft), the land falling away in a long spur down into the Lickle valley at Bank End. West of the Duddon the fells are more open and even wilder, climbing steadily from the Great Worm Crag at 1400ft, south across Ulpha Fell, up to Whitefell at 1881ft, before descending, as usual, to the south, past craggy Black Combe and down to Whitbeck. From the high western face of these fells, where the ground falls away in a great sweep towards the sea, a place blazing with golden bracken in the autumn, there are fine views out into the Irish Sea, to the Isle of Man, and even across to Ulster if the weather is kind and clear.

The picture of this southern region of Lakeland then, is one of a mixed but always attractive countryside, rising steadily to the south and west before toppling over sharply and finally into the Irish Sea. The great natural attractions for the visitor hereabouts are the peak of the Old Man of Coniston and the two great lakes, Coniston Water and Windermere. To these add the splendid road which runs along the coast under the lee of the high fells from Millom up to Ravenglass.

Country parks & nature reserves

Bardsea Country Park   G7
Just off the A5087 at Bardsea. A coastal park with sea views, woodlands and picnic areas. *Open all year.* **Free.**
Fell Foot Country Park   I4
Im NE of Newby Bridge off A592. Tel Newby Bridge (0448) 31273. An 18-acre National Trust lakeside park at the south end of Windermere. Fishing, rowing boats for hire. *Open all year.* **Free.**
Ravenglass Gullery & Nature Reserve A1
Drigg, Holmbrook. Tel Carlisle (0228) 23956. Set close to the B5344 road. This famous, coastal seabird sanctuary near Ravenglass shelters a wide variety of nesting gulls and terns; also natterjack toads. *Senior ornithologists only, viewing by appointment.*
South Walney Nature Reserve   E10
Walney Island, Barrow-in-Furness. Tel Barrow (0229) 41066. Europe's largest gullery and eider duck colony. *Open Nov–Mar 10.00–16.00; Apr–Oct 10.00–17.00.* **Charge.**

Forests & nature trails

Brantwood   H1
On NE of Coniston Water, 3m E of Coniston reached by unclassified road. The trails from Brantwood House are a good way to see Ruskin country, and offer good views of the lake. The gardens and woods are a riot of flowers in the spring. Total distance 3½m.
Grizedale Forest   H2
Between Windermere and Coniston. Much of this vast woodland is owned by the Forestry Commission but there are splendid way-marked walks and views. Full information can be obtained from the Grizedale Forest Visitors' & Wildlife Centre in Grizedale.

Hampsfield Fell   **J6**
This starts in Windermere Rd.
Grange-over-Sands and runs for two miles
to the top of Hampsfell. Good views over
the fells and Morecambe Bay.

Millwood Forest   **H2**
This one-mile trail through the woods
starts at the Grizedale Forest Visitors'
Centre in Grizedale.

Serpentine Woods   **L2**
This trail begins in Queens Rd, Kendal,
and runs for one mile, mostly through
woodland. Details on flowers and trees
from the tourist information centre,
Highgate, Kendal.

Islands

Belle Isle   **J1**
Set in Lake Windermere opposite
Bowness-on-Windermere. This large

island has the only really round Georgian
house in England and a two-mile long
nature trail. *Open late Mar–early Sep.*

Walney Island   **D9**
This is the southern tip of Cumbria, a long
windswept island, shaped like an anchor
fluke, and reached across a causeway. See
Piel Castle, a medieval fortress in the
Channel, and follow the nature trail for
some bird-watching on the sands.

Lakes

Coniston Water   **H2**
Coniston is famous as the setting for
attempts on the world's waterspeed
records and the place where Donald
Campbell died in 1967 while making yet
another attempt to regain the record once
held by his father, Sir Malcolm Campbell.
Peel Island, to the south of the lake,
featured as 'Wild Cat Island' in Arthur
Ransome's famous book 'Swallows and
Amazons', although the islands on

Windermere were used for the television
film. The best view of the lake, with the
Old Man rising up behind, is from
Brantwood, John Ruskin's old home on
the eastern shore.

Devoke Water   **D1**
2m S of Eskdale Green, west of the road
to Ulpha. This small attractive tarn is set
on the moors below Rough Crag and can
be reached on foot along the drove road
across Birker Fell.

Tarn Hows   **H1**
2m N of Coniston. A 'tarn' is a small lake
or a large pond and Lakeland is full of
them, but Tarn Hows is probably the
prettiest, and now belongs to the National
Trust. It is in fact artificial, caused by a
dam built before the Great War, but the
setting is quite superb – a little paradise
but best avoided on summer weekends
when the crowds here flock to see it.

Windermere   **I4–J1**
This is the largest and most popular of the
lakes, 10½m long and 1m wide at most.
It is a centre for all kinds of watersports
from sailing to waterskiing. Boat trips
around the lake leave from Bowness and a
car ferry operates across the lake to Far
Sawrey for visits to Hill Top Farm
at Near Sawrey, and Coniston.

Mountains, valleys & fells

Black Combe   **C4**
This great round-topped fell, set with
crags along the eastern slope, lies in the
south-western corner of the region,
overlooking the coast road from Millom
to Bootle. The 1970ft summit offers views
so marvellous that they were featured in
a poem, 'View from the Top of Black
Combe' by Wordsworth. A footpath leads
to the summit from Bootle.

Coniston Old Man   **G1**
This famous peak, 2635ft high, can be

reached on foot along a fairly well-defined track and is a pleasant walk from the village of Coniston far below, but this should not be attempted in poor or uncertain weather. Good footwear is necessary. Details on local walking from the Visitors' Centre in Coniston.

Duddon Valley E3
The Duddon Valley, or as it is often called, Dunnerdale, runs up into the fells from near Broughton-in-Furness to Seathwaite. Birks, at the north end, is very picturesque.

Viewpoints

Black Combe C4
Wonderful views to Ravenglass, the coast of Cumbria and even to the Isle of Man.

Corney Fell C3
3½m N of Black Combe, just off the minor road which leads across the fells from Corney to Beckfoot in the Duddon Valley, and offers great views to the Isle of Man on a clear day.

Coniston Old Man G1
From the summit, fine views over Coniston Water and the nearby southerly lakes and fells.

Gummers How J4
This viewpoint lies at 1054ft at the southern end of Lake Windermere, just to the north of Lakeside, and offers marvellous views over the lake and the high fells to the north and west.

Orrest Head J1
½m N of Windermere. This viewpoint offers one of the finest views of the Central Fells and the lake below.

Oubas Hill G6
Just NE of Ulverston. A low hill, only 435ft high, yet easy to reach and giving great views over Cartmel Sands to the east, and south to the sea.

Visitors' & wildlife centre

Grizedale Forest Visitors' & Wildlife Centre H2
Grizedale, Hawkshead. Tel Satterthwaite (022984) 273. This excellent centre contains displays featuring the geological, botanic and wildlife characteristics of this part of Cumbria. *Open daily.*

The Coast

This southern section of the Lake District has a marvellous diversity of coastline, overlooked by fells but largely flat along the shore.

From Grange-over-Sands the visitor can look out on a vast stretch of sand when the tide is out, over the great expanse of Morecambe Bay. North of Grange-over-Sands the estuary of the River Kent nudges inland and much of this southern corner of Cumbria is similarly indented with deep, attractive river valleys running far north or east into the fells, past Ulverston and Millom, which lies on the beautiful Duddon Channel. Millom itself is best seen from the Furness peninsula on the eastern side. North of Millom the fells run down to the coast and overlook the sea all the way up to the attractive and bustling little port of Ravenglass. A tour around this shoreline will show the visitor some of the attractive, very different and much less frequented parts of Lakeland.

Beaches & sea bathing

Sea bathers on the coast of Cumbria must beware of tides and offshore currents, bathing only on secure beaches at approved times. The ebb tides are particularly strong and floating out to sea on airbeds or air-mats is a practice to discourage, especially among children. That said, there is sea bathing available at the following.

Grange-over-Sands J6
On the beach below the esplanade.

Haverigg D6
On Haverigg beaches by Haverigg Point.

Silecroft C5
On Silecroft beach by the golf course.

Vickerstown, Walney Island D9
On Walney beach.

Towns & villages

Arnside K6
3m SW of Milnthorpe. *EC Thur.* Arnside is a little village on the south side of the Kent Channel opposite Grange-over-Sands; pleasant to visit and a paradise for bird-watchers. Arnside Tower, a ruined pele tower, offers great views over the estuary of the River Kent.

Backbarrow I4
2m S of Newby Bridge. A small village, which used to be a thriving centre for iron smelting and the production of washday 'blue' (once a popular method of whitening clothes). The 'Dolly Blue' factory closed in 1981 and the site is now being developed as a leisure and holiday complex.

Barrow-in-Furness   **E8**
8m S of Ulverston. *EC Thur. MD Mon,
Wed, Fri, Sat. Pop 64,000.*Barrow is a
shipbuilding centre. That much can be
seen even from a distance, for the entire
town is dominated by the giant cranes
which overlook the yards. The shipbuilding industry is currently in decline,
but much of the town dates from its
heyday in the last century, with long
narrow streets of Victorian houses and two
fine 19thC churches, one dedicated to St
George and the other to St James. There
is a good museum, The Furness Museum,
in Ramsdon Sq and two fine medieval
ruins, Piel Castle out in the estuary,
which can be visited by boat from Roa
Island, and Furness Abbey, just outside
the town, which is now in the care of the
Department of the Environment.

Blawith   **G3**
3m S of Torver. Blawith lies at the
southern end of Coniston, and is a
popular departure point for rambles along
the lake. The main historic site in the
village is the ruin of the 16thC church of
St John the Baptist beside the A5084.

Bootle   **B3**
6m S of Ravenglass. Lying between the
fells and the coast, Bootle is just a small
village but it has a good beach nearby and
is a centre for walks towards Black
Combe. St Mary's Church has a good brass
of Sir Hugh Askew, the local squire who
died in 1562.

Booth   **H4**
1½m N of Haverthwaite. Set on the
southern side of the Furness Fells, the
hamlet of Bouth is noted for the Hay
Bridge Deer Conservation Centre, which
aims to protect and preserve the native roe
and red deer which were once plentiful in
Cumbria.

Broughton-in-Furness   **E4**
6m N of Millom. *Pop 480. EC Thur. MD
Tue.* Broughton lies at the head of the
Duddon Channel, with the sea at the front
door and Dunnerdale at the back. It was
one a thriving port but has now declined
into a quiet little village, with an
impressive Market Square to remind
visitors of former glories. The Market
Hall houses the Hadwin Lakeland
Motorcycle Museum. Other sights in this
small town – or large village – include St
Mary's Church, a much restored building
with Norman elements, Broughton Tower,
a 19thC mansion built around a medieval
keep and now a school, and Duddon
Forge, now a ruin by the river, just
outside the town.

Burneside   **L1**
1½m N of Kendal. Burneside is a large,
unremarkable village on the minor road
from Kendal to Windermere, a centre for
paper-making with several mills, the
oldest of which dates from 1750. Note the
memorial erected in 1814 to the memory
of William Pitt, which was a somewhat
premature celebration of the end of the
Napoleonic Wars.

*Priory Church
of St Mary, Cartmel*

Cartmel   **I6**
3m N of Grange-over-Sands. A small but
most attractive village, crowned by the
attractive Gothic outlines of the Priory
Church of St Mary which, because of its
size, is often referred to as the 'Cathedral
of the Lakes'. Apart from its size this is
a beautiful church and a very necessary
visit for any lover of Lakeland. The
Priory was founded in the late 12thC by
the famous knight, William Marshal, later
Earl of Pembroke, but the monastic
buildings were demolished at the orders
of Henry VIII at the Reformation. All that
remains is the 14thC gatehouse and the
Priory Church, which was saved to serve
as the parish church, and although much
restored is still full of the former medieval
glory. The 14thC Harrington tomb is
magnificent, as is the East window, and
among other memorabilia, note the
memorial to those drowned attempting the
hazardous crossing of the sands from
Grange to Morecambe. The village itself is
set out attractively around a charming
square full of hotels, the Cavendish Arms,
the Royal Oak, the King's Arms or the
Priory Hotel. There is even one called the
Pig and Whistle.

Coniston   **G1**
7m S of Ambleside. *Pop 870. EC Wed.*
Coniston is a small, grey little village
saved from mediocrity by its setting, which
is magnificent, positioned as it is at the
foot of the Old Man of Coniston and the
edge of the lake. The village is a great
walking centre and one almost entirely
devoted to tourism, with cafes, bed &
breakfasts, small hotels, most notably the

Black Bull, a number of gift shops and a Visitors' Information Centre. Two worthwhile attractions are the Ruskin Museum and the National Trust's little steam launch, 'The Gondola', which takes visitors on cruises around Coniston Water during the summer.

Crosthwaite   **K3**
4m SE of Windermere. Late spring is the time to visit Crosthwaite, for while the village is small, the country round about is devoted to the cultivation of damsons, and is a sheet of white fruit blossom in April and May.

Dalton-in-Furness   **F7**
5m S of Ulverston. *Pop 11,000*. Dalton is now very much of a suburb for the shipbuilding centre of Barrow-in-Furness, 3m to the south. Once a market centre for the lands of Furness Abbey, and Dalton Castle, (now a National Trust property), the town was built to protect the Abbey and its lands from the marauding Scots and Irish pirates. The painter George Romney was buried in St Mary's Church in 1802.

Grange-over-Sands   **J6**
12m S of Kendal. *EC Thur*. Grange-over-Sands looks what it is, a typical Edwardian seaside resort, set on the low cliffs overlooking the vast sandy expanse of Morecambe Bay. In fact the sands are rather too muddy for good bathing, but are therefore very popular with birds and birdwatchers. Guided walks across the Bay (this walk should *not* be attempted without a guide) are still popular and details can be obtained from the tourist information centre.

Finsthwaite   **I4**
1m N of Newby Bridge. The chief attraction of Finsthwaite is the Stott Park Bobbin Mill, built in 1836, and recently restored by the Heritage Commission. The tarn behind the mill is most attractive and there are good walks in the wooded countryside round about.

Great Urswick   **F7**
3m S of Ulverston. Great Urswick is only a little place, made up of two hamlets set about a small tarn. It is notable because the villagers hold one of the Cumbria rushbearing ceremonies here on the Sunday nearest to St Michael's Day (29 Sep), when flowers and rushes from the tarn are carried around the village and then strewn on the floor of St Mary's and St Michael's Church.

Greenodd   **H5**
5m SW of Newby Bridge. This little village lies on Morecambe Bay on the

small estuary created by the rivers Leven and Crake. It was once a port and the old quays still remain, but today Greenodd is chiefly noted as a centre for birdwatchers studying the birds of Morecambe Bay.

Haverthwaite   **H5**
3m SE of Newby Bridge. Haverthwaite, on the banks of the River Leven, marks one end of the Lakeside & Haverthwaite Railway, although the terminal lies a little to the east of the village centre. The steam engines and carriages can be inspected in the sidings, and the village, a rather scattered place, is a good centre for walks.

Hawkshead   **I1**
4m S of Ambleside. *Pop 530. EC Thur*. Hawkshead stands at the northern end of Esthwaite Water. It is chiefly noted for being one of the prettiest villages in the Southern Lakes and the place where Wordsworth went to school. The centre of the village is jammed with tourists in the summer, when crowds flock to see the timber-framed Jacobean buildings in the village centre. St Michael's Church dates back to the mid 15thC as does the Old Courthouse. Wordsworth lodged in the village with Ann Tyson and attended the old grammar school by the church, where visitors can still inspect a desk with his name carved upon it. The best way to reach Hawkshead is across Lake Windermere by ferry from Bowness, but the queues in the summer months can be very long.

Kendal   **M2**
8m E of Windermere. *Pop 23,000. EC Thur. MD Wed, Sat*. Kendal is a busy, bustling market town, hellish to drive in until you get used to the one-way system. It has a long history, dating back to Roman times, and existing historic relics include the castle, built at the end of the 11thC by William Rufus, and notable as the place where Henry VIII's sixth wife, Catherine Parr, was born; the castle is now in ruins but there are fine views over the town from Castle Hill. In the Middle Ages Kendal flourished in the wool and cloth trade and the period endowed the town with some splendid churches – Holy Trinity by the river is one of the largest parish churches in England with a nave only a little narrower than that of York Minster, and full of good tombs and brasses.

Abbot Hall, an 18thC building now houses an art gallery, and the Hall stables contain a very fine Museum of Lakeland Life and Industry. The Museum of Natural History is well worth a visit, as is the Castle Dairy, a 16thC building which is

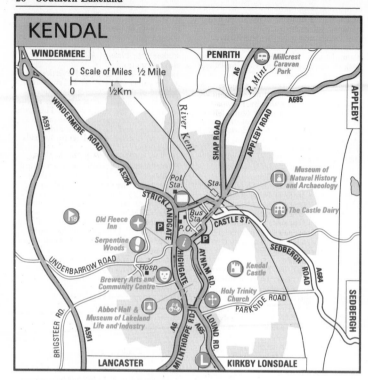

KENDAL

WINDERMERE

PENRITH

Millcrest Caravan Park

Scale of Miles ½ Mile
0
0   ½Km

WINDERMERE ROAD

A591

A5284

River Kent

SHAP ROAD

APPLEBY ROAD

A6

A685

R. Mint

APPLEBY

SEDBERGH

Museum of Natural History and Archaeology

Pol. Sta.

Sta.

STRICKLANDGATE

The Castle Dairy

Old Fleece Inn

Bus Sta.

P.O.

CASTLE ST.

Serpentine Woods

HIGHGATE

AYNAM RD.

Kendal Castle

SEDBERGH ROAD

A684

UNDERBARROW ROAD

Hosp.

Brewery Arts and Community Centre

Holy Trinity Church

PARKSIDE ROAD

LOUND RD.

Abbot Hall & Museum of Lakeland Life and Industry

BRIGSTER RD.

A591

A6

MILNTHORPE RD.

A65

LANCASTER

KIRKBY LONSDALE

now a restaurant. The Old Brewery in Highgate contains an Art Centre and the Townhall contains a tourist information centre where all visitors should stop to pick up details of walks around the town. The town has plenty of interesting architecture and is built in a series of squares or 'yards' of which Dr Marney's Yard and the Old Shambles, once the butchers' quarter, are the most interesting. The town has a number of good pubs, notably the Old Fleece Inn in Strickland Gate, or the Woolpack, but is not too well off for good restaurants, except for the Riverside Restaurant, where a huge bow window looks out over the river. Kendal is one of the liveliest towns of the Lake District, and although a place which clearly benefits from tourism, it is not over-touristic and has a life and style all its own.

Lindale   **J6**
1m N of Grange-over-Sands. A little north of Morecambe Bay, Lindale lies on the very edge of the National Park. In the centre visitors can see the Wilkinson Monument, a cast-iron memorial to a local iron craftsman, who so loved his trade that he was buried in a cast-iron coffin.

Millom   **D6**
8m S of Broughton-in-Furness. *EC Wed.* Small town set on the Duddon Channel opposite Furness. Millom was once an iron-working centre. Millom Castle, a 13thC castle 1m to the north, is half in ruins and half a farmhouse. The town has a tourist information centre and an excellent Folk Museum illustrating the local mining industry.

Milnthorpe   **L5**
7½m S of Kendal. *EC Thur. MD Fri.* A village best visited on market day when it

really comes alive. Local sights include the Manor House at nearby Preston Patrick, and the cornmill at Beethan which still grinds flour.

Natland M3

2m S of Kendal. Pretty village, where old whitewashed houses cluster round a church and village green. It is a fine setting for a good deal of modern development. There are walks along the canal towpath, and pony trekking out to the gentle fells nearby.

Newby Bridge I4

7m S of Bowness-on-Windermere. Newby Bridge is barely a hamlet, but it has several fine hotels and inns, notably the Swan, and it is also the railhead for the Lakeside & Haverthwaite Railway, a picturesque 3½m line. A good centre for walking, cruising the lakes or touring about.

View of Newby Bridge

Ravenglass B1

Perched on the western coast, Ravenglass lies on the estuary formed by the rivers Esk and Mite, and has been a port since Roman times. Today it is little more than a small village, the houses lining the street up to the little harbour by the foreshore. But it is well worth visiting for it has some unique attractions – notably the 12ft high walls of the Roman fort at Walls, Muncaster Castle, home of the Pennington family since the 13thC, which has marvellous gardens, and the Ravenglass & Eskdale Railway, built in 1875 to bring iron ore to the port and now a popular 7m tourist route. There is also a Railway Museum. Tourists may visit parts of the controversial atomic power station at nearby Sellafield (or Windscale). The Pennington Arms is the most interesting and historic pub in the main street, and serves good food. Full information on Ravenglass from the Tourist Information Centre's Mobile Unit,

Ravenglass & Eskdale Railway Station, Tel Ravenglass (065 77) 278.

The Sawreys I2

2m W of Bowness (by ferry). The Sawreys – Far Sawrey and Near Sawrey – are little hamlets on the road

Beatrix Potter's house

from the ferry to Hawkshead. They are famous because Beatrix Potter lived here and wrote her tales of Peter Rabbit, Jemima Puddleduck, Tom Kitten and the rest, at Hill Top Farm at Near Sawrey. The house is now owned by the National Trust and is open to the public from Easter till the end of Oct.

Silecroft C5

1m NW of Millom. Silecroft lies on the south coast of Cumbria, just inside the Park boundary, close to Black Combe. There is a good sand and shingle bathing beach and many sheltered spots for picnics.

Ulpha E2

5m NW of Broughton-in-Furness. Ulpha is a little place, barely a hamlet but it lies in a beautiful setting, overlooked by a small church.

Ulverston G6

3½m S of Penny Bridge. *Pop 12,000. EC Wed. MD Thur, Sat.* The most unusual, or at least the most unexpected thing about Ulverston is the discovery that this is the UK centre for the Laurel & Hardy cult, mainly because Stan Laurel, the downtrodden one of the duo, was born here on 16 June 1890. There is a 'Stan Laurel' pub, and a small Laurel & Hardy Museum in Upper Brook St. That apart, modern Ulverston is a rather dull little town with confusing narrow streets, but a good Saturday market. The other famous local was Sir John Barrow, who founded the Royal Geographical Society, and George Fox, founder of the Quaker sect in the 17thC, who lived at Swarthmoor Hall, which still belongs to the Society of Friends.

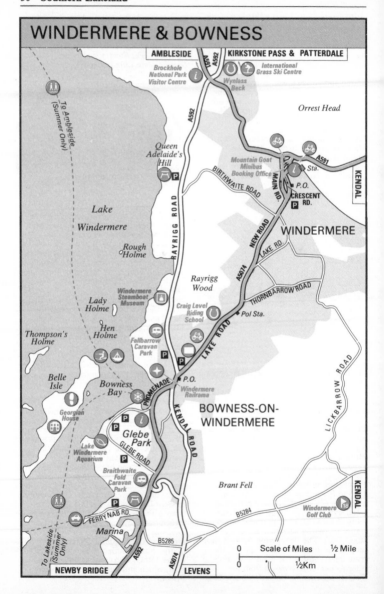

WINDERMERE & BOWNESS

AMBLESIDE

KIRKSTONE PASS & PATTERDALE

Brockhole
National Park
Visitor Centre

Wynlass
Beck

International
Grass Ski Centre

To Ambleside
(Summer Only)

Orrest Head

A591

KENDAL

Queen
Adelaide's
Hill

A552

Mountain Goat
Minibus
Booking Office

Sta.

P.O.

CRESCENT
RD.

BIRTHWAITE ROAD

MAIN RD.

Lake
Windermere

RAYRIGG ROAD

WINDERMERE

Rough
Holme

NEW ROAD

LAKE RD.

Rayrigg
Wood

A5074

Windermere
Steamboat
Museum

THORNBARROW ROAD

Lady
Holme

Craig Level
Riding
School

Pol Sta.

LAKE ROAD

Hen
Holme

Thompson's
Holme

Fallbarrow
Caravan
Park

P.O.

Windermere
Railrama

Belle
Isle

Bowness
Bay

PROMENADE

BOWNESS-ON-
WINDERMERE

LICKBARROW ROAD

Georgian
House

KENDAL ROAD

Glebe
Park

Lake
Windermere
Aquarium

GLEBE ROAD

Brant Fell

KENDAL

Braithwaite
Fold
Caravan
Park

Windermere
Golf Club

B5284

FERRY NAB RD.

Marina

A592

B5285

A5074

Scale of Miles
0   ½ Mile

0   ½Km

To Lakeside
(Summer Only)

NEWBY BRIDGE

LEVENS

Windermere and Bowness-on-Windermere   **J1**

8m W of Kendal. *Pop (with Bowness) 8500. EC Thur*. Windermere and Bowness were once separate places, the one on the hill, the other by the lake, but they have now grown together so that it is hard to say where one ends and the other begins. Both combine to form the most popular and most visited town of the region, the one place which everybody visits, which means it has plenty of hotels, cafes, bars, excursions, shops – and crowds.

Bowness is the older, a medieval lakeside village built around St Martin's Church; Windermere came later and was originally called Birthwaite. The railway was the making, or the ruin, of Windermere, for it brought both the trippers and the wealthy industrialists who built their country houses around the shore. Visitors today will find plenty to do in and around Windermere and Bowness; good shopping, excursions by boat or Mountain Goat minibus, the Steamboat Museum, Belle Isle out in the lake, and the Beatrix Potter country on the far shore. The National Park Centre at Brockhole lies 2m to the north.

Places of interest

Barrow-in-Furness   **E8**

Furness Abbey
1m N of Barrow-in-Furness on road to Dalton. Tel Barrow (0229) 23420. The ruins of this once famous abbey lie in a beautiful green and lush valley, and are, all things considered, in excellent preservation. The buildings now belong to the Department of the Environment. *Open 15 Mar—15 Oct, Mon–Sat 09.30–18.30. 16 Oct–14 Mar, Mon–Sat 09.30–16.00, Sun 14.00–16.00.* **Charge**.

The Furness Museum
Ramsden Sq. Tel Barrow (0229) 20600. In the same building as the library, an interesting local museum illustrating life and history in the Furness peninsula, with a bird collection, various historic exhibits, a model ship collection and various prehistoric implements and weapons. *Open Mon–Wed & Fri 19.00–17.00, Thur 10.00–13.00, Sat 10.00–16.00. Closed Nat hols.* **Free**.

Beetham   **L6**

The Heron Corn Mill
Tel Milnthorpe (04482) 3363. This much restored but still working flour mill dates back to the Middle Ages and can be reached along a footpath from the car park at Beetham. *Open 1 Apr–30 Sep Tue–Sun, Nat hols 11.00–12.30, 14.00–17.00.* **Charge**.

Heron Corn Mill

Broughton-in-Furness   **E4**

The Jack Hadwin Motorcycle Collection
Old Town Hall, The Square. Tel Coniston (09664) 494. Opened only in 1981, this unique local museum contains a large collection of post-vintage and post-war motorcycles.

Burton-in-Kendal   **M7**

Dalton Deserted Village
¾m S of Burton-in-Kendal. This abandoned medieval village is the first example of its type in the country and especially interesting to history lovers. It lies in a field to the left of the private road to Dalton Old Hall. *Open 6–14 Apr, 25 May–29 Sep, Mon–Wed, Fri & Sat 10.00–17.00, Thur 10.00–16.30, Sun 13.00–17.00.* **Charge**.

Cartmel   **I6**

Cartmel Priory Church
This magnificent medieval church dates from the late 14th and 15thC, with fine choir stalls, a huge East window, and a 17thC rood screen. Often called the 'Cathedral of the Lakes', it is a splendid example of an English Gothic church and well worth a diversion. *Open at all times, services permitting, 1 Jan–30 Mar 08.00–15.30, 31 Mar–27 Oct 08.00–17.30, 28 Oct–31 Dec 08.00–15.30.*

Note also the medieval gatehouse, which with the church is all that remains of the Priory destroyed by the commissioners of Henry VIII. Key obtainable from the Manager of the Priory Hotel in return for a small deposit – contributions towards upkeep welcome. *Gatehouse open Apr–Xmas.*

1658 Gallery
Grammar School Rd. Tel Cartmel
(044854) 392. This original art gallery, set
in a 17thC 'cruck' barn, contains a
remarkable collection of huge and
intricate wood sculptures by the artist-
proprietor. *Open daily and by request.*
Charge.

Coniston   **G1**
Brantwood House
Brantwood. 3m E of Coniston. Tel
Coniston (09664) 396 or 263. This was
John Ruskin's home and he lived here for
nearly 30 years. The house contains much
Ruskin memorabilia, including his art
collection and personal possessions. *Open
Mar–Nov daily 11.00–17.30. Nov–Mar
11.00–13.00.* **Charge.**

John Ruskin's home at Brantwood

The Gondola Steam Launch
Far End. Tel Coniston (09664) 41288.
Now owned by the National Trust, this
well-restored craft makes regular cruises
taking visitors on Coniston Water during
the summer months and is open to view at
other times. *Open 4 Apr–24 May, 9 Sep–
13 Oct daily 12.45–17.00. 25 May–8 Sep,
Sun–Fri 11.15–17.00, Sat 12.45–17.00.*
Charge.
Ruskin Museum
Yewdale Rd. Tel Coniston (09664) 359.
This is just a museum and not Ruskin's
home, but it contains many interesting
items relating to Ruskin, Coniston and
the nearby lakes and fells. *Open 31 Mar–31
Oct daily 09.30–dusk.* **Charge.**

Dalton-in-Furness   **F7**
Tytup Hall
1m N of Dalton-in-Furness off A590. Tel
Dalton-in-Furness (0229) 62929. A small

17th–18thC manor house with original
interior panelling and very fine gardens.
Visits by appointment only, so phone ahead
as it is well worth the effort.

Finsthwaite   **I4**
Stott Park Bobbin Mill
1¼m NW of Newby Bridge. Tel Newby
Bridge (0448) 31087. Restored 19thC
bobbin mill with working machinery, a
good place for those interested in
industrial archaeology. *Open 1 Apr–30 Sep
Mon–Sat 09.30–18.30, Sun 14.00–18.30.*
Charge.

Graythwaite Hall & Gardens   **I3**
3m N of Newby Bridge. Tel Newby
Bridge (0448) 31248. This fine private
house is only open in the early summer,
mainly to display the marvellous garden
containing rhododendrons, azaleas and
shrubs. *Open 1 Apr–30 Jun, daily
10.00–18.00.* **Charge.**

Haverthwaite   **H5**
Lakeside Railway Museum
Haverthwaite Railway Station. Tel Newby
Bridge (0448) 31594. A small but
interesting collection of steam and diesel
locomotives and carriages. Steam trains
run daily in summer on the Lakeside &
Haverthwaite Railway. *Open summer only.*
Charge.

Hawkshead   **I1**
The Courthouse
Now a National Trust property, this 15thC
building is all that remains of the medieval
Hawkshead Manor. Key to view available
from National Trust Centre in
Hawkshead or *open daily 1 Apr–31 Oct
10.00–17.30.* **Charge.**
Grammar School
This school dates from 1585 and is noted
as the setting of Wordsworth's
schooldays. See the main classroom, the
exhibition room and the library; also a
desk with Wordsworth's name. *Open 5
Apr–31 Oct, Mon, Tue, Thur, Sat
10.00–17.00, Sun 12.30–17.00.*

Holker   **I6**
Holker Hall
Cark-in-Cartmel, Grange-over-Sands. Tel
Flookburgh (044853) 328. This Victorian
mansion is surrounded by fine floral
gardens, noted for rhododendrons, and
the grounds contain a deer park and a
motor museum. Well worth a family visit.
Open 7 Apr–27 Oct Sun–Fri 10.30–18.00.
Charge.

Holker Hall

Lakeland Motor Museum
Holker Hall, Cark-in-Cartmel, Grange-over-Sands. Tel Flookburgh (044853) 509. This interesting collection, which includes a fully-fitted replica of a pre-World War II garage, contains a varied selection of cars, motorcycles, tricycles and bicycles. *Open 7 Apr–27 Oct Sun–Fri 10.30–17.30.* **Charge.**

Kendal   **M2**

Abbot Hall
Tel Kendal (0539) 22464. This Georgian building contains a fine display of Lakeland industries in the Museum of Lakeland Life and Industry, which occupies the old stable block and won the Museum of the Year Award in 1973. There is also a good collection of 18thC furniture, porcelain, glass and silver in the house itself. *Open Mon–Fri 10.30–17.30, Sat & Sun 14.00–17.00. Closed two weeks at Xmas & Good Fri.* **Charge.**

Castle Dairy
26 Wildman St. Tel Kendal (0539) 21170. This medieval building, the oldest stone-built house in Cumbria, was once the dairy for Kendal Castle. It is now a restaurant but the older parts can be visited on *Wed afternoons only throughout the summer, 14.00–16.00.* Exhibits include a hand-carved four-poster bed. **Charge.**

Kendal Castle
Only the ruins remain of this 12thC castle which was once the home of Catherine

Parr, sixth wife of Henry VIII. Set in a public park to the east of the town centre.

Kendal Museum of Natural History & Archaeology
Station Rd. Tel Kendal (0539) 21374. A rather unusual and very fine museum to find in such a town, with displays of African big game, Egyptology and Prehistoric man, as well as the expected local life and history. Well worth an extended family visit. *Open all year Mon–Fri 10.30–17.00, Sat 14.00–17.00. Closed two weeks at Xmas & Good Fri.* **Charge.**

Levens   **L4**

Levens Hall
2m S of Sedgwick. Tel Sedgwick (0448) 60321. Levens Hall is noted for the topiary garden first laid out in 1675. The Hall was built in the 12thC as a pele tower and was converted to the present mansion in the 16thC. The interior is very fine, with good furniture, plasterwork and porcelain. More modern attractions include a collection of model steam engines as well as full-sized versions which are fired up on summer Sundays. *Open 7 Apr–29 Sep, Sun–Thur 11.00–17.00. Steam Collection open 14.00–17.00.* **Charge.**

Levens Hall

Millom   **D6**

Millom Folk Museum
St Georges Rd. Tel Millom (0657) 2555. This is a museum of industrial archaeology, with a miner's cottage, a blacksmith's forge and the reconstruction of an old drift iron mine. *Open 6–14 Apr, 25 May–14 Sep, Tue–Sat 10.00–17.00, Sun–Mon 14.00–17.00.* **Charge.**

Near Sawrey   **I1**

Hill Top Farm
2m SE of Hawkshead. Tel Hawkshead

(09666) 269. This famous little farm where Beatrix Potter wrote her books is now in the hands of the National Trust. The contents are very much as she left them and there is still no electric lighting inside the cottage. Many of the original drawings for her books are on display. The cottage is not large, so be prepared to queue for admission during the summer months. *Open Apr–Oct, Mon–Sat 10.00–17.30, Sun 14.00–17.00. Closed Fri & Good Fri.* **Charge.**

Piel Castle F10

Situated by the headland off Roa Island. A rather spectacular ruin set on a small offshore island. Piel Castle was built to defend Furness Abbey and is a typical motte and bailey fortification. Visits by boat from Roa Island. *Open Easter–Sep.* **Charge.**

Ravenglass B1

Muncaster Castle
Tel Ravenglass (06577) 614. Built round a 14thC pele tower, the garden of the medieval Muncaster Castle can boast the finest display of rhododendrons in Europe, splendid views of the Esk Valley, while the castle has a fine interior which contains furniture from the 16th and 17thC. *Open spring and summer months only 5 Apr–29 Sep Tue–Sun.* Grounds 12.00–17.00. House 13.50–16.30. **Charge.**

Muncaster Mill
Ravenglass. Tel Ravenglass (06577) 232. A working water mill on the A595, now fully restored and producing fine stone-ground flour from restored Victorian machinery. Open to visitors in summer months only; the complete tour takes 45 mins. *Open Apr, May, Sep, Sun–Fri 11.00–17.00. Jun, Jul, Aug, Sun–Fri 10.00–18.00.* **Charge.**

Ravenglass Railway Museum
Station Yd. Tel Ravenglass (06577) 226/7. This little museum contains displays of trains and railway equipment, illustrating the history of the Ravenglass & Eskdale Railway. Called 'The Ratty' locally and still in operation, it is a narrow gauge track running for seven miles from Ravenglass to Dalegarth. *Open 30 Mar–3 Nov 9.00–17.00.* **Charge.**

Rusland H3

Rusland Hall
3m NW of Newby Bridge. Tel Satterthwaite (022984) 276. This Georgian manor contains an exhibition of

vintage photographic equipment, a steam car and mechanical musical instruments. *Open 20 Apr–30 Sep Mon–Sat 11.00–17.30.* **Charge.**

Sizergh Castle L3

4m S of Kendal. Tel Sedgwick (0448) 60285. This castle was built in the 14thC as a simple pele tower. The Great Hall was added a 100 years later and other buildings followed in succeeding centuries to create the present castle which now belongs to the National Trust. The interior contains fine furniture and the gardens are beautiful, especially in the spring. *Open Apr–Oct Mon, Wed, Thur, Sun & Nat hols 14.00–17.45. Last entry 17.15. Closed Good Fri.* **Charge.**

Sizergh Castle

Swinside D3

Swinside Stone Circle
1¾m W of Duddon Bridge. A large stone circle of 95 stones set beside Swinside Fell, north of Thwaite Mill.

Ulverston G6

Conishead Priory
Priory Rd. Tel Ulverston (0229) 54029. In spite of the medieval sounding name, this is a Victorian house, in the Gothic style, and now a centre for Buddhists. The interior has fine plasterwork and panelling. Attractive gardens. *Open summer only.*

Laurel & Hardy Museum
4c Upper Brook St. Tel Ulverston (0229) 52292. The world's most comprehensive collection of Laurel & Hardy memorabilia and a small 30-seat theatre showing their films. *Open Easter–end Oct 10.00–16.30. Winter by appointment only.* **Charge.**

Swarthmoor Hall
Swarthmoor, Ulverston. Tel Ulverston (0229) 53209. Elizabethan house and the birthplace of the Quakers, for George Fox lived here. Period 17thC furniture, and still used by the Society of Friends. *Visits by appointment only.*

Windermere   **J1**

Belle Isle
Lake Windermere. Tel Windermere
(09662) 3353. The largest island on
Windermere and the only one with a
permanent population. It contains the
only Georgian Round House in the
country, which contains portraits by
Romney. Belle Isle can be reached by boat
from Bowness. No dogs or very young
children. *Open summer only.* **Charge.**

Lake Windermere Aquarium
Glebe Rd, Windermere. Tel Windermere
(09662) 4585. Unique close-up display of
fascinating lake and river fish, such as
pike, perch and trout. The Aquarium
Shop has tropical shells, shell novelties,
fishing tackle and bait. *Open 1 Mar–31
Oct 10.00–18.30. 1 Nov–31 Apr Sat & Sun
10.00–17.00. Parties by arrangement.*
Charge.

Steamboat Museum
Rayrigg Rd. Tel Windermere (09662)
5565. This rare and marvellous museum
contains a collection of ancient craft and
working steamboats which used to ply on
the lakes in Victorian and Edwardian
times. *Open 1 Apr–10 Nov, Mon–Sat
10.00–17.00, Sun 14.00–17.00.* **Charge.**

Local events & attractions

Craft centres

Coniston   **G1**

The Fell Workshop
Brocklebank, Grid Tower. Tel Coniston
(09664) 449. An attractive workshop and
display centre selling pottery, sculpture
and woodwork. *Open 1 Mar–31 Oct only.*

Kendal   **M2**

Kendal Glass Engravers
177 Highgate. Tel Kendal (0539) 21883.
Beautiful engraved glasswork, produced
in the workshop or locally and displayed
in the nearby gallery.

Susan Foster
9 Windermere Rd. Tel Kendal (0539)
26494. A working craft shop with
spinning and weaving looms which
produce a wide range of clothing, bags,
rugs and shawls for sale in the shop.

Ulverston   **G6**

Cumbrian Crystal
Lightburn Rd. Tel Ulverston (0229) 5440.
Visitors can tour the glass factory between
08.00–16.00 weekdays, and then buy from
the factory shop. **Charge.**

Windermere   **J1**

Craftsmen of Cumbria
The Craft Centre, Fallbarrow Rd,
Bowness-on-Windermere. Tel
Windermere (0966) 2959. A large shop
selling a wide range of locally produced
craft goods, pottery, leather, jewellery and
stone work. A glass-engraver, potter and
leather-worker can usually be seen at their
crafts and there's the opportunity to try
your own hand at copper-rubbing and
spiral arts, too. A good place to buy
souvenirs or presents for the folks back
home. *Open Easter–Oct Mon–Sun
09.30–18.00.*

Pots & Engines
40A Main Rd, Windermere. Tel
Windermere (09662) 4849. Pottery,
stoneware and a fine collection of model
steam engines.

Stonecraft Designs
Longlands, Bowness-on-Windermere. A
range of products in Lakeland green
stone. *Workshop open 08.00–16.00.*

Fairs & country shows

Cartmel Show   **I6**
A country show with pony club events,
show jumping and competitions for the
local farmers. Held on the *second Wed in
Aug.*

Great Urswick Rushbearing   **F7**
Flowers and rushes from the nearby tarn
are carried around the village and then
laid on the floor of St Mary's and St
Michael's Church. *On Sat nearest to St
Michael's Day* (27 Sep).

Hawkshead Show   **I1**
A country show with hound trailing, show
jumping, as well as stock competitions for
the local farmers. Details from all tourist
information centres or Tel Hawkshead
(09666) 409. *First Tue in Sep.*

The Kendal Gathering   **M2**
A mixture of country fair and folk festival,
with everything from roundabouts to a
torchlight procession, brass band contests,
dances in the hotels, exhibitions – the lot.
Details from tourist information centres or
Tel Kendal (0539) 20040. *Two weeks from
late Aug to early Sep.*

Westmorland County Show   **M2**
This event, a relic from the old county of
Westmorland, now absorbed by Cumbria,
is held on the County Showground at
Kendal. It offers the complete day out,
with stock competitions, show jumping,

Westmorland and Cumbrian wrestling, and dog shows. Details from all tourist information centres. Tel Kendal (0539) 23459. *On second Thur in Sep.*

Festivals

Kendal Folk Festival   M2
More than just a music festival, this event also features displays of local crafts and competitions for folk music. Centred on the Brewery Arts Centre, Kendal, and local pubs. Details from tourist information centres. *Usually late Aug.*

Kendal Jazz Festival   M2
A must for all lovers of jazz from trad to mainstream, attracting top performers and usually held at the Brewery Arts Centre, Kendal. Details from tourist information centres. *Sep.*

The Lake District Festival
This arts festival takes place every year at theatres and public halls all over the Lake District, with main events taking place in the Kendal Leisure Centre. Full details are published well in advance, or can be obtained from tourist information centres. *Sep or early Oct.*

Flower shows

Lakeland Rose Show   I6
Holker Hall, near Cartmel. A big social event as well as a splendid flower display, plus brass bands, parachute jumping, and all the fun of the fair. *Second weekend in Jul.*

Sheepdog trials

The Lake District Trials   J1
Usually held on Applethwaite Common near Windermere. Tel Ambleside (0966) 32468. *First Tue after first Mon in Aug.*

Sports

Cartmel Races   I6
This is a National Hunt course. Details are advertised in the local press. *Races held spring and summer Nat hols weekend.*

Cumberland and Westmorland Wrestling
Visit any of the main county shows in Cumbria, and you can be fairly certain of seeing some local wrestling, an exclusively Cumbrian sport in which the competitors, clad in vests and long-johns, lock their hands behind each other's back and then attempt to break loose – the secret is all in the balance.

Fell Racing
Fell racing is a Lakeland sport designed for local people only, or the fittest cross-country runner. The idea is to race up a footpath to the top of the fell and back down to the sports field below. The fell racing at the Grasmere Show is said to be the finest in Cumbria.

Hound Trailing
A variation on fox hunting, but without the fox. The dogs and their followers chase an aniseed trail for 10 miles or more across the fells. Details on these events from tourist information centres, though you can usually find one held at any of the local shows *between Apr and Oct.*

Steam Engine Rallies   M2
Cumbria Steam Gathering on the County Showground, Kendal, with traction engines, steam cars, threshing machines, a fair and a market. Details from tourist information centres or Tel Kirkby Lonsdale (0468) 71584.
Last weekend in Jul.

Leisure & entertainment

Boat hire

Bowness-on-Windermere   J1

Bowness Bay Boating Company
The Promenade, Bowness-on-Windermere. Tel Windermere (09662) 3360. Motor boats and rowing boats.

Windermere Lake Holidays Afloat Ltd
Shepherds, Bowness Bay. Tel Windermere (09662) 3415. Motor boats, day sailers, sailing cruisers.

Coniston   G1

Coniston Boating Centre
Lake Rd. Tel Coniston (09664) 366. Motor, rowing and sailing boats.

Newby Bridge   **I4**
National Trust Fell Foot Park
Tel Newby Bridge (0448) 31273. Rowing
boats and yachts.

Car tours

**1. The West Cumbria Shore:
Kendal to Ravenglass.**
This interesting car tour wil take the
visitor along the coast and through some
of the lesser known as well as the more
popular parts of the Southern Lakes.
Leave Kendal on the minor road west for
Underbarrow (3½m) and Crosthwaite
(2½m), turning south along the River
Winster towards Witherslack (6m) before
running through more open country and
into Grange-over-Sands (8m) for views of
the vast sandy expanse of Morecambe Bay.
From here visit Cartmel to the west (2m)
to see the Priory before heading further
west onto the B5278, and turning north
for Haverthwaite (5m), and then south to
Ulverston (6m) in the Furness peninsula.
Turn west at Kirkby moor to the A595 at
Soutergate (5m) for good views to
Millom, following this road back north to
Broughton-in-Furness (5m) and Duddon
Bridge (1m). Stay on the A595 heading
south to Silecroft on the coast (6½m)
before turning north along the coast under
Black Combe for Ravenglass (12m). After
visiting the Pennington Arms return past
Muncaster Castle to Ellerbeck and take
the minor road first north-west and then
south over the fell to Ulpha (9½m) in the
Duddon Valley. Continue south through
the valley back to Broughton before
following the A593 north-east to Torver
(6½m), then taking the A5084 back south
along the western shore of Coniston Water
to Penny Bridge (7½m), from which the
A590 leads back to Lakeside (6½m).
From the Fell Foot Country Park at
Lakeside minor roads lead back across
country to Crosthwaite and so back to
Kendal (12m). *Total distance: 104½m.*
**2. A Tour to Coniston:
Tarn Hows & Windermere from
Bowness-on-Windermere.**
Leave Bowness for the south on the A592,
along the eastern edge of the lake for
Newby Bridge (7½m), and then on to
Penny Bridge (5½m) before turning
north for Coniston, first to Lowick Bridge
(3m) on the A5092, then forking right
onto a minor road to the eastern shore of
Coniston Water, and so to Ruskin's home
at Brantwood (6m). After a visit here,
press on to Coniston (2½m) and then

follow the sign-posted route to Tarn Hows
(3m); this road will be very crowded in
summer and on any fine, dry weekend.
From Tarn Hows, where there is a small
car park, return to Hawkshead (3m), then
take the road around Esthwaite Water to
see Hill Top Farm at Near Sawrey, then
back to Bowness (4m) via the ferry. Long
queues may be anticipated here in
summer. *Total distance: 34½m.*

Cinemas

Royalty Cinema
Lake Rd. Tel Windermere (09662) 3364.

Kendal   **M2**
Palladium Cinema
Sandes Av. Tel Kendal (0539) 29907.

Coach trips

Barrow-in-Furness Transport   **E8**
Hindpool Rd, Barrow-in-Furness. Tel
Barrow-in-Furness (0229) 21325. Coach
trips throughout the Lakes. **Charge.**
Mountain Goat   **J1**
Victoria St. Windermere. Tel Windermere
(09662) 5161. Mountain Goat is a
uniquely Cumbrian institution. Their
white-painted minibuses can be seen all
over the Lake District offering transport
from place to place, dropping people off
for walking excursions or collecting them
at the end of the day. **Charge.**
Post Buses
Broughton-in-Furness Post Bus; Duddon
Valley Post Bus; Grizedale Post Bus. Post
buses offer passengers a seat in the van –
or minibus – which carries and collects
the Royal Mail. Details from local post
offices. **Charge.**
Ribble Coaches & Coach Tours
Ribble run excursions from Bowness,
Ambleside, Keswick, Windermere,
Grange-over-Sands, Kendal, Ulverston.
Details can be obtained from local Ribble
bus depots, tourist information centres or
Tel Kendal (0539) 20932. **Charge.**

Cycle hire

Arnside   **K6**
South Cumbria Cycles
'Santon', Silverdale Rd. Tel Arnside
(0524) 761929.

Bowness-on-Windermere   **J1**
Rent-a-Bike
117 Craig Wlk. Tel Windermere (09662)
3270.

Kendal   **M2**
Brucie's Bike Shop
187 Highgate. Tel Kendal (0539) 27230.
Lakeland Cycles
104 Strickland Gate. Tel Kendal (0539)
23552.

Windermere   **J1**
Rentacamp Leisure House
Station Buildings. Tel Windermere
(09662) 4780.

Entertainment centres

Barrow-in-Furness   **E8**
Barrow Civic Hall
28 Duke St. Tel Barrow-in-Furness (0229)
21250. Year-round programme of
exhibitions, local shows, antique fairs,
concerts. Full details from the tourist
information centre in the same building or
the local press.

Grizedale   **H2**
Theatre in the Forest
2m SW of Hawkshead. Tel Satterthwaite
(022984) 291. Art and craft exhibitions
during the day. The theatre runs a full
evening programme of concerts, plays and
variety shows. Details from local press or
tourist information centres. *Open all year.*
Charge.

Kendal   **M2**
Brewery Arts Centre
122A Highgate. Tel Kendal (0539) 25133.
A community centre with shows and
displays of arts and crafts, and a
continuous programme of plays and
theatrical events.

Ulverston   **G6**
Renaissance Theatre Trust, The Centre
17 Fountain St. Tel Ulverston (0229)
52299. More a coffee shop and arts and
crafts centre, but also the centre for the
performing arts in South Cumbria.
Events usually held in the Civic Hall.

Fishing

Listed below are places where rods may
be hired and fishing permits obtained.

Barrow-in-Furness   **E8**
Angling & Hiking Centre
62 Forshaw St, Barrow-in-Furness. Tel
Barrow-in-Furness (0229) 29661.

Broughton-in-Furness   **E4**
The Post Office
Broughton-in-Furness. Tel Broughton
(06576) 220.

Coniston   **G1**
National Park Information Centre
1 Yewdale Rd, Coniston. Tel Coniston
(09664) 41533.
Coniston Gift & Sports Shop
Yewdale Rd, Coniston. Tel Coniston
(09664) 41412.

Grange-over-Sands   **J6**
Tourist Information Centre
Victoria Hall, Grange-over-Sands. Tel
Grange-over-Sands (04484) 4026.

Grizedale
Fern Cottage
Near Hawkshead. Tel Satterthwaite
(022984) 257.

Hawkshead   **I1**
The Post Office
Hawkshead. Tel Hawkshead (09666) 201.

Kendal   **M2**
T. Atkinson & Son
19 Stricklandgate, Kendal. Tel Kendal
(0539) 20300.
Carlson Fishing Tackle
64/66 Kirkland, Kendal. Tel Kendal
(0539) 24867.
Kendal Sports Shop
28/30 Stramongate, Kendal. Tel Kendal
(0539) 21554.

Levens   **L4**
Low Levens Farm
Levens. Tel Sedgwick (0448) 60435.

Millom   **D6**
Duddon Sports & Leisure
52 Queen's St, Millom. Tel Millom (0657)
3155.

Milnthorpe **L5**
Hart's Cabin
12 The Square, Milnthorpe. Tel
Milnthorpe (04482) 2532.

Newby Bridge **I4**
The National Trust Fell Foot Park
Newby Bridge. Tel Newby Bridge (04483)
31273.

Ravenglass **B1**
Pennington Arms Hotel
Main St, Ravenglass. Tel Ravenglass
(06577) 222.

Ulverston **G5**
Harvey Jackson
Market Pl, Ulverston. Tel Ulverston
(0229) 52247.

Windermere **J1**
The Lake Warden's Office
Ferry Nab, Windermere. Tel Windermere
(09662) 2753.
National Park Information Centre
The Glebe, Bowness-on-Windermere. Tel
Windermere (09662) 5602.
The Record & Gift Shop
Ash St, Bowness-on-Windermere. Tel
Windermere (09662) 3750.
Tourist Information Centre.
Windermere. Tel Windermere (09662)
4561.

Golf

Askham-in-Furness **E6**
Dunnerholme Golf Club
Tel Dalton-in-Furness (0229) 6275. 10
holes only. Booking advisable. Meals
available on Suns only by contacting the
treasurer, tel (0229) 63135. **Charge.**

Barrow-in-Furness **E8**
Barrow Golf Club
Rakesmoor La, Hawcoat. Tel Barrow-in-
Furness (0229) 25444. 18 holes, booking
advisable. Ladies day on Fri. Pro shop,
bar, lunches and dinner available.
Charge.

Grange-over-Sands **J6**
Grange Fell Golf Club
Fell Rd. Tel Grange-over-Sands (04484)
2536. 9 holes. Visitors welcome, bar.
Charge.
Grange-over-Sands Golf Club
Meathop Rd. Tel Grange-over-Sands
(04484) 3180. 18 holes. Visitors with a

handicap welcome, if members of a golf
club. Pro shop, bar. Meals daily except
Tue. Trolleys available. **Charge.**

Kendal **M2**
Kendal Golf Club
The Heights. Tel Kendal (0539) 24079. 18
holes, pro shop, bar. Meals available daily
except Mon by arrangement with the
steward. Clubs and trolleys for hire.
Charge.

Millom **D6**
Silecroft Golf Club
9 holes, booking advisable. No visitors on
Nat hols, Sat, Sun or Mon. Bar. **Charge.**

Ulverston **G6**
Ulverston Golf Club
Bardsea Pk. Tel Ulverston (0229) 52824.
18 holes, shop, bar. Meals daily except
Mon. Trolleys available. **Charge.**

Walney Island **D9**
Furness Golf Club
Tel Barrow (0229) 41232. 18 holes,
booking advisable, shop, bar. Bar meals
available or full meals by arrangement with
the steward. **Charge.**

Windermere **J1**
Windermere Golf Club
Cleabarrow, Windermere. Tel
Windermere (09662) 3132. 18 holes,
shop, bar, meals available. Trolleys and
clubs for hire. **Charge.**

Grass skiing

Windermere **J1**
International Grass Ski Centre
Limefit Pk. Tel Ambleside (09663) 2564.
Equipment and instruction available. Ski
lift. *Open summer only 10.00–dusk.*
Charge.

Lake cruises

Coniston **G1**
Steam Yacht Gondola
The Pier. Tel Coniston (09664) 288. First
launched in 1859 and recently restored by
the National Trust, the elegant Gondola
steam launch offers a fine way to see and
enjoy Coniston Water and the views to the
high fells set around the shore. Cruises
Sun–Fri. Operates from Good Fri–late Oct.
Charge.

Lakeside   I4
Sealink Windermere
Tel Newby Bridge (0448) 31539. An ideal
way to get about on Lake Windermere is
by these Sealink ferries. Full details of
sailing times are posted at all tourist
information centres and by the shore.
Operates Easter, then end Apr–Oct.
Charge.

Windermere   J1
Bowness Bay Boating Company
Bowness Bay. Tel Windermere (09662)
3360. Launch cruises around
Windermere on the 'Miss Cumbria'.
Available in two directions, north and
south, the complete cruise lasts three
hours. *Operates 15 May–end Sep.* **Charge.**
Steam Launch Trips
Windermere Steamboat Museum, Rayrigg
Rd. Tel Windermere (09662) 5565. Trips
on some of the museum's unique collection
of steam launches – 'The Lady Elizabeth',
'The Osprey' – for up to 40 minutes,
subject to weather. *Operates Apr–Oct.*
Charge.

Leisure centre
Kendal   M2
South Lakeland Leisure Centre
Burton Rd. Tel Kendal (0539) 29777.
Squash, badminton, swimming, sports
and fitness training available. **Charge.**

Riding & pony trekking
Backbarrow   I4
Bigland Hall Riding Centre
1m SW of Newby Bridge. Tel Newby
Bridge (04483) 31728. Instruction,
trekking and hacking. Indoor school.
Minimum age 6 years for instruction, 7
years for hacking. Hats provided. *Open all
year.* **Charge.**

Bardsea   G7
Well House Farm Riding Establishment
Well House Farm. Tel Bardsea (022988)
278. Instruction, hacking and trekking.
Minimum age 5 years. Hats provided.
Open all year. **Charge.**

Barrow-in-Furness   E8
Park Road Riding Stables
Schneider Rd. Tel Barrow-in-Furness
(0229) 22006. Hacking and pony
trekking. Adults catered for, hats
provided, no experience necessary. *Open
all year.* **Charge.**

Bootle   B3
Beckside Farm
Tel Bootle (06578) 736/695/694. Trekking
only, hats provided. Minimum age 4
years. *Open Easter–Oct.* **Charge.**

Cartmel   I6
Birkby Cottage
Tel Cartmel (044854) 319. Instruction and
hacking available for all ages. *Open all
year.* **Charge.**

Coniston   G1
Spoon Hall Stables
Tel Coniston (09664) 41391. Trekking
only for ages from 10 years old. No
experience necessary. Hats provided.
Charge.

Dalton-in-Furness   F7
Greenscoe Riding Centre
Greenscoe Quarry. Tel Barrow-in-Furness
(0229) 26307. Trekking and hacking for
which some experience is required. Ages
5 plus for instruction, 10 plus for hacking.
Hats provided. *Open all year.* **Charge.**

Grange-over-Sands   J6
Guides Farm
Cart La. Tel Grange-over-Sands (04484)
2163. Trekking and hacking, with some
experience required for hacking. Ages 6
plus. Hats provided. *Open Easter–end
Sep.* **Charge.**

Holme   M6
Elmsfield Park Equestrian Centre
2m SE of Milnthorpe. Tel Milnthorpe
(0448) 2891. For instruction and
experienced riders. Indoor school. *Open
all year.* **Charge.**

Natland   M3
Larkrigg Stables
Tel Sedgwick (0448) 60245. Instruction
and hacking. Minimum age 5 years. Some
experience required for hacking. Hats
provided. *Open all year.* **Charge.**

Staveley   K1
Park Hall Riding Centre
Tel Staveley (0539) 821200. Instruction
and hacking. All-weather arena available.
Minimum age 4 years for instruction, 6 for
hacking. *Open all year.* **Charge.**

Ulverston   G6
Ghyll Farm Riding Stables
Pennington, Ulverston. Tel Ulverston
(0229) 6312. Instruction and hacking.

Minimum age 5 years. Hats provided. *Open all year.* **Charge.**

Windermere   J1
Craig Level Riding School
Lake Rd. Tel Windermere (09662) 3572. Trekking, hacking and instruction. Minimum age 5 years, beginners welcome. Hats provided. *Open all year.* **Charge.**
Limefill Park.
Tel Ambleside (0966) 32300. Trekking, no experience necessary. Minimum age 10 years. Hats provided. *Open Easter–end Oct.* **Charge.**
Wynlass Beck Stables
Tel Windermere (09662) 3811. Instruction, hacking and trekking. All ages welcome, no experience required. Hats provided. *Open all year.* **Charge.**

Swimming

A number of hotels also have pools open to residents or diners. Contact tourist information centres for details.

Barrow-in-Furness   E8
Abbey Baths
Abbey Rd. Tel Barrow-in-Furness (0229) 20706. Indoor pools, solarium, sauna and keep fit area, refreshments. Ring first for opening times to the public. *Open all year.* **Charge.**

Grange-over-Sands   J6
Grange-over-Sands Pool
Tel Grange-over-Sands (04484) 305. Outdoor pool, with car parking available. *Open summer only.* **Charge.**

Kendal   M2
South Lakeland Leisure Centre
Burton Rd. Tel Kendal (0539) 29777. Indoor pool as part of the leisure/sports complex. Also sauna, bar, cafeteria. Parking available. *Open all year.* **Charge.**

Ulverston   G6
Indoor Pool
Priory Rd. Tel Ulverston (0229) 54110. Heated indoor pool with viewing area. *Open all year.* **Charge.**

Train trips

Haverthwaite   H5
Lakeside & Haverthwaite Railway Company
Haverthwaite Station. Tel Newby Bridge (0448) 31594. A short three-and-a-half-mile journey by steam train between Haverthwaite and Lakeside. Can be linked with Sealink ferries on Lake Windermere to make a round trip. *Operates Easter, then Mon–Sun 21 Apr–6 Oct.* **Charge.**

Ravenglass   B1
The Ravenglass & Eskdale Railway
Ravenglass Railway Station. Tel Ravenglass (06577) 226. A seven-mile

steam train journey on the popular 'Ratty' to or from Ravenglass and Eskdale is an essential family excursion on any visit to the Southern Lakes. Operates *Mon–Sun 30 Mar–end Oct; curtailed service in winter.* Ring first for details. **Charge.**

Walks

1. Devoke Water   D1
Devoke Water serves as the reservoir for Millom. Commence the walk at the old schoolhouse by Dalegarth Station on the road over the river to Dalegarth Hall. After passing the Hall the road climbs through Low Ground Farm and High Ground Farm and then arrives at a crossroads. Cross over the road and continue along a fell road to Devoke Water. Continue along the fell side on the right of the lake until the head is reached. Cross the beck at the point where it leaves the lake and follow the footpath down to the left of Linbeck Ghyll to join the road in the valley. Turn right at the farm and follow the road back to the George IV Hotel. Continue beyond the hotel for ¼m to the station. From the station there is a frequent train service to Boot. *Total distance: 6m.*

2. Esthwaite Water   I1
Commence the walk at Near Sawrey from Hill Top Farm, where Beatrix Potter wrote many of her books. This is now

owned by the National Trust and is open to the public. After a visit here, take the road by the side of Esthwaite Water to Hawkshead, where Wordsworth was educated. Continue along the road towards Coniston, taking the righthand fork at Hawkshead Hall, now a Folk Museum. Within a short distance the road forks right again along a lane. Take the second lane on the right to Crag and continue along the footpath which starts on the left and crosses to Belle Grange on the shores of Windermere. Follow the shore road down the lake back towards the ferry and cross by ferry to Far Sawrey, returning along the road to Near Sawrey. This is an easy walk, part of it running through a marked Nature Walk. *Total distance: 10m.*

3. Old Man of Coniston   G1

Commence the walk at the Black Bull Hotel by the road signposted to the YHA. Follow the course of the Church Beck for over a mile to the Copper Mines. The old mineworkings are currently the subject of a restoration programme, details of which can be inspected by the YHA building. From the hostel keep left and follow the well-marked track to Low Water. The footpath from Low Water bears left beneath the Old Man, then ascends sharply to the top. The view from the top is spectacular, taking in Coniston Lake and to the south, Morecambe Bay. To the north and east on a fine day Scafell, Skiddaw, Helvellyn and many other principal fells can be seen. To return to Coniston there is a choice. Either bear

due south by Cove Quarries to join the Walna Scar road, or descend to Goats Water to the west for more magnificent views. A footpath from the tarn follows the course of the beck and joins the Walna Scar road; turn left along this road for Coniston. This is a fairly strenuous walk and should not be attempted in poor weather conditions. The mists can descend very quickly, and good footwear is essential. *Total distance: 6m.*

4. Tarn Hows   H1

This is an artificial lake, which takes its name from that of a nearby farm. The walk commences at Coniston village and follows the footpath round the head of the lake. Take the first road on the left signposted Hawkshead for ¼m to the foot of a hill. Follow the narrow road on the left for a few yards only, then take the bridle track on the right leading up to Tarn Hows. The shores of the lake are wooded and in the background are the Langdale Pikes, the Fairfield Fells, and Wansfell. Follow the road round to the right for a short distance and cross a stone wall up a small fell for marvellous views of Coniston Water and the fells. A track round the east side of the lake joins the road from Borwick Lodge into Oxenfell main road, but a more pleasant route is to return to the tarn from the viewpoint, continue round the foot to the dam, then descend down Glen Mary by Tom Gill, and cross the latter halfway down where there is a footbridge. The main road lies at the bottom. Turn left along the road and look for the first farm on the right, where there is a footpath by the gateway signposted Coniston. The footpath continues through fields before joining the road just outside Coniston. *Total distance (with diversions): 5m.* There is also a bus service from Tom Gill to Coniston. This is an easy walk but can be muddy in wet weather.

5. Tilberthwaite Ghyll   G1

From Coniston take the road towards Tilberthwaite (1½m). There is a bus service to Tilberthwaite but the footpath is good and leads through woods to the left of the road. Join the main road at Tilberthwaite and then take the smaller road on the left (west) for 1½m. Look for the second footpath on the left, leaving the road and ascending past slate quarries. This then descends to cross the beck, known as Tilberthwaite Ghyll, by a footbridge. To reach the top, climb up the bank on the right until a well-defined path is reached, leading along the fell side, above the Ghyll. Continue along this path to a footbridge over the falls. Return by the same path to Tilberthwaite Cottages and back to the main road. There is a bus service back to Coniston or you can retrace the walk through the woods. *Total distance: Tilberthwaite Cottages to Tilberthwaite Ghyll 4m.* This walk is fairly easy, but can be muddy in wet weather.

6. Windermere to Ings   J1

The walk commences opposite Windermere railway station, where there is a signposted footpath by the bus stop leading to the top of Orrest Head. Towards the top of the Head a path leads off to the left towards Causey Farm. Turn right to follow the lane to Ings, where there is a church. Look round the church and take the lane over the River Gowan to Ings Hall. Continue under the railway and then turn right to Hag End. Cross the

common to a lane on the right past Droomer Farm. This lane leads back to Windermere Station. A very easy walk. *Total distance: 6½m.*

Eating & drinking

Bardsea   G7

Ye Olde Mill

Coast Rd, Bardsea, near Ulverston. Tel Bardsea (022988) 262. An attractive, licensed restaurant built around an old corn mill. Morning coffees, lunch snacks, afternoon teas and high teas. Features a special children's menu and a proper roast beef lunch on Sunday. *Open end May–mid Sep Tue–Sun to 18.00.* **££**.

Barrow-in-Furness   E8

Ambassador Restaurant

Dalton Rd. Tel Barrow-in-Furness (0229) 23823. This first-floor coffee lounge and restaurant, with delightful Georgian decor, serves good scones, sandwiches, a wide range of snacks, morning coffee and afternoon tea (the tea itself is especially recommended). English cooking in the restaurant proper, where in the evening you can choose from either a five-course table d'hôte menu or go à la carte. Set menu and à la carte at lunch too. *Open all year LD Mon–Sat. Coffee lounge open 10.00–17.00. Closed Sun & Nat hols.* Dc.V. **£–££**.

Broughton-in-Furness   E4

Beswicks Eating House

The Square, Broughton-in-Furness. Tel Broughton (06576) 285. Useful little restaurant right in the centre, with local food and children's portions. Offers game as a speciality, and vegetarian dishes too. Set price menu. *Open all year D only Tue–Sun.* **£**.

High Cross Inn

On A595, Broughton-in-Furness. Tel Broughton (06576) 272. An attractive pub just on the northern end of the village, with fine views over the Duddon Valley. Bar meals, home cooking and a huge Sunday lunch. Children welcome. *Open all year LD Mon–Sun during normal licensing hours.* **£**.

Cark-in-Cartmel   I6

The Engine Inn

Cark-in-Cartmel. Tel Flookburgh (044853) 589. Pleasant local pub which dates back to 1689. Bar menu available

during licensing hours. A comprehensive choice of English dishes and home cooking in the restaurant, where the prices are moderate and the service speedy. *Pub open all year. Restaurant open Easter–Oct LD Mon–Sun.* **££.**

The Rose & Crown
Cark-in-Cartmel. Tel Flookburgh (044853) 501. Country inn with whitewashed walls, open fireplaces and plenty of brass. Near Holker Hall and a mile or so from Cartmel Priory. Good food including pâtés, soups, gammon, chicken and fish and an excellent wine list. *Open all year LD Mon–Sun during normal licensing hours.* **£.**

Cafe at Coniston Boating Centre
Tel (0966) 41366. If the village centre is crowded, as it usually is in season, a short walk will take you to this pleasant little cafe by the shore. Light meals and snacks. *Open Mar–end Oct Mon–Sun to 18.00.* **£.**

Crown Hotel
Coniston. Tel Coniston (0966) 41243. The Crown is one of several pub-hotels in the centre of this small village. Like the rest it caters for walkers, but has a large and most useful car park. Provides breakfast, morning coffee, bar lunches, afternoon tea, high teas and bar dinners. *Open all day end Jun–Oct Mon–Sun; Nov–May open morns & LD Mon–Sun. Closed Xmas day.* A.V. **£.**

Wild Boar Hotel
Near Windermere. Tel Windermere (09662) 5225. This attractive hotel on the B5284, close to the Windermere Golf Club, has a fine restaurant which offers wild boar daily, a rare event in England. Table d'hôte menu and à la carte menu includes quail, fish, duck and lamb. Large wine list. *Open all year LD Mon–Sun.* A.Ax. Dc.V. **££–£££.**

At Home Restaurant
Danum House, Main St. Tel Grange-over-Sands (04484) 4400. Small cellar restaurant where you can have anything from an open sandwich to a three-course meal. Fish features strongly on the menu with mussels, prawns, Morecambe Bay shrimps, tuna and smoked salmon, alongside the more regular chicken and meat dishes. *Open LD Tue–Sat. Closed Sun, Mon, two weeks end Nov & mid Jan–mid Feb.* A. **£–££.**

Ormandy Restaurant
Tel Hawkshead (09666) 532. Quiet and secluded restaurant-cum-guest house in the middle of Grizedale forest which offers good solid food in pleasant surroundings. Venison is the house speciality; try the game pie with local fresh vegetables. *Open D Thur–Tue. Closed Jan & Feb.* **££.**

Kings Arms
Village Centre, Hawkshead. Tel Hawkshead (09666) 372. Country pub set on the square in the heart of this attractive village and close to all the sights. Traditional bar snacks during licensing hours. French and English cuisine in the restaurant. Specialities include steaks, pheasant, home-made stews and pies. Eating on the terrace if the weather is fine. Take-away service available. *Open all year LD Mon–Sun.* **£.**

Castle Dairy
26 Wildman St, Kendal. Tel Kendal (0539) 21170. A seven-course all inclusive meal is served in this small, popular restaurant, housed in the oldest inhabited building in Westmorland. Two wings date back to the 12thC and the centre part is Elizabethan. Game and local specialities such as Windermere char are highlights of the menu. Booking is essential. *Open all year D only from 20.00 Wed–Sat.* **££.**

The Moon Restaurant
129 Highgate, Kendal. Tel Kendal (0539) 29254. Charming, cosy and informal bistro-style restaurant in the centre of town. Varied continental menu and a good selection of vegetarian dishes. *Open all year L Tue–Sat, D Mon–Sun.* **££.**

Nutters
Yard 11, Stramon Gate. Tel Kendal (0539) 25135. This coffee shop offers scones, snacks, steak and kidney pie, salads and sandwiches. *Open all year Mon–Sat 09.30–19.00. Closed Sun.* **£.**

The Old Fleece Inn
Highgate. Tel Kendal (0539) 20163. This old pub has no rooms for accommodation but offers a range of fast food, burgers, pizzas, steaks, children's meals, in the first-floor Lofts Diner Restaurant. *Open all year LD Mon–Sun. Closed D Sun & Nov–Easter* A. V. **£.**

Riverside Restaurant
Stramongate Bridge, Kendal. Tel Kendal (0539) 24707. Situated on the Bridge

overlooking the River Kent, a two-tier restaurant with much to offer all tastes and pockets. On the ground floor, there's The Buttery for morning coffee, lunch, afternoon teas and evening meals. The food is moderately priced and includes pies, roast of the day, quiches, steaks and farmhouse grills. *Open all year 10.00–22.00 Mon–Sun.* **£.**
Upstairs, an elegant and relaxing French à la carte restaurant with an expensive wine list including four house wines and 51 bins. Also has table d'hôte menus at lunchtime and in the evening. *Open all year LD Mon–Sun.* **££–£££.**

The Woolpack Hotel & Restaurant
Stricklandgate. Tel Kendal (0539) 23852. This ancient hotel, in what was once the local auction rooms, offers English cooking in the restaurant, with roasts, soups and a good sweet trolley. Snacks and bar lunches in the Crown Bar, and a range of snacks in the coffee shop. *Open all year LD Mon–Sun. Closed Nat hol Mons.* A. Ax. Dc. V. **££.**

Lindale   J6

The Lindale Inn
Near Grange-over-Sands. Tel Grange-over-Sands (04484) 2416. In a small, attractive village this 17thC coaching inn offers bar meals and claims to serve the best 'steaks in the Lakes'. Children welcome. *Open all year LD Mon–Sun during normal licensing hours.* **£.**

Little Chef
Kendal Rd, Lindale. Tel Grange-over-Sands (04484) 2605. A handy spot to find one of these small, clean, fast-food restaurants. *Open all year Mon–Sun. Closed Xmas day.* **£.**

Newby Bridge   I4

The Fellfoot Cafe
Fellfoot Pk. Tel Newby Bridge (0448) 31273. A small but useful cafe, just the place to relax in after seeing the National Trust property or walking down the lake shore. Soups, hot and cold snacks, salads, coffees and teas. *Open 10.30–17.30.* **£.**

Ravenglass   B1

Pennington Arms Hotel
Main St, Ravenglass. Tel Ravenglass (06577) 222. This 17thC inn is recommended for good, wholesome English breakfasts, morning coffee, lunch, cream teas and supper – in fact, the works. An all-English menu. *Open all year LD Mon–Sun.* **£.**

Staveley   K1

Little Chef
Main Rd. Staveley. Tel Staveley (0539) 821543. Set beside a filling station, this useful roadside restaurant is ideal for feeding the children or a quick snack. The Early Starter breakfast is excellent value. *Open all year Mon–Sun to 22.00. Closed Xmas day.* **£.**

Staveley House Restaurant
Windermere Rd, Staveley. Tel Staveley (0539) 821292. On the B5284 between Crook and Windermere, this attractive, whitewashed restaurant occupies a building which was once a barn. Essentially English cooking with a table d'hôte menu and an à la carte menu. Good, fresh food and a respectable wine list. The home-made desserts are the house speciality. Traditional roast lunch on Sunday. *Open LD Wed–Mon. Closed Jan.* **££.**

Windermere & Bowness-on-Windermere   J1

Odana Cafe
14 Church St, Windermere. Tel Windermere (09662) 2894. A useful place to know about, opening at 07.30 for breakfast, then for sandwiches, snacks, fast food and take-aways. Reasonable prices. *Open Easter–Oct Mon–Sun to 19.00; Nov–Easter Thur–Tue.* **£.**

Hedge Row Restaurant
Greenbank, Lake Rd, Bowness-on-Windermere. Tel Windermere (09662) 5002. Vegetarian restaurants are quite common in Lakeland, but this is one of the best and offers morning coffee, lunch, afternoon tea and dinner. The menu includes avocado dishes, bean casseroles, lasagne, crumbles and salads. *Open end May–end Sep LD Mon–Sun; closed Tue & Wed Oct–Apr, Xmas & 1 Jan.* A.V. **£.**

Miller Howe Hotel Restaurant
Rayrigg Rd. Tel Windermere (09662) 2536. A very stylish restaurant on two floors which offers a five-course menu of English country house cooking using fresh local produce. A very wide range of desserts. *Open Mar–Dec D Mon–Sun. Sun–Fri D at 20.00, Sat D at 19.00 & 21.00. Closed Jan–Mar.* A.Ax.Dc. **£££.**

Porthole Eating House
Ash St, Bowness-on-Windermere. Tel Windermere (09662) 2793. The Porthole offers a mixture of Italian and French provincial cooking and such local delicacies as freshly caught char from Lake Windermere, but the chief attraction is

the wide and varied wine list, including a vast number of German vintages. The building dates from the 18thC. *Open D only Wed–Mon. Closed mid Dec–mid Feb.* A.Ax.Dc.V. **££.**

Rogers
4 High St, Windermere. Tel Windermere (09662) 4954. The menu changes daily in this small family-run restaurant. Only fresh ingredients are used in the predominantly French menu with some English dishes, cooked by the proprietor. Good service, adequate wine list. Booking is essential. *Open Apr–Oct LD Mon–Sat; Nov–Mar D only Tue–Sat.* A.Ax.Dc.V. **£££.**

Toby Jug Restaurant
Victoria St, Windermere. Tel Windermere (09662) 3429. Inexpensive cafe-restaurant in the centre of Windermere, offering home cooking and children's portions. Everything from three-course lunches to sandwiches, fry-ups and substantial steak dinners. *Open Easter–Nov LD; Nov–Mar L only. Closed Xmas day & New Yr.* **£.**

Camping & caravanning

Ayside J5
Oakhead Caravan Park
Ayside, Newby Bridge, Nr Ulverston, Cumbria. Tel Newby Bridge (0448) 31475. 2m SE of Newby Bridge, the Oakhead Caravan Park caters equally for campers and caravanners with 30 pitches for each. Good simple facilities, showers, lights, telephone. Shops nearby. *Open Mar–Oct.* **£.**

Bouth H4
Black Beck Caravan Site
Bouth, Nr Ulverston, Cumbria. Tel Greenodd (022986) 274. Just over 2m W of Newby Bridge, NE of Ulverston. A touring site with 45 caravan and 12 tent pitches, it has a shop, showers, children's play area and drying rooms. *Open Mar–Oct.* **££.**

Coniston G1
Coniston Hall Campsite
Coniston, Cumbria LA21 8AS. Tel Coniston (0966) 41223. 1m S of the village, entrance off A593 road. This is a large site with 150 tent pitches and simple facilities; hot showers, a shop. Designed for walkers, climbers and sailors. *Open Apr–Oct.* **£.**

Park Coppice Caravan Site
Coniston, Cumbria. Tel Coniston (0966) 41555. 1½m S of Coniston. This large, fully equipped Caravan Club site has 300 tent or caravan pitches available, but it is best to book any time between Easter and September. Facilities include boating, children's playground, showers and telephones. *Open Apr–Oct.* **£.**

Endmoor M5
Gatebeck Caravan Park
Endmoor, Kendal, Cumbria. Tel Crooklands (04487) 425. Set beside the A65, 5m S of Kendal. This caravan-only site has 30 pitches, a shop, flush toilets, hot showers, children's playground, washing and ironing facilities. *Open Mar–Oct.* **££.**

Flookburgh I7
Lakeland Caravan Park
Moor La, Flookburgh, Grange-over-Sands, Cumbria. Tel Flookburgh (044853) 235. 4m SW of Grange-over-Sands. A pleasant site with 95 caravan and 30 tent pitches for hire as well as static holiday caravans and chalets for rent. On-base facilities include showers, shop, bar, TV room, swimming pool, fish and chip shop. *Open Mar–Oct.* **££.**

Haverigg D6
Butterflowers Holiday Homes
Haverigg, Millom, Cumbria. Tel Millom (0657) 2880. 1m S of Millom. Large, well-balanced camp site with space for 80 static vans, 60 tourers and 50 tents. All modern facilities available including shop, children's play area, riding and swimming close by, washing and ironing room. *Open all year.* **££.**

Hawkshead I1
Croft Caravan & Camp Site
North Lonsdale Rd, Hawkshead, Cumbria. Tel Hawkshead (09966) 374. Lying just on the outskirts of the village, this simple site is more for tents (72 pitches) than caravans (3 pitches). Power points, showers and adequate parking available. *Open Mar–Oct.* **£.**

Kendal M2
Millcrest Caravan Park
Skelsmergh, Kendal, Cumbria. Tel Kendal (0539) 21075. 1m NE of the town. This is for touring caravans only, with simple facilities, children's swings and sand pit, hot showers, telephones. *Open Apr–Oct.* **£.**

Meathop K5

Meathop Caravan Park
Highwood, Meathop, Grange-over-Sands, Cumbria. Tel Grange-over-Sands (04484) 3596. This large site has 85 touring caravan pitches and 40 tent pitches, plus a full range of basic on-site facilities, hot water, showers, electricity, swings, shops in village. *Open Apr–Oct.* **££.**

Newby Bridge I4

Newby Bridge Caravans
Canny Hill, Newby Bridge, Ulverston, Cumbria. Tel Cleveleys (0253) 855989. A small site with 12 static vans and pitches for 15 touring caravans. No tent pitches. Basic facilities, showers, electricity. *Open Apr–Oct.* **£.**

Ravenglass B1

Walls Caravan Park
Ravenglass, Cumbria. Tel Ravenglass (06577) 250. On the outskirts of the village, this site has space for 50 vans, and a full range of basic facilities, hot water and showers, electricity, drying rooms. Shops nearby. *Open Apr–Oct.* **£.**

Staveley K1

Ashes Lane Caravan & Camping Park
Staveley, Nr Kendal, Cumbria. Tel Staveley (0539) 821119. 5m E of Windermere on the A591. This very large site has 100 pitches for touring caravans, and 200 tent pitches. A popular site, it fills up early, and pre-booking is therefore essential. Every facility available including TV room, shop, bar, restaurant, washing and drying room. *Open Mar–Nov.* **££.**

Windermere J1

Braithwaite Fold Caravan Site
Glebe Rd. Bowness-on-Windermere,

Cumbria. Tel Windermere (09662) 2177. A Caravan Club site with 60 touring caravan pitches only, close to the lake. Simple facilities, shops nearby. *Open Apr–Oct.* **££.**

Fallbarrow Caravan Park
Rayrigg Rd, Bowness-on-Windermere, Cumbria. Tel Windermere (09662) 4428. An excellent site close to the town centre yet with every facility; music, TV, restaurant, bar, shop, laundry room. 80 touring caravan pitches. No tents. *Open Mar–Oct* **££.**

Youth hostels

There are plenty of youth hostels in the Lake District, but they tend to get very full in the summer when the walkers and cyclists arrive. Pre-booking is therefore essential, and all reservations should be confirmed in writing. Opening times may vary slightly from year to year, so it is always advisable to check in advance of arrival.

Coniston G1

Coniston Youth Hostel
Holly How, Far End, Coniston, Cumbria LA21 8DD. Tel Coniston (0966) 41323. Superior grade youth hostel with shop and evening meals available at *19.00.* 70 beds. Car parking. *Closed 5 weeks before or after Xmas (alternates each year).*

Coniston Coppermines Youth Hostel
Coppermines House, Coniston, Cumbria LA21 8HP. Tel Coniston (0966) 41261. Simple grade hostel, one mile outside Coniston village on track to Coniston Old Man. Small store in hostel. Evening meal available *19.00.* 33 beds. Parking in village. *Closed 6 weeks before or after Xmas (alternates each year).*

Esthwaite Water I1

Hawkshead Youth Hostel
Esthwaite Lodge, Hawkshead, Ambleside, Cumbria LA22 0QD. Tel Hawkshead (09666) 293. 1m S of Hawkshead. Standard grade youth hostel in Regency style building overlooking the lake. Evening meal available *19.00,* including vegetarian meals. 78 beds. Car parking available. *Closed 5 weeks before or after Xmas (alternates each year).*

THE
CENTRAL FELLS

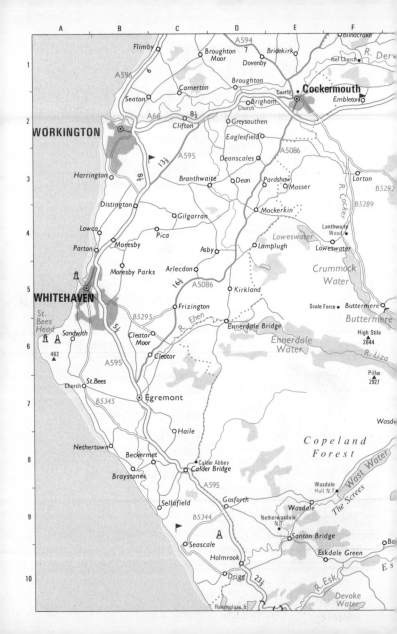

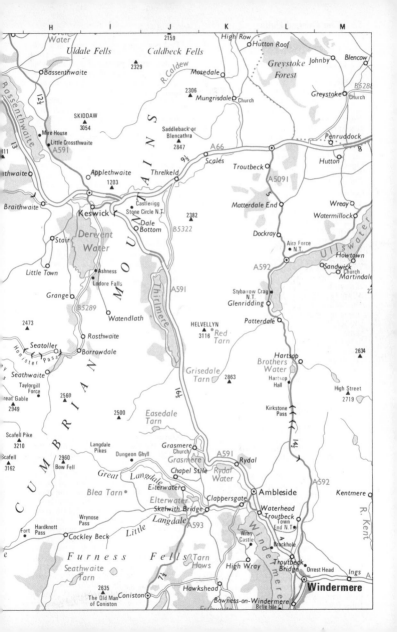

Tourist information centres

Ambleside   **K9**
Old Courthouse, Church St. Tel (0966)
32582. Operates local bed-booking
service. Access for disabled. *Open
Easter–Oct.*

Cockermouth   **E2**
Riverside Car Park. Market St. Tel (0900)
822634. Operates local bed-booking
service. *Open Easter–Oct.*

Egremont   **B7**
Lowes Court Gallery, 12 Main St. Tel
(0946) 8206993. Operates local bed-
booking service. *Open all year.*

Glenridding   **L5**
Main Car Park. Tel (08532) 414. Operates
local bed-booking service. *Open
Easter–Oct.*

Grasmere   **J8**
Red Bank Rd. Tel (09665) 245.
Operates local bed-booking service
and 'Book-a-bed-ahead' accommodation
service. *Open Easter–Oct.*

Keswick   **I4**
Moot Hall, Market Sq. Tel (0596) 72645.
Operates local bed-booking service and
'Book-a-bed-ahead' accommodation
service. Access for disabled. *Open all
year.*

Whitehaven   **A5**
Market Pl. Tel (0946) 5678. Operates local
bed-booking service and 'Book-a-bed-
ahead' accommodation service. Access for
disabled. *Open all year.*

The Countryside

This part of Cumbria, which runs east
from the extreme western promontory of
St Bees Head, across the central fells to
Patterdale and the eastern slopes of Shap
Fell – the countryside that people think of when the
word Lakeland conjures up an image in
the mind's eye. The main physical feature
is the presence of the Cumbrian
Mountains, which run north across
Eskdale up to Scafell Pike, at 3206ft and
on, dividing the lakes of Wast Water,
Ennerdale, Crummock Water, Buttermere
and Derwent Water on the west, from
Thirlmere and Ullswater to the east, up to
Blencartha (2847ft) and High Peak
(2158ft), which overlooks Nether Row and
the village of Caldbeck, famous as the
birth and burial place of the huntsman
John Peel.

This is a region of high peaks and fells, of
hidden valleys, of small lakes and tarns,
of steep-sided passes, of rock and wind
and sky. It is a paradise for climbers and
hillwalkers who have been coming here for
generations and can rightly claim the
central fells as their kind of country. The
map is littered with names which are
never far from the lips of the walking and
climbing community; Skiddaw (3054ft),
Helvellyn (3116ft), Scafell, Striding Edge,
the Langdale Pikes, Watendlath, Red
Tarn, Borrowdale and a score more, each
a mecca for lovers of the outdoors and
therefore routes all too prone to steady
erosion from the constant passing of
countless boots.

As with the country to the south, this
central region has a narrow, fertile coastal
strip, running ever wider to the north
under the high loom of the bare fells,
from Ravenglass to Cockermouth. It is a
region which contains all that remains of
Cumbria's mining and industrial past,
when coal and iron ore were major
contributors to the local economy. From
this coastal strip, great valleys probe up
into and through the fells, some of them
offering good, if steep routes and passes
across the Cumbrian Mountains to the
eastern slopes of the fells; the Hardknott
Pass and Wrynose Pass, east of Eskdale,
and the Honister Pass, south of Derwent
Water, are the most famous and most used
of these old routes. They are impressive
places where the steep, bracken-clad
slopes sweep down to the narrow ribbon
of the road, and few parts of the Lake
District are more lovely or more desolate.
If this dramatic mixture of high fells,
ribbon-like lakes and deep passes is the
general, overall picture of the area, the
countryside does change quite perceptibly
as the traveller ventures north and east.
The change begins placidly enough, on the
level coastline south of St Bees Head, a
place now best known for the presence of

the nuclear power station at Seascale, once better known as Windscale. Heading inland from here the countryside rises gently for a while, until suddenly it soars by Wast Water and above Eskdale before falling again into Ennerdale Water in its deep, half-hidden valley to the north, leaping over Red Pike and Gale Fell to Crummock Water and so east, up and over to Thirlmere and Helvellyn. Littered among these high crags, or tucked away in the top ends of the valley lie other, smaller lakes and tarns; Blea Tarn above Eskdale is a favourite walker's destination, as is Grisedale Tarn north of Grasmere, or Red Tarn cupped by Striding Edge. This may be the popular part of the Lake District for walkers but, in such a wild and jumbled country, those who want to avoid their fellows and the too well-beaten track will have no trouble in finding a footpath where no one else has passed for a week or more.

Apart from the walkers and climbers, who will pick a place to wander off the map, most visitors to this part of the Lake District will enter the region by heading north from Windermere and electing either for the road through Troutbeck, which leads over the steep Kirkstone Pass to Patterdale and Ullswater, or turning off for Grasmere and Wordsworth country. They then have the option of turning off east at Ambleside and heading west across the fells on the old Roman road that leads over the Wrynose and Hardknott passes into Eskdale. Keswick is the main town of these central fells, the focus of many roads.

The reality of the central fells is that it is a wilderness, a place to wander about in on foot, by cycle or car. There are few towns, and the villages tend to be small, scattered hamlets rather than commuter conurbations. The charm of the area lies, as always, in the stark beauty of the landscape, in the sudden views of lake and fell. The hills are now much higher

and more striking than those found further to the south. You could wander here for days or weeks and never see it all, and this is, therefore, a part of Lakeland which draws the visitor back year after year and retains its attractions long after the better-known and more popular Lakeland places like Windermere have been discarded.

Visitors to the central fells should be prepared to leave their cars and tourist coaches and take to those footpaths which lead up the crags and overlook the valleys. On those open, windswept tops, the Lakeland visitor will discover an enchanted land, the like of which exists nowhere else in Britain, and one well worth the hard tramp it often takes to achieve it.

Country parks & nature trails

Buttermere Guided Walk   G5
Buttermere. This short trail begins at the car park close to the village centre and leads through the village and along the lake shore.

Dodd Wood Forest Trail   H2
A short walk that begins at the Mire House car park 3m N of Keswick on the A591 (between Keswick and Bassenthwaite), and offers good views over Bassenthwaite and to Skiddaw and the other peaks of the northern Lake District.

Lake District National Park   L9
Visitors' Centre & Nature Trail
Brockhole. 2m S of Ambleside. Tel Windermere (09662) 2231. Any visitor to the Lake District would be well advised to stop at the Visitors' Centre at Brockhole on the A591 on the shores of Lake Windermere between Windermere and Ambleside. There are gardens, an exhibition centre, a cafeteria and a Beatrix Potter exhibition, apart from nature displays and lectures; also a lakeshore walk. *Open daily 10.00–dusk from late Mar–early Nov.* **Charge.**

Loughrigg Fell Nature Walk   K9
A short two-and-a-half-mile fell walk from the Bridge House, Ambleside, offering marvellous views over Rydal Water and Windermere. *Open all year.*

Mire House Woodland   H2
& Lakeside Walk
Mire House Park offers several walks, but this one of about two miles begins at the car park and leads up beside Bassenthwaite Lake, with a detour to the church of St Bega. Leaflet available.

Nether Wasdale Nature Trail   E9
This walk of three-and-a-half miles begins at the south end of Wast Water, under The Screes, and displays the bird and plant life of this most beautiful of Lake District valleys, which contains the deepest lake in Britain.

Nine Becks Walk   E6
This is a fairly long, nine-mile walk through Ennerdale Forest, along trails and forest footpaths, beginning at Bowness Knott on the north side of Ennerdale Water. Leaflet available from all local TICs and Visitors' Centres. Dogs, if taken, must be kept on a leash, especially during the lambing season of early spring.

St Bees Nature Reserve   A5
1m N of the village of St Bees. Reached by a signposted public footpath along the clifftops at St Bees Head. The cliffs are a breeding ground for seabirds, including puffins and fulmers. *Open all year.*

Smithy Beck Nature Trail   E6
This short, three-mile walk also begins at Bowness Knott and runs along the north shore of Ennerdale Water and into the forest on a waymarked footpath.

Stanley Ghyll Nature Trail   F10
This two-mile waymarked ramble begins at Dalegarth by the eastern terminus of the Ravenglass & Eskdale Railway, and leads the visitor across some very beautiful and varied countryside.

Swirls Forest Trail   J6
This walk begins at the car park halfway down the eastern shore of Thirlmere, just below Helvellyn, and although only three-quarters of a mile long, it displays local flora and the forestry work of the region.

Whinlatter Forest Trail   G3
The route can be shortened or extended by incorporating other foothpaths, but the waymarked length is around one-and-a-half miles, and begins at the Whinlatter Visitors' Centre, 2m W of Braithwaite. A map is available from the Centre.

White Moss Common Nature Walk   K8
A short, low-level, woodland walk of only three-quarters of a mile, perfect in the late spring when the bluebells are out. The walk begins at White Moss Common, ½m S of Grasmere.

Lakes & tarns

Bassenthwaite Lake   G2
Lying east of Cockermouth, this is one of the largest and shallowest lakes in the Lake District; indeed, it is the only true lake, for all the others are either meres (as in Windermere), or waters (as in Ullswater). Bassenthwaite is only 70ft deep at most, but is four miles long and up to three-quarters of a mile wide. Apart from the A66 road which curves along the western shoreline, Bassenthwaite is relatively unspoiled and as such is a popular spot with birdwatchers. It is best viewed either early in the morning, when the mist is rising, or in the evening, when the waters often look very still and eerie. Tennyson had Bassenthwaite in mind when he wrote 'The Idylls of the King', and if the lady's arm bearing Excalibur should still rise from these mysterious waters, it wouldn't be at all surprising!

Blea Tarn   J8
There are three Blea Tarns, but *the* Blea Tarn lies in the Langdales, and is easily reached on foot or down the minor road which runs south off the B5343 from the Old Dungeon Ghyll Hotel. There are walks around the tarn from the cattle grid, and the views from the road or footpath are marvellous.

Brothers Water   L6
Brothers Water lies at Hartsop, just to the south of Ullswater and is best viewed when descending the Kirkstone Pass on the A592. It is rather more of a tarn than a proper lake, but the setting is remarkable.

Buttermere   G6
A small lake just over a mile long and just under a mile wide, Buttermere is a little gem, and one rightly owned by the National Trust. You can walk right round it in a couple of hours from the car park by the road at Gatesgarth or from Buttermere village, but the views all about are quite exceptional so any choice is bound to be good. The view south-east across the lake towards Hay Stacks and High Crag is very dramatic.

Crummock Water   F5
Crummock Water looks as if it might be part of the smaller Buttermere which lies just half-a-mile away to the south-east. They were probably one lake at some time in the distant past, but both are beautiful when seen from the neck of land in the middle, by the village of Buttermere. Crummock Water is a small lake, two-and-a-half miles long, only half-a-mile wide and, like Buttermere, is now owned by the National Trust. The lake setting, surrounded by steep-sided fells is very attractive and one which no visitor should miss.

Derwent Water   I4
Just south of Keswick, Derwent Water has been rightly described as the 'Queen of

the Lakes' and it looks it. Wide, blue and beautifully set, surrounded by woods and crags, this lake and the countryside around is best seen by cruising on one of the launches which ply about the shores from Keswick in summer. One of the islands on the lake only appears every few years or so, and is actually a kind of wandering swamp, a mixture of weeds and branches, thrown up from time to time by marsh gas; hence its name of Floating Island. Derwent Water is fairly shallow, at only 72ft, and therefore freezes over during hard winters, a fact which attracts skaters by the score.

Easedale Tarn J8

A little lake in the Easedale Valley and the objective of a short and popular walk up from Grasmere, along Sour Milk Ghyll – a favourite excursion for visitors on a warm summer day. The path begins near Goody Bridge in Grasmere village.

Ennerdale Water E6

Ennerdale is actually a reservoir but you would hardly notice the fact, for the dam is small and the lake itself is set in some of the wildest Lakeland country. There are no roads around the shore, so visitors have to walk in from Ennerdale Bridge or Beckfoot on the north-west corner of the lake. The facilities hereabouts are minimal or non-existent, no pubs, no cafes. This makes Ennerdale Water the place to go to avoid the summer crowds thronging the more popular lakes to the east.

Elterwater J9

A very little lake, only half-a-mile long, lying between Skelwith Bridge and Elterwater village just off the little B5343 road which runs up into the Langdales. Set there it provides the perfect foreground for photographers taking views of the Langdale Pikes which lie in the fells to the west.

Grasmere K8

No Lakeland visitor can really miss Grasmere, for it lies beside the A591 en route from Rydale to Dove Cottage and since it is, in fact, a very pretty lake, it is well worth a long look. Grasmere is quite a small lake, surrounded by wooded fells and frequently infested with tourists. The central island, where the Wordsworths used to picnic, is now owned by the National Trust.

Grisedale Tarn K7

Grisedale Tarn lies to the south of Dollywaggon Pike, which is itself to the south of Helvellyn. Grisedale is one of the largest of the tarns and set in the splendid scenery of the Grisedale valley. The footpath which runs from the A591 south of Grisedale up Grisedale to the tarn is only for fit and well-shod walkers.

Loweswater E4

Small, remote, quiet, shallow, not spectacular or well known, but still well worth a visit. It lies NW of Crummock Water and was probably once linked to Crummock Water and Buttermere. There is a car park near Waterend on the north-western edge and from here a footpath runs right round the lake through Holme Wood on the south shore; a four-mile circular walk which would make a fine morning excursion.

Red Tarn K6

Red Tarn has a spectacular setting on the eastern slopes of Helvellyn, a spot cupped by Striding Edge. Red Tarn beck flows out of the tarn into Ullswater by Glenridding.

Rydal Water K8

Rydal Water and Grasmere are practically side by side. Rydal is very small and since this whole area is a tourist centre, it is best

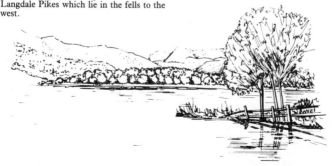

seen out of season or early in the morning during the summer months, preferably from somewhere near Nab Cottage on the A591.

Thirlmere   J5

Lying beside the A591, under Helvellyn, Thirlmere is actually a reservoir formed from two small tarns, and is best viewed from the minor eastern road, rather than the A591.

Ullswater   M4

A long, thin lake, running sinuously north and east from Glenridding for seven-and-a-half miles up to Pooley Bridge, which lies outside this section. It is one of the most attractive of the lakes, and has somehow managed to remain so even though it is also very popular with trippers. The southern end has the finest and most dramatic scenery. All the views from the lake to the fells, or looking down on the lake from the surrounding hills, are never less than splendid. In summer the lake is a great centre for watersports, and it is also possible to cruise down the lake on steamers.

Wast Water   F8

To the north of Eskdale, Wast Water has long been a favourite place for walkers and climbers, who gather to swap lies in the bar of the Wasdale Head Inn. The lake, only three miles long but very beautiful, is set off by the apparently sheer walls of The Screes, which soar up for 2000ft along the south-eastern shoreline. Wast Water is surrounded by great walking and climbing country and lies close to Scafell Pike, Great Gable, Wasdale Fell, Kirk Fell, and a vast expanse of empty country which runs from the northern tip of the lake, all the way east to Buttermere, Thirlmere and the Langdales. A minor road skirts the north-western shore up to the Wasdale Head Inn, and this route offers good views of The Screes and Great Gable, set in the notch of fells to the north.

Mountains

All the major mountains of the Lake District fall within this section, including the tallest mountain in England, Scafell Pike (3206ft), Scafell itself, Helvellyn and finally Skiddaw, from which the red glare of a beacon once woke the burghers of Carlisle. All are open to walkers and climbers, who flock to the tops by the thousand, but is worth remembering that given the vagaries of the Lakeland weather, any walker should have

hillwalking experience, check the weather, and be well equipped before setting out to 'bag' one of these peaks.

Bow Fell   H8

(2960ft). The Langdales is a wild and attractive place and one good walk, which is not too testing, runs from the National Trust car park in Langdale up Mickleden to Angle Tarn and Bow Fell, which lies to the south.

Hay Stacks   G6

(1750ft). Hay Stacks lies to the SE of Buttermere, above Gatesgarth, and is best reached from Honister. From the top there are marvellous views over Buttermere and the Ennerdale Valley to the south.

Helvellyn   K6

(3118ft). The best route up Helvellyn runs from Glenridding on Ullswater, past Red Tarn and out eventually onto Striding Edge. The narrow path along Striding Edge was once a perfectly viable footpath, but the constant erosion by passing boots has made it something of a scramble and a place to go carefully, especially if there is ice about. There is an alternative and less 'airy' track a few feet below. Tradition has it that serious walkers will welcome the dawn of Midsummer's Day on the top of Helvellyn, and many still manage to do so.

Scafell Pike   G8

(3210ft). Scafell Pike, the highest mountain in England, is not a difficult mountain to scale if the weather stays kind, but it is a long, hard slog to the summit. The shortest, steepest route is from Wasdale Head, the most picturesque from Seathwaite via Sty Head Tarn. Scafell itself is a separate summit, slightly to the south and slightly lower than the Pike.

Skiddaw   I2

(3054ft). The ascent of Skiddaw from Keswick is one of the easiest and most popular of Lakeland walks and why not? It's the views which most people are after and from the top of Skiddaw you can see for miles – or yards if the clouds come down. The route up from Keswick is signposted up Jenkin Hill, but waymarking is hardly necessary; just follow the crowds.

Dales & passes

These central fells are full of dales and passes, too many to list in full, but the finest or most popular are as follows:

Borrowdale   H6

Borrowdale lies to the south of Derwent Water and since it lies on the road that runs over to Buttermere, it gets more than its share of tourist traffic. The first part, between Grange Fell and Castle Crag further south, is known as the 'Jaws of Borrowdale', and here the valley narrows to a slender pass. Most people will stop on this pass to inspect the Bowder Stone, a huge, isolated rock.

Eskdale   **G10**
Running inland from Ravenglass up to the Hardknott Pass, Eskdale is a long, wild and beautiful valley. The road and the 'Ratty' railway display some of it, but the best way to see more is on foot from Dalegarth up to another Blea Tarn, or on to the village of Boot and into the fells.

Hardknott Pass   **H9**
(1291ft). The Romans built the first road over Hardknott when Ravenglass was one of their major ports, and there are still the remains of a Roman fort in the pass just above Eskdale. Even today, it is not an easy road, a low-gear climb with a 1:4 gradient, sharp bends, a nasty drop when coming from the east, and insufficient passing places. Hardknott is a wild spot and best viewed from the east.

Honister Pass   **H6**
(1176ft). Honister Pass, which joins Borrowdale to Buttermere, cannot be compared with Hardknott, Wrynose or Kirkstone, but it does have a good finish in either direction and is the shortest route into the central fells from the north. Besides, from the east it leads into Buttermere, which is one of the prettiest valleys in the Lakes.

Kirkstone Pass   **L7**
The great compensation of the Kirkstone Pass, which leads from Ambleside over to Patterdale and Ullswater, is the inn at the top and the views beyond. The main A592 road which leads up from Windermere through Troutbeck is much easier but not as interesting as the minor Ambleside route, which runs onto the A592 by the Kirkstone Pass Inn.

The Langdales   **J8–9**
The Langdales, Great and Little, are delightful, each a slender valley, winding up into the hills, with streams and little tarns beside the road, then widening out suddenly to give great views across the green fields to the Langdale Pikes. Good walks lie on every side. The two valleys are linked by a road at the Old Dungeon Ghyll Hotel, and a drink at the bar there tops off any day.

Wasdale   **G8**
This is really walking country, virtually inaccessible except on foot anywhere away from the lakeshore, but it is well worth the effort if you want to get away from the summer crowds and attempt the routes around Great Gable or Black Sail Pass, or even Scafell. If the eastern lakes are crowded, try Wasdale.

Wrynose Pass   **I9**
2m NE of Cockley Beck. Wrynose Pass is, if anything, steeper and narrower than the Hardknott Pass, but if you can lift your eyes from the road, the views are worth the risk, especially to the north towards the Langdales. Just west of the actual pass, to the north of the road, stands the Three Shires Stone, which marks the meeting place of Westmorland, Cumbria and Lancashire, three counties now largely embraced by Cumbria.

Waterfalls

In Cumbria and Yorkshire a waterfall is usually known as a 'force'. The finest of these lie in the central fells and are:

Aira Force   **L4**
Set off the A5097 road on the north shore of Ullswater, 3m S of Watermillock, the force falls 70ft from under a footbridge and can be viewed from the path that runs from the car park.

Scale Force   **F5**
This force, at 172ft, the longest in Cumbria, is hard to see, for it lies in a narrow wooded gorge in a valley south of the western edge of Crummock Water, but it may be reached on foot from Buttermere village on a well-trodden footpath.

Taylorgill Force   **H7**
About 3m SW of Borrowdale, near Stockley Bridge south of Seathwaite. This is a long, 140-foot fall, best seen from the river at Stockley Bridge below, and reached on foot from Seathwaite.

Viewpoints

To pick out the best viewpoints in the central fells is an invidious task, for beauty is in the eye of the beholder and beautiful views abound hereabouts. However, some views are held to present classic Lakeland vistas and among these are the following:

Buttermere   **G6**
A view to rival Wast Water is Hay Stacks and High Crag, seen across Buttermere from any point on the B5289 south of Buttermere village.

Castle Crag, Borrowdale   **H6**
This crag, the southern 'Jaw of Borrowdale', gives good views over a wide

sweep of country to Derwent Water,
Grange Fell to the east, and down to
Rosthwaite and the River Derwent.

Crummock Water   F5
Crummock Water is the perfect setting
when seen from the car park on the
B5289, on the north shore, with the lake
in front and the high fells behind.

Loughrigg Terrace   K8
Set to the south of Grasmere, Loughrigg
Fell overhangs Rydal Water and
Grasmere, giving marvellous views over
this picturesque part of Lakeland, and the
villages below. An opposing view can be
obtained from White Moss Common on
the far shore of Grasmere.

St Bees Head   A6
Seen from the car park by the railway
station in St Bees village, this headland
soars up above the pounding waves of the
Irish Sea.

Wast Water   F8
From the small turning place just past
Wasdale Hall on the north shore of Wast
Water, there is a superb, highly
photogenic view up the lake, where Great
Gable is framed by Scafell, Kirk Fell and
High Fell, with the lake as foreground.

Visitors' centres

Brockhole National Park Centre   L9
On A591 between Windermere and
Ambleside. Tel Windermere (09662)
2331. This main centre offers a complete
insight into the National Park and
contains, apart from a permanent
exhibition, a bookshop, a cafeteria, nature
trails, and offers lake cruises and garden
tours. *Open daily 10.00–dusk, Mar–Nov.*

*Visitor's centre
Brockhole*

Lake District National Park Centre   H6
Dale Head Base, Seatoller. Tel Borrowdale
(059684) 294. Off the B5289 road, to the
south of Borrowdale, this Centre has
displays of Lakeland life, industry, flora
and fauna. *Open daily Easter–Oct.*

Whinlatter Visitors' Centre   G3
Beside the B5292 road, 2m W of
Braithwaite. Tel Braithwaite (059682)
269. A centre for the study of forestry and
local wildlife, with audio-visual displays,
films, working models, and a forest trail to
Thornthwaite. *Open daily Easter–Oct.*

The Coast

The Cumbrian coastline, west of the
central fells, begins among the sand dunes
across the estuary of the River Esk by
Ravenglass, where the land levels out
under the northern edge of Muncaster
Fell, and changes from high peak and fell
into gentle rolling farming country. The
towers and chimneys of the nuclear power
station at Seascale are the only real hint of
industry here. Doomsday thoughts apart,
it is worth remembering that this coast all
the way north through Whitehaven and
Workington contains much of the area's
industrial inheritance, in the now largely
disused iron, coal and slate industries.
The fells still butt in from the east, but
gradually the coastal plain widens as it
shifts to the north, between Egremont and
St Bees, and wider still between
Workington and Cockermouth, but always
with the watchful fells offering a
backdrop.
For most of the way the coastline itself is
flat, with a sand and shingle beach rising
gradually to the western promontory at St
Bees Head, and then continuing as a
mixture of cliffs and open sand or shingle
beaches, all the way up to Workington.
The farmland is interspersed with
stretches of moor and seamed with a
number of small rivers; the Eben, the
Keckle, the Cocker, the Marron. The
largest of these is the Derwent, which
flows out of the fells from Bassenthwaite
Lake and into the sea at Workington.

Natural features

St Bees Head   A6
This red sandstone headland, rising to
over 300ft is a nature reserve, a breeding
ground for seabirds, including guillemots
and puffins. There are magnificent views
over the Irish Sea and the Solway Firth
from the clifftops by the lighthouse. A
path leads down to the beach, and this is
the start, or finish, of a path which spans
the North of England, running over to the
North Sea coast in Yorkshire.

Towns & villages

Ambleside   **L9**
4m N of Windermere. *Pop 2560. EC Thur.
MD Wed.* Ambleside is generally
considered to be the finest touring centre
for the Southern Lakes. There is good
access from Ambleside to all the main
beauty spots of the region, and plenty of
attractive walks and excursions into the
fells and by the lakes close to the village
itself. It was once a mill town but has been
popular as a tourist centre for a 100 years
or so. Historically, the little town dates
back to Roman times when there was a
fort in what is now Borrans Field by the
lake. The most notable building in the
town today is the much photographed
Bridge House, a tiny cottage, set right on
the bridge which spans the River Rother.

Bridge House

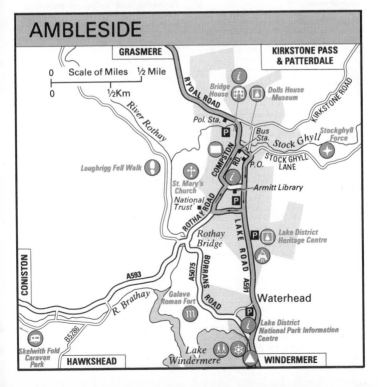

This little house was once a family home and has since been a shop, a cobbler's, even a tearoom, before it became the first information centre for the National Trust. St Mary's Church, a Victorian building, contains the Wordsworth Chapel and a fine mural depicting the annual Ambleside rushbearing ceremonies, which take place on the last Saturday in July.

Other attractions are the notable collection of books in the Armitt Library, the Dolls House Museum on Kirkside Road, and the Lake District History Centre in the town museum on Lake Road. Do not miss the splendid Stock Ghyll Force waterfall behind the Royal Yachtsman Hotel, or the Ambleside Sports in August. Such attractions and events apart, Ambleside is full of pubs, cafes and outdoor shops – and rather over full of people in the summer.

Applethwaite   **I3**
1m N of Keswick. A small village on the slopes of Skiddaw, offering marvellous views over Derwent Water. Ghyll House, built in 1867, stands on land originally given to William Wordsworth so that he could live near his fellow poet Samuel Coleridge, who lived in Keswick. Although Wordsworth never actually lived here, he wrote a poem 'At Applethwaite', immortalising the view.

Bassenthwaite   **H1**
7m NW of Keswick. Bassenthwaite village lies to the north-east of Bassenthwaite Lake on a minor road off the A591. The village surrounds a pleasant green and is a popular centre for walks along the north shore of the lake or up towards Skiddaw.

Blindcrake   **F1**
4m N of Cockermouth. Blindcrake is a small, unspoilt village just inside the National Park boundary. The chief attraction, apart from the scenery, is Isel Church, which lies two miles away, but in the same parish, on the banks of the Derwent. This church dates from Norman times, and was carefully restored in the last century. It contains carved stones bearing Viking runes.

Borrowdale   **I6**
7m S of Keswick. The villages of Borrowdale lie along the valley floor just east of the Honister Pass. The main population centres are Grange-in-Borrowdale, which is one of the prettiest villages in the Lakes, and the hamlet of Rosthwaite. In the first half of this century, Borrowdale was the home of Hugh Walpole (d.1941) who set his 'Herries Chronicles' in this area. Today

tourists flock to climb or crawl around the Bowder Stone.

Braithwaite   **H4**
2m W of Keswick. Braithwaite lies at the foot of the Whinlatter Pass, close to Noble Knott, which offers good views over Skiddaw and the Whinlatter Forest Centre.

Bridekirk   **E1**
2m N of Cockermouth. Small Lakeland village with a notable church. St Bride's (or St Bridget) has suffered from Victorian reconstruction, but the Norman-style church erected in 1870 retains elements of the original building and is attractive in its own right. The rare feature is the 12thC font, carved and signed by a medieval craftsman, Richard of Durham. This is a superb example of Early English craftsmanship, intricately carved with scenes from the Old and New Testaments, and bearing the inscription: 'Rikarth he me I wrokt and to dis mehr gernr me brokte'. Richard made me, and brought me to this glory. Such signed examples are very rare indeed.

Buttermere   **G5**
8m SW of Keswick. *Pop 255.* Lying on the neck of land on the B5289 between Buttermere and Crummock Water, Buttermere village is the perfect centre for walking and climbing in the surrounding fells, and for visiting the Scale Force waterfall on the western shore of Crummock Water. In 1802 the Fish Inn at Buttermere was the centre of the famous Lakeland 'Beauty of Buttermere' scandal, when the innkeeper's daughter, Mary Robinson, married a man who claimed to be an MP and the brother of the Earl of Hopetown, but turned out to be an imposter and, even worse, a forger. He was therefore hanged, after which Mary married again, had many children and now lies buried in Caldbeck churchyard. Today, pretty Buttermere is a walker's centre, and offers wonderful views over two lakes and many fells.

Calder Bridge   **C8**
4m SE of Egremont. The chief attraction at Calder Bridge, apart from the bridge over the Calder, is the ruins of Calder Abbey half-a-mile to the east, built in 1134 and destroyed in 1536. The ruins are in private hands and cannot be visited, but they are in plain view from the road to Priorling.

Cleator Moor   **C6**
4m S of Whitehaven. *MD Fri.* Cleator Moor was once a mining centre and since that industry declined, has become a

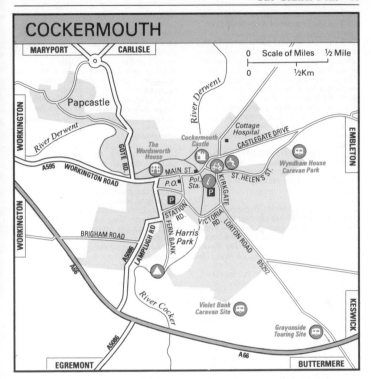

COCKERMOUTH

MARYPORT   CARLISLE

Scale of Miles   ½ Mile

Papcastle

River Derwent

WORKINGTON

River Derwent

GOTE RD.

A595   WORKINGTON ROAD

The Wordsworth House

Cockermouth Castle

Cottage Hospital

CASTLEGATE DRIVE

EMBLETON

MAIN ST.

ST. HELEN'S ST.

KIRKGATE

Wyndham House Caravan Park

P.O.

Pol. Sta.

WORKINGTON

STATION RD.

LAMPLUGH RD

FERN BANK

BRIGHAM ROAD

A5086

A66

VICTORIA RD.

LORTON ROAD

B5292

Harris Park

River Cocker

A5086

Violet Bank Caravan Site

Grayonside Touring Site

KESWICK

EGREMONT

A66

BUTTERMERE

market centre for the surrounding farms. The church has a Norman chancel and a 17thC font, while the Square, in the village centre, has a number of good country shops and cafes.

Cockermouth   **E2**
8½m E of Workington. *Pop 7000. EC Thur. MD Mon.* A rather fine and unfairly neglected little town, set on the River Derwent, where it is fed by the River Cocker. It has good shops and pleasant restaurants, and is well worth a visit. There is a late 13th but mostly 14thC castle, which is still in private hands, but the most popular attraction for visitors is Wordsworth's House, at the western end of Main Street, where the poet was born in 1770. The building is now owned by the National Trust and offers an audio-visual display and a souvenir shop. One of the town's other famous sons was

Fletcher Christian, who led the Mutiny on *The Bounty*. He was born in Moorland Close in 1764, and later attended the same school as William Wordsworth. On the River Cocker, three miles outside the

Wordsworth's birthplace

town, stands Lorton Hall, a 17thC house built on the remains of a medieval pele tower.

Cockermouth is a real Lakeland town and market centre rather than a tourist mecca, offering a great change from the summer bustle found in the more popular places. The attractive main street is lined with shops and the fells to the west provide an attractive backdrop. The Cockermouth Show, on the Saturday before the first Sunday in August, is well worth a stop, for among the other events are Cumberland wrestling and hound-trailing.

Drigg   **D10**
1m N of Ravenglass. *Pop 600.* A rather jumbled village on the coast, where the main street winds down to the dunes. The advantages are easy parking and a good sandy beach.

Eaglesfield   **D2**
2m SW of Cockermouth. Eaglesfield is just a little place but it has produced some famous sons: John Dalton, who discovered the Theory of the Atom, was born here in 1766; Fletcher Christian, of *The Bounty*, was born at nearby Moorland Close in 1764; and Robert of Eaglesfield, founder of Queens College, Oxford, is yet another local personage. He died in 1349.

Egremont   **B7**
6m S of Whitehaven. *EC Wed. MD Fri.* Egremont is a small, pleasant town, a little off the normal tourist route. Its most striking feature is the extremely wide main street, the site of an open market in days gone by. The biggest draw, however, is the ruins of Egremont Castle over the River Eben, built by the Normans, fought over during the wars with the Scots, rebuilt in the 12thC, and then falling into ruins in the 16thC, although enough remains to make an interesting visit. Wordsworth tells the story of the Egremont Horn, an instrument which could only be blown by that Lacy who was the true Lord of Egremont. The Egremont Crab Fair, held each September, dates back to the 13thC, and the crabs in question are crab apples. Apart from shows, displays and a procession, events held during the Fair include a 'gurning' or face-pulling competition.

Elterwater   **J9**
5m SW of Grasmere. Elterwater is just a hamlet on the B5343 road which leads up into the Langdales, just before the dale opens out to give great views to the Pikes. The old gunpowder mill, which was once powered by the tarn, has now been replaced by the Pillar Hotel, and a timesharing development. The Britannia Inn is a popular spot for lunch or a drink on a summer evening.

Eskdale Green   **F10**
4m NE of Ravenglass. Eskdale Green, although only a hamlet, is the main village of Eskdale, through which the road leads up to or down from the Hardknott Pass. This is the home of the Eskdale Outward Bound School, and a good centre for exploring the dale itself up to Dalegarth and Boot.

Glenridding   **L5**
11m SW of Penrith. Lying at the foot of Glenridding Beck, this is a popular holiday centre on the western shore of Ullswater and the best departure point either for a walk on Helvellyn, or for a lake cruise north to Pooley Bridge. There are several hotels, shops, cafes and a garage. In season there is a TIC in the car park. Glenridding was once a mining centre, and has begun to develop forestry plantations on the nearby fells, but tourism remains the main occupation for the present inhabitants. It was near Glenridding that Dorothy Wordsworth saw those daffodils which later inspired her brother's best-known poem.

Gosforth   **D9**
7m SE of Egremont. Gosforth is rather larger than a village and it is well worth visiting, if only to see the rare 10thC Viking cross carved with Christian and pagan symbols which stands in St Mary's churchyard beside the road. The Gosforth Show, in August, is one of Lakeland's most popular events.

Grasmere   **J8**
4m NW of Ambleside. *Pop 1030. EC Thur.* The favourite village for the Lake poets, which remains a popular spot with their admirers and countless, less poetically-endowed tourists. Wordsworth came to live in Dove Cottage in 1789 when it was described as a rustic, unsuspected paradise. Grasmere may now be crowded but it remains a little paradise, and cannot be missed by any visitor to the Lake District. Dove Cottage and the Grasmere and Wordsworth Museum can be visited at Town End, which lies by the main road a few hundred yards to the south-east of the village. William and Dorothy Wordsworth are buried in St Oswald's churchyard, and the church has a rushbearing ceremony on the Saturday nearest to 5 August. Grasmere is also the centre for the largest of all the Lakeland sports days, held every August, when

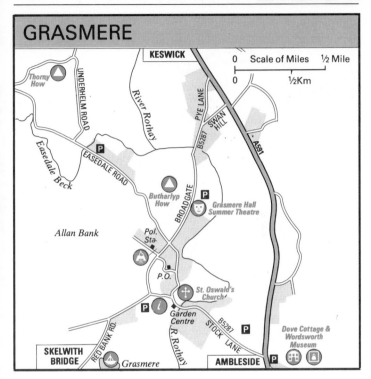

GRASMERE

KESWICK

Scale of Miles   ½ Mile

0   ½Km

Thorny How

UNDERHELM ROAD

River Rothay

PYE LANE

SWAN HILL

B5287

A591

Easedale Beck

P

EASEDALE ROAD

Butharlyp How

BROADGATE

P

Grasmere Hall Summer Theatre

Allan Bank

Pol. Sta.

P.O.

St. Oswald's Church

P

i

Garden Centre

R. Rothay

STOCK LANE

B5287

P

Dove Cottage & Wordsworth Museum

P

SKELWITH BRIDGE

RED BANK RD.

Grasmere

AMBLESIDE

events include Cumberland wrestling and fell racing. That apart, the village is an excellent centre for walking, and a good centre for touring to the south and central fells. There are fine local walks to Red Bank and High Cross, and great views across Grasmere from Loughrigg Terrace, south of the lake.

Greystoke   **M2**
12m NE of Keswick. Well worth visiting, for although it is quiet and rather tucked away, the village contains pleasant stone houses, and a very attractive and surprisingly large medieval church, with effigies, and a sanctuary stone by the gate.

Keswick   **I4**
17m W of Penrith. *Pop 4700. EC Wed. MD Sat.* Keswick is the metropolis of the central fells, and has been referred to, probably with reason, as 'The Queen of Lakeland'. However, it owes the title more

to location than to architecture for, with the exception of a rather pleasing main street, where the 19thC townhall dominates the scene with its notable one-hand clock, and St Kentigern's Church in the suburb of Crosthwaite, half-a-mile from the centre, the town is not remarkable. On the other hand, it lies between Derwent Water and Bassenthwaite, Borrowdale lies just to the south, and the main spine of the Cumbrian Mountains runs just to the east. As a fell walking and climbing centre then, Keswick is superb.

It was originally a market town, and a centre for the local copper and lead mines. The tourists arrived in 1865 with the opening of the Penrith to Cockermouth railway, and although this has long gone, the tourists still flock in, for there are a number of good museums, including the

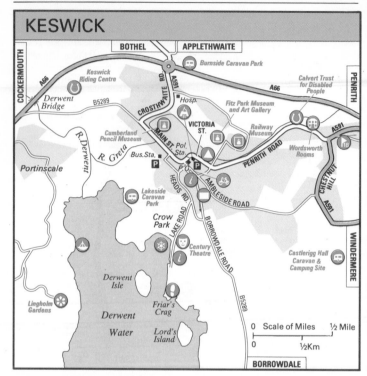

KESWICK

BOTHEL APPLETHWAITE

COCKERMOUTH

Burnside Caravan Park

Keswick
Riding Centre

Calvert Trust
for Disabled
People

PENRITH

A66

A66

*Derwent
Bridge*

B5289

Hosp.

Fitz Park Museum
and Art Gallery

CROSTHWAITE RD.

VICTORIA
ST.

Railway
Museum

*Cumberland
Pencil Museum*

MAIN ST.

A591

R. Derwent

R. Greta

Bus. Sta.

Pol.
Sta.

P.O.

PENRITH ROAD

Wordsworth
Rooms

CHESTNUT HILL

A591

Portinscale

P

P

i

AMBLESIDE ROAD

*Lakeside
Caravan
Park*

WINDERMERE

HEADS RD.

LAKE ROAD

*Crow
Park*

BORROWDALE ROAD

*Castlerigg Hall
Caravan &
Camping Site*

*Century
Theatre*

i

*Derwent
Isle*

*Lingholm
Gardens*

Derwent

B5289

Friar's
Crag

Water

Lord's
Island

0   Scale of Miles   ½ Mile

0   ½Km

BORROWDALE

Fitz Park, which contains many of the
Lake poets' manuscripts and a stone
xylophone, and the Keswick Railway
Museum. The Century Theatre, built from
several caravans, stands by the lake, and
it is possible to hire craft and cruise about
Derwent Water with the Keswick Launch
Company. The Keswick Show is held
annually on the late summer bank holiday
Monday.

The town lies in the ideal position to serve
as a tourist centre, with bus and Mountain
Goat tours, plenty of hotels and, from any
viewpoint, the most striking scenery in
the countryside round about. The walk
from Keswick centre to the top of
Skiddaw is a Lakeland visitor's 'must'.

Lamplugh   **D4**
8m NE of Whitehaven. A scattered village
on the western boundary of the National
Park near Loweswater, this place is

famous locally for a tasty dish, Lamplugh
pudding, made with spiced ale, raisins and
crushed biscuits. The Church of St
Michael has a twin-bell belfry, and there
is good walking in the fells around the
village.

Lorton   **F3**
6m S of Cockermouth. Lorton lies in two
parts, Low and High, beside the River
Cocker, close to Crummock Water.
Lorton Hall is built around a medieval
pele tower, and the village hall in High
Lorton is known as the Yew Tree Hall
because it stands in front of the huge yew
under which George Fox, the Quaker,
preached to Cromwell's soldiers.

Mungrisdale   **K2**
9m NE of Keswick. Reached by a minor
road north, off the A66, Mungrisdale has
some fine houses and a whitewashed
church, built in 1756 and dedicated to St

Kentigern or St Mungo, who gave his name to the village.

Patterdale L6

8m N of Ambleside. Two attractions draw the visitors to Patterdale, over the long steep climb of the Kirkstone Pass. Firstly, it offers the best departure point for the ascent of Helvellyn via Striding Edge, although those who come by car will have a parking problem. Do not leave Patterdale though, without visiting the second great attraction, St Patrick's Church, where there are the marvellous modern tapestries worked by Ann McBeth, who died here in 1948. The views over the fells from the churchyard are also notable. The Patterdale Sheepdog Trials, held over the late summer bank holiday are fascinating to watch.

Rydal Mount

Rydal K8

1m NW of Ambleside. *Pop 500.* Rydal is a small, quiet little village set at the eastern end of Rydal Water and is significant because Wordsworth lived at Rydal Mount for the last 37 years of his life, from 1813 to 1850. The house where he entertained friends and admirers is now owned by one of his descendants and is open to visitors; the gardens are still as he planned them. The meadow behind Rydal Mount is 'Dora's Field' which Wordsworth planted with daffodils to please his daughter. St Mary's Church contains memorials to Thomas Arnold and his family, and the Wordsworth pew still stands before the pulpit.

St Bees A7

4m S of Whitehaven. A somewhat modernised and rather scattered village of white houses. St Bees takes its name from St Bega, a 7thC Celtic saint who is supposed, on no evidence whatsoever, to have built a nunnery here. The present church of St Mary and St Bega dates from the 12thC and is all that remains of a Benedictine priory destroyed time and time again by the Scots. This church is

interesting, with a very fine Norman door, but that apart, the village has little to offer except a long sand and shingle beach and the nearby presence of St Bees Head, which offers great views over the Solway Firth.

Seascale B10

4m N of Ravenglass. A small village now completely dominated by the (formerly Windscale) nuclear power station.

Seatoller H6

1m W of Borrowdale, 6m S of Keswick, A small but picturesque village in Borrowdale at the eastern foot of the Honister Pass, now a centre for slate mining. The Dale Head Base Visitors' Centre in Seatoller displays local history and geology.

Troutbeck L9

3m N of Windermere. Troutbeck is an unusual village, for the centre consists of various 17th and 18thC buildings, each gathered round a well dedicated to a saint. The wells were in regular use until the recent introduction of piped water. The village church is set by the stream, the Trout Beck, below the village and has glass by William Morris and Edward Burne-Jones. Townend, at the south of the village, is a 17thC yeoman's cottage, now owned by the National Trust, full of beautiful carved oak furniture and open to the public. An ever-more popular attraction is the main pub, The Mortal Man, once famous for selling Sally Birkett's potent ale. The whole village is now a conservation area.

Wasdale Head G8

5m N of Wasdale. Set at the head of Wast Water, Wasdale Head is barely a hamlet, but the parish is said to contain the tallest mountain, the deepest lake, and the smallest church in England, in Scafell Pike (3206ft), Wast Water (250ft deep), and the church of St Olaf, where the walls are just 6ft 6in high. Ritson's Bar at the Wasdale Head Hotel is also the scene for the annual Biggest Liar contest.

Watendlath I5

5m S of Keswick. Watendlath is a rather remote little village of old farmers' cottages, reached up a narrow road off the B5289, south of Derwent Water. This road offers splendid vistas at Ashness Bridge, which gives a classic glimpse of Derwent Water and the famous 'Surprise View' over the lake from the cliff edge. Watendlath Tarn is picturesque and the beck tumbles down over the Lodore Falls. The hamlet is now owned by the National Trust, and is well worth a visit.

Whitehaven   **A5**
Pop 26,000. EC Wed. MD Thur & Sat. It
seems odd to find an industrial town and
port in Cumbria, but in the 18thC
Whitehaven ranked second only to
London as a port, handling coal and iron
ore with an annual tonnage twice that of
Liverpool and Bristol. All that was long
ago, and although the town is still a
mining and manufacturing centre and
handles coastal shipping, it is now a very
pleasant example of a town laid out during
the Georgian period and the Industrial
Revolution. The streets form a grid pattern
with one square open for the church of St
Nicolas, which dates from the last century.

The other main church, St James, is
Georgian. There are many fine buildings,
especially along the quays and around
Duke Street. The town is best inspected
by following the route suggested in the
Whitehaven Walkabout leaflet offered by
the TIC, which leads from the centre,
down to the harbour and along South
Beach. Whitehaven is worth a visit and
do not leave without at least inspecting the
local history exhibits in the Whitehaven
Museum and Art Gallery in the Market
Place, or spending an evening at the Sir
Nicolas Sekers Theatre at Rosehill, a mile
to the north.

Workington   **B2**
Pop 29,000. EC Thur. MD Wed & Sat.
Workington, on the Derwent, looks like
a 'working town'. Like Whitehaven, it
began life as a coal and iron ore port, and
then developed into a manufacturing town.
The town has known hard times in recent
years with the decline of the steel industry,
but still retains relics of a former
prosperity. Although Whitehaven is nicer,
Workington has some attractive
buildings, notably around Portland
Square, which was laid out in 1775. The
centre has been somewhat modernised, but
the one-way system leads past the vast
columns and portico of the Parish Church

of St John the Evangelist, to the
Workington Central Hotel and the new
shopping centre. Perhaps the most
striking building in the town is the 19thC
green and white painted brewery by the
river. The Helena Thompson Museum in
Park End Road is an 18thC building
which contains displays illustrating the
history of the town.

Places of interest

Ambleside   **L9**
Dolls House Museum
Junction of Kirkstone Rd and North Rd.
Tel Ambleside (0966) 32358. An unusual
museum featuring a dozen Victorian dolls'
houses, and a large collection of dolls.
Parking nearby. *Open 20 Apr–28 Sep
Wed–Fri 10.30–13.00 & 14.00–17.00.*
Charge.
Lake District Heritage Centre
Lake Rd. Tel Ambleside (0966) 32336. An
essential stop for all those who want to
know more about the life and history of
the Lake District, well displayed here
with exhibits in 12 subject areas. The
exhibits include a model of Galava Fort.
Parking. *Open 1 Apr–31 Oct Mon–Sat
10.00–17.00.* **Charge.**

Blindcrake   **F1**
Isel Church
2m S of Blindcrake but in the same parish
lies the Norman church of St Michael at
Isel. Carved stones incorporated in the
restored Norman structure reveal
evidence of an earlier Viking or Danish
building. Among these is the Triskele
Stone, carved with a swastika and Thor's
thunderbolt. The chancel arch, which
dates from 1130, supports the Royal Arms
of 1721 which show the White Horse of
Hanover, and were presented to the
church in 1721 by the local squire, Sir
Wilfrid Lawson.

Bridekirk   **E1**
St Bridget's Church
Off the B594 road. The glory of this much
restored church is the 12thC font carved
by a medieval craftsman, Richard of
Durham, with scenes from the Old and
New Testaments and bearing his name.

Boot   **G10**
Eskdale Cornmill
Tel Eskdale (09403) 335. A working
cornmill dating from 1778, although there
has been a cornmill on this site since the

13thC. Well restored, with original machinery, two waterwheels and a farming exhibition. Picnic areas and a 17thC packhorse bridge complete the scene. *Open 7 Apr–30 Sep Sun–Fri 11.00–17.00 & Nat hol weekends.* **Charge.**

Calder Bridge   C8
Calder Abbey
By the river, 1m E of Calder Bridge. The ruins of this 12thC abbey are now in private hands and cannot be visited, but they are within easy view from the minor road to Priorling which runs close by.

Castlerigg prehistoric stone circle

Castlerigg   I4
Castlerigg Stone Circle
Beside the A66 road, 1m SE of Keswick. Only about 40 stones remain of this prehistoric stone circle, which is now owned by the National Trust.

Cockermouth   E2
The Wordsworth House
Main St. Tel Cockermouth (0900) 824805. This house, now owned by the National Trust, is the building where Wordsworth was born. The house, which overlooks the River Derwent, is Georgian and still contains 18thC furniture and the poet's personal effects, set out in displays over nine rooms. Visitors can also see his childhood garden. Audio-visual presentations. Light refreshments and lunches available. National Trust parking. *Open 1 Apr–31 Oct Fri–Wed 11.00–17.00, Sun 14.00–17.00. Closed Thur.* Free admission for NT members. Otherwise **Charge.**

Egremont   B7
Egremont Castle
The ruins of this 12th–14thC castle are set in a public park. *Open all year.*

Embleton   F2
Wythop Mill
S of the A66, 1m W of the village. Tel Bassenthwaite Lake (059681) 394. A fascinating timber mill, still powered by an overshooting waterwheel. Contains the original machinery and a display of hand

tools. *Open 5 Apr–27 Oct Tue–Sun 10.30–18.00.*

Gosforth   D9
Gosforth Church
Gosforth churchyard contains a very rare 10thC Viking cross, carved with Nordic runes.

Grange-in-Borrowdale   H5
The Bowder Stone
Beside the B5289 road, 1m S of Grange-in-Borrowdale. This huge, balancing stone is unique in Lakeland. It is possible to climb to the top (30ft) by ladder, or crawl under the overhang to shake hands with someone on the other side.

Grasmere   J8
Dove Cottage & Wordsworth Museum
Town End. Tel Grasmere (09665) 544. Wordsworth lived at Dove Cottage from 1799 to 1808, and his daily life there has been recorded in the journals of his sister Dorothy. After Wordsworth left, Dove Cottage became the home of the writer Thomas de Quincy. The cottage was completely restored in the late 1970s and the new Grasmere & Wordsworth Museum in the garden contains a vast display of Wordsworth memorabilia and the recently discovered collection of his papers. Other attractions include a bookshop and a research centre for Wordsworth scholars. *Open Apr–Sep Mon–Sat 09.30–17.30, Sun 11.00–17.30; Mar & Oct Mon–Sat 10.00–16.30, Sun 11.00–16.30; Dec–Jan Mon–Sat 10.00–16.30, Sun 11.00–16.30. Closed Nov.* **Charge.**

Dove Cottage, Grasmere

Greystoke   M2
St Andrew's Church
This large collegiate church is late
medieval and was established as a 'college
for a group of priests'. There is a sanctuary
stone by the gate and several good 13th
and 14thC effigies inside the church.

Hardknott Pass   H9
Roman Fort
Situated beside the road which leads over
Hardknott Pass, 5m W of Little
Langdale. This 1stC Roman fort still
retains the stone foundations, the
granary, and an extensive parade ground.

Keswick   I4
**Cumberland Pencil Museum &
Exhibition Centre**
Southey Works, Greta Bridge. Tel
Keswick (0596) 73626. Set only a short
distance from the town centre, this
unusual museum records the history of
pencil making and contains, among other
exhibits, the world's largest pencil. *Open
1 Mar–31 Oct Mon–Fri 09.30–16.30;
Sat–Sun 14.00–17.00.* **Charge.**
Lingholm Gardens
Tel Keswick (0596) 72003. Beautiful
formal and woodland gardens best visited
in late spring for the azaleas and
rhododendrons. A one-and-a-half-mile
garden walk gives views to Borrowdale and
Skiddaw. Garden centre, tearoom,
parking available. *Open 1 Apr–31 Oct daily
10.00–17.00.* **Charge.**
Museum & Art Gallery
Fitzpark. Tel Keswick (0596) 73263. A
very interesting museum with varied
collections of exhibits, which include
manuscripts by Wordsworth, Southey,
Coleridge and Hugh Walpole, as well as
displays of butterflies and birds. Also
features geology and local industry,
including the stone xylophone made from
local stones. *Open 1 Apr–31 Oct Mon–Sat
10.00–12.30 & 14.00–17.00.* **Charge.**
Railway Museum
Railway Station, Station Rd. Tel
Braithwaite (059682) 265. A display of
railway travel, life and artifacts, with
models illustrating the railways of the
north-west. *Open 6 Apr–27 Oct Sat
10.00–17.00, Sun 14.00–17.00, also
Mon–Fri 10.00–17.00 during school
holidays.* **Charge.**
Wordsworth Rooms
Old Windebrowe, Brundholme Rd. Tel
Keswick (0596) 72254. This exhibition
consists of two rooms, kitchen and
parlour, restored to the style they were in
when Wordsworth stayed there. Also
exhibits on the other Lakeland poets. Old
Windebrowe is now a Riding for the
Disabled Centre, *but the rooms are open
any time by appointment only.* **Charge.**

Little Crosthwaite   H3
Mire House
Under Skiddaw. Tel Keswick (0596)
72287. 3m N of Keswick on the A591
road. Mire House is a 17thC manor, set in
its own woodland. The house contains a
Victorian playroom and nursery and many
manuscripts and portraits of the poets
Wordsworth, Southey and Tennyson, who
were friends of the Speddings of Mire
House. Modern attractions include a
tearoom in the Olde Saw Mill and lakeside
walks. *Open 1 Apr–31 Oct. House open
Wed, Sun & Nat hol Mon 14.00–17.00.
Grounds & tearoom open Mon–Sun
10.00–17.30.* **Charge.**

Rydal   K8
Rydal Mount
Rydal Hill. Tel Ambleside (0966) 33002.
Rydal Mount was Wordsworth's home for
37 years, and contains many first editions
of his work as well as manuscripts,
portraits and other memorabilia. The
gardens are still very much as he laid them
out in the 1840s. Facilities include
information translated in 27 languages
and a bookstall. *Open 1 Nov–29 Feb
Wed–Mon 10.00–12.30 & 14.00–16.00;
1 Mar–31 Oct daily 10.00–17.30.* **Charge.**

Seatoller   H6
Seatoller Barn
Dale Head Base. Tel Borrowdale (059684)
294. Displays featuring the life and
history of Borrowdale. Crafts displayed on
periodic craft days, usually on Tue or
Wed every fortnight. Refreshments
available. Parking. *Open Easter–end Sep
daily 10.00–17.00.* **Free.**

Sellafield   C9
British Nuclear Fuels Ltd
Exhibition Centre, Calder Hall, Seascale.
Tel Seascale (0940) 27735. Better known
as Windscale or Calder Hall, this nuclear
power station stands on the Cumbrian
coast just off the A595 near Calder Bridge.
The Exhibition Centre and its staff exist
to answer questions on the future of
nuclear power. *Open Apr–Oct daily
10.00–16.00. 1 Nov–30 Mar Mon–Fri only.*
Free.

Townend Museum, Troutbeck

Troutbeck   **L9**

Townend
South end of village. Tel Ambleside (0966)
32628. Set in a 17thC farmer's house built
about 1626, this museum contains
carvings, books, furniture and domestic
implements illustrating the history of the
Browne family who lived in this house
from the day it was built until 1944. *Open
Apr–end Oct Good Fri, Sun & Tue–Fri
14.00–18.00 or dusk. Closed Sat & Mon.*
Charge.

Troutbeck Bridge   **L9**

Holehird Gardens
On A592, N of Windermere. Tel for
information Carlisle (0228) 23456. Owned
by the Cumbria County Council, these
formal gardens are famous for their rare
plants, rhododendrons and shrubs, and
offer good walks and fine views over the
nearby fells. *Open all year.* **Free.**

Waterhead   **L9**

Galava Roman Fort
Borrans Field. Many remains excavated
from this Roman fort can be seen in the
Brockhole Visitors' Centre between
Ambleside and Windermere. The fort
dates from about AD100 but only the
foundations remain by the lake.
Stagshaw Gardens
Tel Ambleside (0966) 32109. ½m S of
Ambleside on the A591. This National
Trust woodland garden is situated on a
steep slope overlooking Lake
Windermere and is especially noted for
spring flowers and shrubs. *Open 1 Apr–30
Jun daily 10.00–18.30, and by appointment
only from 1 Jul–31 Oct.* **Charge.**

Whitehaven   **A5**

Whitehaven Museum & Art Gallery
Market Pl. Tel (0946) 3111. A local history
museum, illustrating the town's
individual past. Among the most
interesting exhibits are: the shroud of the
St Bees man, a perfectly preserved body

from a medieval burial ground; a
collection of 19thC Whitehaven-made
pottery; a 1740 painting, 'A Bird's Eye
View of Whitehaven', by Matthias Read.
*Open all year Mon, Tue, Thur–Sat
10.00–17.00. Closed Wed, Sun & Nat hols.*
Free.

Workington   **B2**

Helena Thompson Museum
Park End Lane. Tel (0900) 62598. Set in
an 18thC house, standing in its own
grounds, this attractive museum contains
collections of costume, art, and local
history. *Open Easter–Oct Mon–Sat
11.00–15.00.* **Free.**

Local events & attractions

Competitions

Whitehaven   **A5**

The Biggest Liar in the World Contest
This contest actually takes place *either* at
the Bridge Inn at Santon Bridge, or in
Wasdale at the Wasdale Head Inn, but it
is organised from Whitehaven. Would-be
competitors can obtain details from
Copeland District Council, Catherine St,
Tel Whitehaven (0946) 3111. It owes its
origins, or so they say, to Will Ritson, a
19thC publican who was a terrible liar. It's
great fun and well worth stopping for if
you are in the area at the right time.
Third Thur in Nov.

Craft centres

Ambleside   **K9**

Adrian Sankey Glass
Rothay Rd. Tel Ambleside (0966) 33039.
A small workshop producing functional
and lead crystal glass, with the craftsmen's
work on view to the visitor. *Open
Mon–Sun 09.00–17.30. Closed Jan.*

Grasmere   **J8**

Allan Ellwood
White Bridge Forge. Tel Grasmere
(09665) 414. A working blacksmith who
produces wrought iron, doorstops, signs,
escutcheons etc. *Open normal shop hours.*
Heaton Cooper Studio
Village Centre. Tel Grasmere (09665) 280.
Watercolour paintings and prints. *Open all
year, normal shop hours.*
Chris Reekie
The Old Coach House. Tel Grasmere
(09665) 212. Weaving of all kinds, shawls,

blankets, tablecloths, from local wool.
Open normal shop hours.

Keswick   I4
Lakeland Stonecraft Ltd
13 High Hill. Tel Keswick (0596) 72994.
All kinds of stonecraft worked from local
stone. *Open normal shop hours.*

Skelwith Bridge   K9
Kirkstone Galleries
Tel Ambleside (09663) 3296/7/8. Working
in local stone, this craft workshop
produces tiles, fireplaces, building slabs,
slates. *Open normal shop hours.*

Thornthwaite   H3
Thornthwaite Galleries
Tel Braithwaite (059682) 248. In the
village centre, this gallery claims to offer
the best selection of local crafts in the Lake
District, including paintings, pottery,
crystal and bronzes. Cafe and licensed
restaurant, too. *Open Mon–Sun
10.00–17.00. Closed last two weeks in Nov.*

Whitehaven   A5
Whitehaven Workshop
48/49 Roper St. Tel Whitehaven (0946)
63310. Pottery and batik-weaving
workshop, with a large selection of both
for sale. *Open normal shop hours.*

Rushbearing

Ambleside Rushbearing   K9
Led by the town band, the children carry
rushes around the town to the market
place and then to St Mary's Church.
Details available on Ambleside (09663)
3205. *First Sat in Jul.*
Grasmere Rushbearing   J8
Preceded by a procession round the village
led by the village band, the clergy and
children carry 'bearings' of flowers and
rushes. Details on Grasmere (09665) 245.
Sat nearest to 5th Aug.

Sheepdog trials

Patterdale Sheepdog Trials   L6
St George's Playing Fields. First held in
1901, these long-established trials and
competitions display the high level of skill
and communication required between
shepherds and their dogs when working
sheep. Details on Glenridding (08532)
266. *Held on late summer Nat hol Sat.*
Rydal Sheepdog Trials   K8
Rydal Park. Apart from the sheepdog
competitions, other attractions at these

trials include hound trailing and a display
of shepherds' crooks and sticks. Details
from Hawkshead (09666) 264. *On or about
15th Aug.*
Threlkeld Sheepdog Trials   J3
Burns Field. A typical Cumbrian sheepdog
trial. Details from Threlkeld (059683)
393. *Held on third Wed after the first Mon
in Aug.*

Sports days & shows

Ambleside Sports   K8
A full range of field and track events with
such local competitions as Cumberland
and Westmorland wrestling and fell races.
Details from Coniston (09664) 564. *On the
Thur before the first Mon in Aug.*
Cockermouth Show   E2
A truly Cumbrian day out with livestock
and produce displays, mixed with craft
exhibits, fell races, hound trailing and
Cumberland and Westmorland wrestling.
Details on Maryport (090081) 2925. *On the
Sat before the first Mon in Aug.*
Egremont Crab Fair   B7
This Fair has been held annually except
for the war years, since 1267. A colourful
event with such rare attractions as
climbing the greasy pole (£1 to the
winner), a pipe-smoking contest, and a
'gurning' or face-pulling competition.
The crab apple cart parades down the main
street at *12.30* and apples are thrown to
the crowd. Other competitions include fell
races, track and field events, and hound
trailing. Details from Egremont (0946)
820376. *Third Sat in Sep.*
Ennerdale Show   D6
Held at Bowness Knott, this event began
in the last century as a flower show. The
profits go to provide a Christmas party for
the local children. Details from
Lamplugh (094686) 391. *Last Wed in Aug.*
Eskdale Show   G9
Between Boot and Cockley Beck. Now
over 100 years old, this show is mainly a

sheep fair, set in the magnificent surroundings of the Hardknott Pass, and well worth a visit to see the local breeds and mix with local people. Details from Eskdale (09403) 269. *Last Sat in Sep.*

Gosforth Show D9

Dating back to 1876, this annual event is a traditional Cumbrian show with sheep, cattle and horse classes, as well as hound and terrier racing, and wrestling. Details: Seascale (09402) 3411. *Third Wed in Aug.*

Keswick Show I4

This is a large agricultural show which offers the lot! Cattle, sheep and produce classes, a horse show, plus hound trailing and Cumberland and Westmorland wrestling. Details from Keswick (0596) 73180. *Held on summer Nat hol Mon.*

Wasdale Show E9

The Wasdale Show is primarily a shepherds' meet and sheep fair, one of the largest in Cumbria. Details from Gosforth (09405) 340. *Second Sat in Oct.*

Leisure & entertainment

Boat cruises

Derwent Water I4

Derwent Water Launch Co
29 Manor Rd, Keswick. Tel Keswick (0596) 73013 or 72263. The craft used here are launches not steamers or ferries, but the service leaves the various piers around Derwent Water every half-hour or so, and a complete trip round the lake takes just under an hour.

Ullswater L5

Ullswater Navigation & Transit Co
13 Maud St, Kendal. Tel Kendal (0539) 21626 or Glenridding (08532) 229. The UNTC run two cruisers, the 'Raven' and the 'Lady of the Lake' up and down Ullswater from Glenridding to Howton and Pooley Bridge. Both craft are over 100 years old, but both are in excellent working order. The end-to-end cruise lasts about one hour and is one of those essential lakeland excursions.

Boat hire

Grasmere J8

J. D. Allanby
Padmire, Pavement End. Tel Grasmere (09665) 409. Rowing boats.

Keswick I4

Keswick-on-Derwent Water Launch Co
29 Manor Rd. Tel Keswick (0596) 72263 or 73013. Motor boats, rowing boats.

Nicol End Marine
Portinscale, 1m W of Keswick. Tel Keswick (0596) 73082 or 73013. Motor boats and rowing boats.

Waterhead L9

Ambleside Motor Launch Co Ltd
Tel Ambleside (09663) 3187. Motor boats and rowing boats for hire.

Watermillock M4

Ullswater Sailing School
Landends. Tel Pooley Bridge (08536) 438. Sailing cruisers.

Car tours

The central fells of Lakeland are really places to explore on foot. That said, there are a number of roads and routes which no wise motorist would want to miss, for they offer the visitor marvellous views, a wide selection of attractive villages, and somewhere to escape to when the more popular places are crowded with summer visitors. Be warned though that in summer, even the minor roads are full of traffic.

1. Ambleside to Wasdale Head

This route is a spectacular and exciting drive and takes the traveller east to west, across, or rather round, the spine of the Cumbrian Mountains and over two of the great passes that lie along the old Roman road which leads to Ravenglass. Leave Ambleside on the A593 road for Skelwith Bridge, where you can stop for a visit to Skelwith Force where the River Brathay tumbles over a 20-foot-high ledge. Turn left here and follow the B4343 road up to Elterwater, where there is a series of little lakes, and then turn south, through the village towards Little Langdale and then west, past Little Langdale Tarn to Fell Foot where the road starts to climb towards the Wrynose Pass. The gradient reaches 1:4 here, so it pays to use low gears and keep the engine from overheating. One useful stop, with great views, is at the Three Shires Stone, which stands on the north of the road and marks the meeting place of the former counties of Cumberland, Westmorland and Lancashire, now combining to form the present Cumbria.

Once across this pass, the road descends sharply to Wrynose Bottom and Cockley Beck, before ascending steeply again to the Hardknott Pass, where, on the top, another worthwhile stop is for a visit to the remaining vestiges of the 1stC Roman fort which once guarded the top of the pass. From the col, the road falls away very sharply, a vertiginous drop down into Eskdale, but the views are superb on a clear day. Then head past Boot and Dalegarth, where the road follows the line of the little 'Ratty', the Ravenglass & Eskdale Railway, to Eskdale Green, The road then veers off to Gubbergill and onto the A595, where a short run to the south will bring the traveller to Ravenglass, just in time for lunch at the Pennington Arms, Here the visitor has a choice of delights, including a visit to the Gullery or Muncaster Castle.

In the afternoon, follow this road back to Gubbergill, before turning east and forking left for Stanton Bridge, then heading north-east for Nether Wasdale and Wast Water. From Wasdale Hall, which is now a Youth Hostel, the road runs beside the north-western shore of the lake, and offers marvellous views across the water to the steep plunging side of The Screes and the high fells to the north-east.

Follow this road up the western shore of the lake and it will bring you at last to the Wasdale Head Hotel, a favourite spot with walkers and climbers, with good views up the valley to Great Gable, and a fine spot for tea.

Return down this valley to the 'Ratty' station at Irton Bridge, and re-cross the mountains in the late afternoon or early evening when the westering sun will cast great shadows across the peaks and light up the hills ahead, as the road skirts the Langdale Pikes and leads at last back to Ambleside. *Total distance: 40m.*

2. A circular tour of the Central Fells from Ambleside

The route is a classic journey, which takes in most of the finest sights of central Lakeland, although opinions on what exactly the finest sights are may vary with the individual. Even so, this is a very enjoyable journey which begins at Ambleside.

Leave Ambleside, heading south on the A591 road along the eastern shore of Lake Windermere, stopping for a visit at the National Park Centre at Brockhole, which is just beside the road. A mile past Brockhole, a road on the left, signposted to Troutbeck, turns to the north-east and follows the little Trout Beck stream up to the village of Troutbeck, which is well worth a visit. Then, follow this minor road up onto the main A592 road, which is reached just by the Kirkstone Pass Inn, and turn left here for the Kirkstone Pass.

The Kirkstone Pass, at 1476ft is the highest pass accessible to motorists in Lakeland. The road falls away through some very wild and rugged country. A pause at the top for a look around and a drink at the Inn might be welcome, before the descent past Brotherswater on the left, to the village of Patterdale for a look at the church, and down to Glenridding and the lake of Ullswater. Glenridding is one of the stops for the Ullswater steamers, so, if time permits, why not park here and take a cruise around the lake?

North of Glenridding turn left, onto A5091, climbing up through Dockray and Matterdale and yet another Troutbeck to the main A66 road which lies just north of Great Mell Fell, where the route turns left towards Keswick. The road runs under Saddleback, or Blencathra Fell, leaving Threlkeld to the right, after which our route turns south onto the B5322 and along St John's Beck through pretty St-John-in-the-Vale and down to the northern

edge of Thirlmere, from which the great
bulk of Helvellyn can be seen looming up
to the left above the lake.
Take the unmarked road which turns off
the A591 at the head of the lake, and
follow this along the western shore of
Thirlmere rejoining the A591 at
Wythburn Fells. Turn south here onto the
main road, and follow this down to
Grasmere, and then round Rydal Water
and so back into Ambleside, to complete
a varied and delightful run along the
eastern part of the fells. *Total distance:
55m.*

**3. A circular tour from Keswick through
Cockermouth**
This short tour takes in a number of the
lakes, and runs through more of the
attractive areas of central Lakeland. Leave
Keswick for the south on the B5289,
which soon runs down to the eastern edge
of Derwent Water, and on into lovely
Borrowdale. Pause to climb the Bowder
Stone and then on through the 'Jaws of
Borrowdale' to Rosthwaite. The road veers
west, past the turning to Borrowdale
village and into Seatoller, where it begins
to climb over the Honister Pass, which
lies at nearly 2000ft at the coll, before
descending to Buttermere and Crummock
Water. This is one of the most spectacular
places in Lakeland, a long valley filled by
two separate lakes and surrounded on
every side by steep-sided fells. There are
numerous parking places, so stop, look
around, and take photos. Scale Force
waterfall, which falls 120ft on the far side
of Crummock Water, is a good walk from
Buttermere village, or from the rambling
centre at Hassness on the shore of
Buttermere. Crummock Water and
Buttermere are surrounded by attractive
fells, and from the northern edge of these
two lakes the B5292 leads on into more
open country out of the fells and through
Lorton Vale to Cockermouth.
Cockermouth is a pleasant town, the
birthplace of William Wordsworth. It is
well worth exploring and makes a good
stop for lunch before leaving again for the
east. First, out on the B5292, and then
east onto the main A66, past the golf
course at Lambfoot, to the vast lake at
Bassenthwaite, which lies between the
great forest of Thornthwaite and the peaks
of Skiddaw to the east. These can be seen
at their best from the western shoreline
which the A66 road follows down towards
Derwent Water and then back into the
east and into Keswick. *Total distance:
55m.*

Cinemas
Ambleside L9
Zeffirellis Cinema
Compston Rd. Tel Ambleside (0966)
33845. A recently renovated and
redecorated cinema, with old projectors in
the foyer and a slightly arty feel about it.
Late night screenings in summer and up-
to-date films. There's a good restaurant
attached where it is possible to have a
candlelit dinner and go to the cinema for
an all-inclusive price.

Keswick I4
Alhambra Theatre
Tel Keswick (0596) 72195. A small cinema
situated off the High Street. *Opening times
vary.*

Whitehaven A5
Gaiety Cinema
Tangier St. Tel Whitehaven (0946) 3012.

Workington B2
The Ritz Cinema
Murray Rd. Tel Workington (0900) 2505.

Coach trips
Both Ribble and Cumberland Coaches
(listed below) sell a joint 'Tour-Cumbria'
ticket which offers unlimited travel for
seven days over both networks.

Ambleside L9
Browns Coaches
Market Pl. Tel Ambleside (0966) 32205.
This company has an office at the TIC in
Grasmere and will pick up passengers at
points all round Ambleside, Grasmere
and Troutbeck.

Keswick I4
Cumberland Coaches
Bus Station. Tel Keswick (0596) 72791.
Mountain Goat
Market Sq. Tel Keswick (0596) 73962.
Ribble Coaches
Bus Station. Tel Keswick (0596) 72791.

Workington B2
Cumberland Coaches
Bus Station. Tel Workington (0900) 3080.

Cycle hire
Brothers Water L7
Sykeside Cycle Hire
Brotherswater, Patterdale. 2m S of
Patterdale. Tel Glenridding (08532) 239.

Cleator   C6
Cleator Cycle Shop
Jacktrees Rd. Tel Cleator Moor (0946)
812427.

Cockermouth   E2
Derwent Cycle Sports
Market Pl. Tel Cockermouth (0900)
822113.

Keswick   I4
Keswick Cycle Hire
Pack Horse Ct. Tel Braithwaite (059682)
273.

Cycle repairs & spares

Whitehaven   A5
Mark Taylor
21 King St. Tel Whitehaven (0946) 2252.

Workington   B2
Mark Taylor
4 Murray Rd. Tel Workington (0900)
3280.
The New Bike Shop
Market Pl. Tel Workington (0900) 3337.
Traffic Lights Bike Shop
35 Washington St. Tel Workington (0900)
3283.

Fishing

Licences, rods and local information can
be obtained from the following places and
tourist centres:

Ambleside   L9
King Side Cycles
The Slack. Tel Ambleside (0966) 33592.

Buttermere   G5
Rannerdale Farm
Tel Buttermere (059685) 232. Contact Mrs
J. Beard.

Cockermouth   E2
D. Lothian
35 Main St. Tel Cockermouth (0900)
322006.
Tourist Information Centre
Riverside car park. Tel Cockermouth
(0900) 822634.

Egremont   B7
W. N. Holmes & Son
45 Main St. Tel Egremont (0946) 820368.
W. N. Nixon
10 The Knoll, Thornhill. 1m S of
Egremont. Tel Egremont (0946) 822785.

Ennerdale Bridge   D6
High Bridge Farm
Cleator. Tel Lamplugh (0946) 861339.
Contact Mrs P. Humphreys.

Glenridding   L5
St Patrick's Boat Landing
Lakeside. Tel Glenridding (08532) 393.

Keswick   I3
Temple Sports
9 Station St. Tel Keswick (0596) 72564.
Field & Stream
79 Main St. Tel Keswick (0596) 74396.

Loweswater   F4
Scale Hill Hotel
Tel Lorton (090085) 232.

Seatoller   H6
The National Park Information Centre
Seatoller Barn, Dale Head Base. Tel
Borrowdale (059684) 294.

Waterhead   L9
National Park Information Centre
Waterhead. Tel Ambleside (09663) 2729.

Whitehaven   A5
The Compleat Angler
4 King St. Tel Whitehaven (0946) 5322.
Coarse fishing permits.
Mark Taylor
21 King St. Tel Whitehaven (0946) 2252.

Workington   B2
Simpson Sports
1 South William St. Tel Workington
(0900) 2774.
Mark Taylor
4 Murray Rd. Tel Workington (0900)
3280.

Golf

Embleton   F2
Cockermouth Golf Club
Embleton. 3m E of Cockermouth. Tel
Bassenthwaite Lake (059681) 223. 18-hole

course; booking advisable. Bar. Meals available at weekends by arrangement with the club stewardess. **Charge.**

Seascale C10
Seascale Golf Club
The Banks. Tel Seascale (0940) 28494. 18 holes, pro shop, bar. Snacks only on Mon and Tue; meals available on other days by arrangement with house manager. **Charge.**

St Bees A7
St Bees School Golf Club
St Bees School. Tel St Bees (094685) 254. 9-hole course belonging to the local public school. Parties welcome by arrangement with the bursar; some restrictions during term time. **Charge.**

Threlkeld J3
Keswick Golf Club
Threlkeld Hall. Threlkeld. Tel Threlkeld (059683) 324 or Keswick (0596) 72147. 18 holes. Visiting parties accepted. Bar; meals by arrangement with secretary. **Charge.**

Workington B2
Workington Golf Club
Branthwaite Rd. Tel Workington (0900) 3460. 18 holes. Visitors must be members of a golf club and produce a handicap certificate. Parties accepted by appointment. Pro shop, bar, meals available daily except Mon and Thur evening, by arrangement with steward's wife. **Charge.**

Riding & pony trekking

Bassenthwaite G2
Hill Farm
Tel Bassenthwaite Lake (059681) 498. Trekking. Minimum age 7 years. No experience required. Hats provided. *Open all year.* **Charge.**

Keswick I4
The Calvert Trust for Disabled People
Old Windebrowe, Brundholme Rd. Tel Keswick (0596) 74395. All ages; no experience required. Indoor school. Hats provided. The Trust caters mainly for disabled riders but others are welcome, especially out of season. *Open all year.* **Charge.**
Keswick Riding Centre
Swanfield Stables, adjacent to Crosthwaite Church. Tel Keswick (0596) 73804. Instruction and hacking. Minimum age 5

for instruction, 12 for hacking. No experience required except for hacking.Exam and competition instruction, and cross-country schooling jumps, too. All-weather school. Hats provided. *Open all year.* **Charge.**

Lamplugh D4
Kerbeck Fell Ponies
North Fell Dyke. Tel Lamplugh (0946) 861302. Instruction, hacking and trekking. No experience required. Minimum age 6 years. Hats provided. *Open all year.* **Charge.**

Mosser E3
Wood Farm Stables
Mosser. 3m S of Cockermouth. Tel Cockermouth (0900) 823403. Trekking, trail riding and hacking by arrangement. Pony and trap driving available also. Minimum age 7 or 13 for trail riding. No experience required for trekking. Hats provided. Riding inside the National Park. *Open all year.* **Charge.**

Patterdale L6
Side Farm Trekking Centre
Tel Glenridding (08532) 337. Trekking. No experience required. Hats provided. *Open Apr–Oct.* **Charge.**

St Bees A7
Stonehouse Riding Centre
Stonehouse Farm. Tel Egremont (0946) 822224. Instruction, trekking and hacking. All ages welcome; no experience required. Hats provided. *Open all year.* **Charge.**

Workington B2
Oldside Equestrian Centre
Dock Rd, Oldside. Tel Workington (0900) 65323. Instruction, trekking and hacking. All ages welcome; no experience required. Hats provided. Two all-weather ménages available for show-jumping and dressage. *Open all year.* **Charge.**

Swimming

Hotel pools open and available to non-residents are The Gosforth Hall Hotel, Gosforth, and the Castle Inn, Bassenthwaite.

Cockermouth E2
Sports Centre Pool
Castlegate Drive. Tel Cockermouth (0900) 823596. Indoor pool, with sauna and solarium available. *Open Mon–Sun.* **Charge.**

Egremont   B7
Wyndham School
Tel Egremont (0946) 820463. Indoor pool.
*Open to the public Wed & Fri evenings, all
day Sat, Sun morning and weekdays during
school holidays.* **Charge.**

Troutbeck Bridge   L9
Windermere Pool
Tel Windermere (09662) 3243. Indoor
heated pool, used for school parties but
otherwise open to the public. Telephone
first. Parking available. *Open to the public
all year eves & Mon–Sun during school
holidays.* **Charge.**

Whitehaven   A5
Whitehaven Pool
Duke St. Tel Whitehaven (0946) 5021.
Small 25-metre indoor pool and teaching
pool. *Open to the public 12.00–13.30 &
16.00–18.40 Mon–Fri & all day Sat; also
weekdays during school holidays.* **Charge.**

Workington   B2
Moorclose Swimming Pool
Newlands La South. Tel Workington
(0900) 61771. Indoor pool with separate
learner pool. *Open Mon–Sun.* **Charge.**

Theatres

Grasmere   J8
Wordsworth Summer Conference
Dove Cottage. Tel Grasmere (09665) 544.
This is an annual event for poetry lovers,
and usually takes place in *Jul or Aug.*
Details from Dove Cottage.

Keswick   I4
The Century Theatre
Lakeside car park. Tel Keswick (0596)
74411. Set by the lake and constructed
from old caravans (with the wheels still in
place), The Century looks a shambles but
it hosts a resident company and an
impressive repertoire. Productions have
included Shaw's 'The Millionairess' and
Feydeau's 'The Birdwatcher'.

Moresby   B4
The Sir Nicholas Sekers Theatre
Rosehill, Moresby. 1m N of Whitehaven.
Tel Whitehaven (0946) 2422. Known
locally as The Rosehill, this popular
theatre, is set in a house at Low Moresby,
and offers a year-round programme of
concerts, recitals and plays. Also a theatre
workshop and a restaurant.

Whitehaven   A5
The Civic Theatre
Civic Hall, Lowther St. Tel Whitehaven
(0946) 67575. Plays, concerts and film
shows are among the attractions of this
well-organised Civic Centre.

Workington   B2
Carnegie Theatre & Art Centre
Finkle St. Tel Workington (0900) 2122. A
varied programme throughout the year.
The Centre also houses the tourist
information centre.

Walks

This central area of Lakeland is walking
country *par excellence.* There are good
walks everywhere, so those which follow
can only be a small, if choice, selection.
Walking in the higher fells does require
good footwear, sensible clothing and an
eye on the weather, but the following
walks are within the reach of any
reasonably fit person and are without
'undue difficulty. A 1:50,000 scale OS
map will certainly be useful, and in these
high fells, time rather than distance is the
main factor to consider.

1. Around Buttermere   G5
The Cumbria Tourist Board describes this
walk around Buttermere as 'an absolute
must', and they are almost certainly right,
although they don't allow enough time for
it. Pausing to marvel at the views will add
time to your travels, so choose a clear day
and allow a full morning or afternoon for
this delightful ramble.
From the square in Buttermere village,
take the track which runs beside The Fish
Inn, down the left side of the beck towards
the lake. Keep left, through a gate, and
then right between fences past the footpath
to Scale Force, heading towards another
waterfall which can be clearly seen on the
far hillside.
Go through another gate and cross a stile
to a footbridge, and follow the path on
the left side along the beck, down to the
lakeside. A wide track leads along the lake
shore to Gatesgarth at the southern end,
where the path leads out into a minor
road. Turn left and follow this road back
to the lake where another path,
signposted 'Lakeshore Walk' leads over a
stile and through a small tunnel cut in the
rock. The views at this point up the lake
or south towards Hay Stacks will eat up
your camera film.
From here the path lies ahead over a stile,

and yet another beck, along the shore, and back into Buttermere village at last; the end of a glorious walk which is a definite 'must' indeed. *Time: 3½hrs.*

2. A Walk in Eskdale   G9

This is a well-favoured walk and set in the most attractive country. Parts of the route are steep and, inevitably, it can be muddy, so boots and gaiters are advisable unless the weather has been very dry for several days, an unusual event in the Lake District.

Park by the 'Ratty' rail terminus at Dalegarth, and walk up the road towards Boot. Press on up the main street of Boot past the Post Office, over the bridge by the watermill, and onto the cobbled track which leads directly up to Eskdale Moor. After about an hour this track arrives by the beck which runs out of Burnmoor Tarn, which lies to the left. Take a break and a few photographs here. Then return down the track, with the beck on the right hand, to a cairn where the minor footpath veers off to the left, over usually muddy ground but supplied with flat, helpful stepping stones, and across a bridge over the beck, with the rocks of Eskdale Fell directly ahead. Follow the contours around the southern slopes of this fell, on a route waymarked with white crosses on the stones. This path leads to another small tarn, Eel Tarn.

The path turns sharp right here and curves south onto a wider, drier path, which eventually runs onto a metalled farm track which will lead back into Boot and so to the car park at Dalegarth; an excellent walk to start a holiday in the high fells. *Time: 4hrs.*

3. A Short Walk from Keswick   I4

Leave Keswick on the B5289 road for Borrowdale, but after about a mile, stop at the Great Wood car park on the left and pick up the footpath on the left which leads to Ashness. After taking in the great views across Derwent Water along this path, return down the path, forking right for a kissing gate onto the road and right for Falcon Crag. The path leads through the farmyard and along the stream, past Lady's Rake, to a signpost pointing right for Rakefoot Farm over a ford and back into Great Wood. Following this well-trodden path leads eventually to the car park. Cross the car park to a stile in the wall and then turn right along a footpath, which runs beside the road, to a track from where another path leads down along the shores of Derwent Water. *Time: 3hrs.*

4. Ullswater – Howtown to   M5
   Glenridding

A walk combined with a trip on a lake steamer must appeal to all visitors. This one can be made in either direction but begins at Howtown on the eastern shore of Ullswater. From the pier turn south, and pick up the lakeshore pass, to a point opposite Skelly Neb, where the lake narrows. From here proceed through Hallinhag Wood into the hamlet of Sandwick, keeping right over the bridge, climbing steadily, with vast views opening up across the lake. The path contours round, over a bridge, and descends under Birk Fell to the lake shore, past Silver Bay and so into Patterdale at the head of the lake. Cross the beck, and follow the footpath or the road back to Glenridding to pick up a steamer at the pier. *Time: 3½hrs.*

5. Wasdale   E9

There is walking around Wasdale for every kind of walker, but this walk offers the rambler fine views without great effort, and begins by the church at Nether Wasdale. Walk from here down the road towards Wast Water for about 500 yards before turning right over the bridge and picking up the farm track that leads past the weir to Easthwaite Farm, at the southern edge of The Screes. Turn left, past the farm buildings and follow the clear path which leads down to the bridge and through Low Wood to the eastern shore of the lake. This is a real beauty spot, with the lake as foreground, The Screes behind, reflected in the water, while Kirk Fell and Great Gable serve as a backdrop at the head of the lake.

From here, a clear path leads along the side of the lake, passing in front of Wasdale Hall, and finally emerges onto the minor road which leads to Wasdale Head. Follow this road north to the first track junction, where the walk turns left, away from the lake, to the scattered hamlet of Greendale. Here, a signposted footpath on the left leads between stone walls through Roan Wood, across fields and then back onto the minor road, where the route turns left and brings the walker back to Nether Wasdale. *Time: 3hrs.*

6. A Walk from Wasdale Head   G8

The fells around Wasdale Head are really best suited to climbers and serious fell walkers. However, to drive up here and then not set foot in the countryside would be a real shame, and this short two-hour stroll will, at the very least, give you a taste of the high country and whet your appetite for walking in the Lake District.

Park by the green at Wasdale Head, and then walk back down the road towards Wast Water, over the bridge and then turn right over a stile to the banks of a small beck. Follow up the beck until you come to the small hump of an old packhorse bridge. Just above this lies Ritson Force, another attractive waterfall, but the path from the bridge is rocky, so cross the bridge and follow the opposite bank of the beck, picking up another path on the right, along a smaller beck. Follow this, crossing and recrossing the stream several times to the farm at Burnthwaite. The path leads through the farmyard over a cattle grid and back past the church into Wasdale Head. This is quite a well-trodden route, and it can get very muddy, so a change of footwear might be advisable before entering the Wasdale Head Hotel or your car. *Time: 2hrs.*

Eating & drinking

Ambleside   L9

De Quincey Bistro & Wine Bar
Waterhead, Ambleside. Tel Ambleside (0966) 32254. Typical bistro with good food and a wide selection of wines including English and South African, among the more usual selection of French, Italian, German and Spanish. 1985 winner of the AA Wine Bar of the Year Award for the Northern Region. *Open May–Sep LD Mon–Sun; Oct–Apr Fri & Sat D only, Sun L only. Closed last two weeks in Dec & all Jan.* A.Ax.V. ££.

Kirkstone Foot Country House Hotel
Kirkstone Pass Rd, Ambleside. Tel Ambleside (0966) 32232. Once a manor house, now a country house hotel set in two acres of grounds. The well-appointed restaurant (complete with old oak beams and polished mahogany tables) looks out over the stream that runs through the gardens. Five-course dinner, with a single sitting at *20.00*, includes some unusual starters, a roast, home-made desserts and English cheeses. *Open Feb–mid Nov & 10 days before Xmas D only Mon–Sun.* Dc.V. £££.

Rothay Manor Hotel & Restaurant
Rothay Bridge, Ambleside. Tel Ambleside (0966) 33605. Delightful Regency hotel with a formal and highly recommended restaurant. Especially noted for the five-course set dinner, including good soups, game and local lamb dishes. The hotel provides a very fine tea with all the

trimmings – scones, home-made jam, sandwiches, quiche, treacle tart, cakes, etc. *Open LD Mon–Sun. Closed Jan–first week in Feb.* A.Ax.Dc.V. **£££**.

Sheila's Cottage
The Slack, Ambleside. Tel Ambleside (0966) 33079. A good country restaurant, tea and coffee shop, often crowded in summer when hungry visitors enjoy the delicious cakes, or the ham or kipper pâté on toast. The proper lunchtime menu features a few Swiss-influenced dishes, as well as hot Solway shrimps and Stilton pâté. Interesting teas. *Open Mon–Sat 10.15–17.30. Closed Sun, Nat hols, Jan & first half Feb.* **££**.

Stock Ghyll Snacks
Central Bldgs, Ambleside. Tel Ambleside (0966) 33334. Recommended by Hunter Davis as offering 'the best sausage, egg and chips in the Lake District'. Just the place to eat after a wet day out on the fells. *Open May–end Oct Mon–Sun 09.00–18.00; Nov–Apr 09.00–18.00 six days only.* **£**.

Zeffirellis Pizzeria & Garden Room Cafe
Compston Rd, Ambleside. Tel Ambleside (0966) 33845. Upstairs in a striking, Japanese art deco setting, you can enjoy wholefood pizzas, pastas and various interesting vegetarian dishes, as well as omelettes and pancakes. The restaurant is attached to the town's cinema and offers a three-course candlelit dinner with a cinema ticket for an all-inclusive price. On the lower level, a cheerful cafe for soups, salads, tea, coffee and home-made cakes. *Pizzeria open all year LD Mon–Sun 12.00–15.30 & 17.00–21.45. Cafe open Easter–end Oct & Xmas 10.00–17.00.* **££**.

Bassenthwaite Lake G2

The Pheasant Inn
Wythop, Bassenthwaite Lake. Tel Bassenthwaite (059681) 234. Attractive pub/restaurant in a 16thC coaching inn with mellow tobacco-stained walls lending a cosy atmosphere. Offers breakfasts and bar lunches, restaurant lunches and dinners. Good food includes home-made pâtés and quiches, pheasant in season and Silloth shrimps. *Open all year Mon–Sun 08.30–09.45 for breakfast; LD 12.00–14.00 & 19.00–20.15. Closed Xmas day.* **££**.

Buttermere G5

Bridge Hotel
Buttermere. Tel Buttermere (059685) 252/254. Close to Buttermere Lake and Crummock Water, this tastefully-decorated hotel restaurant and bar offers Cumbrian hot-pot, black pudding and home-made sausages for bar snacks lunch and evening during the week. French cooking in the restaurant. Menu changes daily. Patio for outdoor eating in fine weather. *Open D Mon–Sun, L Sun only. Closed Dec & Jan.* **££**.

Cockermouth E2

Old Court House
2 Main St, Cockermouth. Tel Cockermouth (0900) 823871. On the site of its namesake, this pleasant restaurant provides both lunch and dinner with a continental emphasis. Lunchtime dishes include German soups, open sandwiches, scampi and chops. Set menu in the evening. *Open all year LD Mon–Sat. Closed Sun & Nat hols.* **££**.

Dockray L4

The Royal Hotel
Dockray, Ullswater. Tel Glenridding (08532) 356. On the A5091. One of the oldest inns in Cumbria and so-called because it carries Mary Queen of Scots' coat of arms. The scene of a biennial shepherds' meet, where the farmers gather to sort out their flocks. A good walker's pub, with extensive bar meals including T-bone steak, Cumberland sausage, plaice and chips, soups and even 'tattie pot' on special occasions. Four-course set dinner in the restaurant. *Open all year LD Mon–Sun.* **£**.

Elterwater J9

The Britannia Inn
Elterwater. Tel Langdale (09667) 210. Off the B5343. A traditional English inn with low beams and oak furniture, set in beautiful country. Lunchtime and evening bar meals include pizzas, ploughman's, steak and kidney pie. Also provides full restaurant dinners with a good choice of wines. Children welcome. *Bar meals all year during licensing hours Mon–Sun. Open Easter–mid Nov D Mon–Sun; mid Nov–Easter D Sat only.* **££**.

Embleton F2

Wythop Mill
Embleton. Tel Bassenthwaite Lake (059681) 394. This converted sawmill, which houses a museum of vintage wood-working machinery powered by a water-wheel, also contains an attractive tearoom. In local terms, this means meals and snacks from morning to early evening. Everything is home-made from soups and

salads, to pâtés, flans, meringues and scones. *Open Easter–Oct Tue–Sun 10.30–17.30. D Thur only (essential to reserve). Closed Mon.* **££.**

Eskdale Green F10

Bower House Inn
Eskdale Green. Tel Eskdale (09403) 244. Very much a village pub, always full of locals at lunchtime. Bar snacks and a separate restaurant for evening meals.

Menu changes daily but may feature venison, duck, guinea fowl or pork and home-made sweets. Real ale available and children welcome. *Open all year during normal licensing hours. D Mon–Sun 19.00–20.30. Closed Xmas.* **££.**

Grange-in-Borrowdale H5

Grange Bridge Cottage
Grange-in-Borrowdale, Keswick. Tel Borrowdale (059684) 201. This tearoom by the bridge over the Derwent in the 'Jaws of Borrowdale' serves delicious home-made cakes, sponges, sandwiches and scones. Also light lunches and morning coffees. *Open Tue–Sun 10.00–17.30. Closed Mon & from 1 Nov–two weeks before Easter.* **£.**

Grasmere J8

Michael's Nook Country House Hotel
Grasmere. Tel Grasmere (09665) 496. Formal and beautifully furnished restaurant, full of fine antiques, with the ambience of a private dining room. There are only nine tables. Table d'hôte menu, which changes daily, at lunchtime and in the evening with a good choice of dishes in each course. Quality cuisine and comprehensive wine list. Booking is advisable. *Open all year LD Mon–Sun.* **£££+.**

The Rowan Tree Cafe
Langdale Rd, Grasmere. Tel Grasmere (09665) 528. A small vegetarian restaurant and cafe serving only natural foodstuffs. Some meat dishes, too. Licensed. *Open*

Apr–mid Nov Mon–Sun 10.00–20.00. Closed mid Nov–end Mar Mon–Fri. **££.**

Great Langdale J8

Old Dungeon Ghyll Hotel
Langdale. Tel Langdale (09667) 272. On B5343. No visitor to Lakeland can really miss a visit to this walkers' and climbers' mecca. Not fashionably furnished, with lino on the floors and well-used upholstery on the chairs, but well worth a lunchtime stop. Home-made bar food at both sessions, real ale, children welcome. *Open all year Mon–Sun during normal licensing hours.* **£.**

The Pillar Hotel and Country Club
Great Langdale, Ambleside. Tel Langdale (09667) 302. The restaurant is part of the hotel which in turn is part of a time-sharing complex. Visitors welcome. A wide choice of continental dishes, good wines and, if you can afford it, a £100 cocktail for six, which begins with a base of two bottles of Dom Perignon! There's also a coffee shop for light meals and snacks, as well as a pub-style lunch available.
Open all year LD Mon–Sun. A.Ax.Dc.V. **£–£££.**

Keswick I4

The George Hotel
St John's St, Keswick. Tel Keswick (0596) 72076. An Elizabethan coaching inn, once popular with the Lake poets. Bar lunches feature good snacks and hot dishes. The separate restaurant provides dinner from a table d'hôte menu and an à la carte in season. Real ale and Theakstone's Old Peculiar drawn from the wood; a mecca for lovers of English ale. *Open all year LD Mon–Sun. A.Ax.Dc.V.* **££.**

Greensleeves Restaurant
26–28 St John's St, Keswick. Tel Keswick (0596) 72932. An interesting restaurant which serves a wide range of dishes, mostly French-inspired, but always with fresh, local produce. Run by ex-staff and ex-students from the local catering college. Sees itself as the British version of a French roadside restaurant. Morning coffee with home-made gâteaux, snack lunches and a very reasonable fixed price dinner are offered as well as the excellent à la carte menu. *Open Easter–Oct LD Mon–Sun; Nov–Easter D only Wed–Sat. A.Ax.Dc.V.* **££.**

Mire House H2

The Old Sawmill
Dodd Wood, under Skiddaw. Tel Keswick (0596) 74317. On A591, between Keswick

and Bassenthwaite. This is actually at The Mire House, a 17thC manor house, and forms part of the estate. Serves morning coffee, light lunches and teas. The food is good but simple – soups, salads, sandwiches, home-made scones with cream and jam, apple pie. No licence. There is usually plenty of room. *Open 1 Apr–31 Oct Mon–Sun 10.00–17.30.* **£.**

Rydal   L8
Glen Rothay Hotel
Rydal Water. Tel Ambleside (0966) 32524. Small hotel restaurant overlooking Rydal Water with oak-beamed bar and a patio for summer eating. Full bar meals both at lunchtime and in the evening, as well as a table d'hôte menu for dinner in the restaurant at *19.30*. Home-made soups, pâtés, pies are among the regular fare and the restaurant is developing a good reputation for a variety of vegetarian dishes. *Open LD Mon–Sun. Closed 10 days early Dec & 10 days early Jan.* A.Ax.Dc.V. **££.**

Thornthwaite   H3
Thornthwaite Galleries
Thornthwaite. Tel Braithwaite (059682) 248. A 300-year-old barn which houses a well-known gallery, art shop and tearoom. The gallery contains art and sculpture exclusively by Lakeland and northern artists. The home-cooked lunches and home-made teas are excellent. *Open Mon–Sun 10.00–17.00. Closed last two weeks in Nov.* **££.**

Troutbeck   L8
The Mortal Man Hotel
Troutbeck. Tel Ambleside (0966) 33193. Set in the Kirkstone Pass north of Ambleside. The Mortal Man is another of those necessary stops, a favourite meeting place for the Lake poets, and still a very fine English inn. Bar lunches, table d'hôte restaurant dinner and traditional English lunch on Sunday. Local dishes and good, wholesome food. *Open mid Feb–mid Nov LD Mon–Sun.* **££.**
Queen's Head Inn
Troutbeck. Tel Ambleside (09663) 2174. On A592 N of Windermere. An ancient inn, impossible to miss, set beside the main road but well worth a stop, if only to lean against the bar counter made from a Tudor four-poster bed! Real ale, full bar meals and restaurant service during summer months. *Open all year LD Mon–Sun during normal licensing hours.* **££.**

Ullswater   M4
Sharrow Bay Country House Hotel
Ullswater. Tel Pooley Bridge (08536) 301. 2m S of Pooley Bridge on the E side of Ullswater, opposite Watermillock. This is *the* great hotel of Lakeland, the place for a night out, and a consistent winner of awards for good food, wine and service. Antique furniture, a set five-course meal with a vast choice of expertly prepared dishes. Predominantly English and French cuisine, outstanding wines. Essential to reserve. *Open LD Mon–Sun 13.00 & 20.00 prompt. Closed Dec–early Mar.* **£££+.**

Wasdale Head   G7
Wasdale Head Inn
Wasdale Head, Seascale. Tel Wasdale (09406) 229. Like the Old Dungeon Ghyll in Great Langdale, this hotel is one which cannot be missed by any visitor to the Lake District, if only for the pleasure of getting there. Will Ritson's bar is the centrepiece of the hotel, a slate-floored room named after the celebrated local liar and one-time landlord. The bar is usually packed with fell walkers and provides real ale, Old Peculier. Hearty lunchtime bar snacks – soups, pies, Cumberland ham, local smoked meat platters. The restaurant table d'hôte menu always has dishes based on fresh, local produce. *Open LD Mon–Sun. Closed Nov & Dec.* A.V. **££.**

Watermillock   M4
Leeming-on-Ullswater Hotel Restaurant
Watermillock. Tel Pooley Bridge (08536) 622. Very much the classic hotel restaurant, and very elegant. French and English dishes – ranging from steak chasseur to soup with Stilton, and a notable sweet trolley. Traditional Sunday lunch. *Open LD Mon–Sun 12.30–13.45 & 19.30–20.45. Closed 1st Dec–mid Mar.* A.Ax.Dc.V. **£££+.**
The Old Church Hotel
Watermillock. Tel Pooley Bridge (08536) 204. A small hotel with lawns which run down to the lake. Good quality, fresh food and carefully selected wines. The menu changes daily and everything is home-made. *Open D Mon–Sun 19.30–20.15. Closed 1 Nov–Mar.* **£££.**

Whitehaven   A5
Bruno's Restaurant
9 Church St. Tel Whitehaven (0946) 65270. An Italian restaurant and a good place for lunch or dinner – grills, pastas, steaks, soups and salads. *Open all year LD Mon–Sat, Sun D only.* A.V. **££.**

Camping & caravanning

Camping and caravan sites, especially those in central Lakeland and close to the more famous beauty spots, tend to get very full in summer. Wise campers will phone or write to reserve a pitch well in advance.

Ambleside   L9
Skelwith Fold Caravan Park
Ambleside, Cumbria LA22 0HY. Tel Ambleside (0966) 32277. On B5286 road to Hawkshead. A large park with 125 touring pitches, set in a pleasant woodland. All pitches on hardstanding. Caravans only, no tents. Facilities for shopping, washing, and children. *Open Mar–Nov.* **££**.

Ashness   I5
Ashness Farm
Ashness, Cumbria. Tel Borrowdale (059684) 236. 2m S of Keswick, off the B5289. This tent-only farm site offers simple facilities and 60 tent pitches, but is ideal for walking and touring about Derwent Water. *Open Apr–Oct.* **£**.

Borrowdale   H6
Low Manesty Caravan Site
Borrowdale, near Keswick, Cumbria. Tel Borrowdale (059684) 275. 5m S of Keswick. A Caravan Club site with 60 touring caravan pitches set in beautiful Borrowdale. Static caravans for hire; good on-site facilities. *Open Apr–Oct.* **££**.

Brothers Water   L7
Sykeside Camping Site
Brotherswater, Patterdale, Penrith, Cumbria. Tel Glenridding (08532) 239. 3m S of Glenridding. Set on the south shore of Brotherswater, this well-equipped site offers 80 tent-only pitches at the northern foot of the Kirkstone Pass. Amenities include a shop, washing and ironing facilities, and meals available in the nearby pub. *Open for 80 tents Mar–Nov, for 25 tents Nov–Mar.* **££**.

Buttermere   G5
Dalegarth Campsite
Hassness, Buttermere, Cockermouth, Cumbria. Tel Buttermere (059685) 233. A tent-only site, ideal for walkers or backpackers exploring the local fells, with marvellous views over the lake. 30 pitches and simple facilities. *Open May–Sep.* **£**.

Cockermouth   E2
Graysonside Touring Site
Lorton Rd. Cockermouth, Cumbria. Tel Cockermouth (0900) 823181. A small site with pitches for touring vans only; no tents. Basic facilities. *Open Mar–Nov.* **£**.
Violet Bank Caravan Park
Simonscales La, Cockermouth, Cumbria. Tel Cockermouth (0900) 822169. A little south of Cockermouth centre. This site has 40 pitches for touring caravans or tents. Swings for children, washing and drying rooms, showers, electric light, and easy access to town centre. Full range of on-site facilities. *Open Mar–Nov.* **££**.

Dale Bottom   J4
Dale Bottom Farm
Naddle, Dale Bottom, Cumbria. Tel Keswick (0596) 72176. 2m SE of Keswick, off A591. This site by the Naddle Beck has 30 pitches for caravans and static vans and 30 pitches for tents. Very good facilities for such a small site; electricity, hot showers, shop, telephones etc. *Open Apr–Oct.* **££**.

Glenridding   L5
Gillside Farm Site
Glenridding, Ullswater, Cumbria. Tel Glenridding (08532) 346. A good farm site on the western edge of the village. Ideal for lightweight campers, with 60 tent pitches and 5 caravan pitches. Adequate facilities, close to the lake and good shops and touring connections in Glenridding village. *Open Apr–Oct.* **££**.

Great Langdale   J8
Great Langdale Camp Site
Great Langdale, Ambleside, Cumbria. Tel Langdale (09667) 668. 6m W of Ambleside. On National Trust property, this vast 300-pitch site has good facilities, shop, showers etc and is therefore ideally suited for the climbing and hill walking fraternity. Good pubs close by, notably the Old Dungeon Ghyll. *Open all year.* **££**.
Greenhowe Caravan Park
Great Langdale, Ambleside, Cumbria LA22 9JU. Tel Langdale (09667) 231. A static pitch site for caravans at the head of the Langdale Valley, with first-class units to let, all fully equipped with every luxury. *Open Mar–Nov.* **££**.

Keswick   I4
Castlerigg Hall Caravan & Camping Site
Castlerigg Hall, Keswick, Cumbria CA12 4TE. Tel Keswick (0596) 72437. 1m S of

Keswick. Set on a hillside, overlooking Derwent Water, this well-equipped site offers great views, good walks, fishing and boating nearby, and excellent facilities; 30 caravan pitches and 100 tent pitches. Motor caravans accepted. *Open Apr–Nov.* **££.**

Lakeside Caravan Park
Lakeside, Keswick, Cumbria. Tel Keswick (0596) 72878. Set by Derwent Water, close to the town centre, this site has 18 touring caravan pitches. No tents. Good facilities including a shop, but the town shops are also within easy reach. *Open Mar–Nov.* **££.**

Lamplugh   D4

Inglenook Caravan Park
Lamplugh, Cumbria. Tel Lamplugh (0946) 861240. 6m S of Cockermouth. Set in beautiful countryside, this excellent site is close to Crummock Water, Buttermere and several other lakes. 36 touring caravan pitches and 6 tent pitches. Excellently furnished static vans also available for hire. Well-stocked camp shop, children's play area. *Open Mar–Nov.* **££.**

Rosthwaite   I6

Chapel House Farm
Rosthwaite, Borrowdale, Cumbria. Tel Borrowdale (059684) 633. 6m S of Keswick. This is a tent-only site, with 30 pitches. Ideal for exploring the beauties of Borrowdale. *Open all year.* **££.**

St Bees   A7

Beachcomber Caravan Site
St Bees, Cumbria. Tel Egremont (0946) 822540. 3m W of Egremont. This small but well-equipped site has 18 touring pitches for caravans and a number of static vans. Pre-booking essential in *Jul & Aug. Open Apr–Nov.* **££.**

St Bees Chalet & Trailer Park
St Bees, Cumbria. Tel Egremont (0946) 822335. This large and excellent site has 165 caravan pitches and 100 tent pitches, plus a limited number of static vans for hire. Facilities include a licensed bar, 9-hole golf course nearby, hot showers and well-stocked shop. *Open all year.* **££.**

Troubeck   L3

Gillhead Farm
Troutbeck, Penrith, Cumbria. Tel Threlkeld (059683) 652. *Not* at the Troutbeck near Ambleside, but on a farm site at the other Troutbeck, 8m E of Keswick, on A5091. This site has 21 touring caravan pitches, a camp shop and

good facilities including laundry room. *Open Apr–Oct.* **££.**

Hutton Moor End Caravan & Camp Site
Troutbeck, Penrith, Cumbria. Tel Threlkeld (059683) 615. Close to the A66 road. This small, well-equipped site has 20 touring caravan pitches and 15 tent pitches. Showers; fresh milk from the farm on sale daily. *Open Apr–Oct.* **££.**

Wasdale Head   G8

Wasdale Head Camp Site
Wasdale, Seascale, Cumbria. Tel Wasdale (09406) 220. 9m NE of Ravenglass. There can be few camping grounds in Lakeland with a setting to match this National Trust site, with 120 tent-only pitches close to Wast Water. Good facilities including showers and a shop. Also takes a few caravanettes. *Open Apr–Oct.* **£.**

Watermillock   M4

The Quiet Site
Watermillock, Ullswater, Penrith, Cumbria CA11 OLS. Tel Pooley Bridge (08536) 337. An excellent, family-run site, overlooking Ullswater. Ideal for campers, with good facilities, including an 'Olde Worlde' licensed bar, laundrette and shop; 12 caravan and 50 tent pitches, plus 21 permanent caravans. *Open Mar–Oct.* **££.**

Ullswater Caravan, Camping & Marine Park
Watermillock, Ullswater, Penrith, Cumbria CA11 OLR. Tel Pooley Bridge (08536) 666. 2m SW of Pooley Bridge. Set 1m from the lake, this site has 40 caravan pitches, 115 tent pitches, 13 caravans for hire and 7 holiday homes. Full on-site facilities including a camp shop, children's playground, licensed bar, and lakeside boat launching. *Open Mar–Nov.* **££.**

Youth hostels

The Lake District has plenty of youth hostels, but they tend to get very full in the summer when the walkers and cyclists arrive. Pre-booking is therefore essential, and all reservations should be confirmed in writing. Opening times may vary slightly from year to year, so it is always advisable to check in advance of arrival.

Boot   G10

Eskdale Youth Hostel
Boot, Holmrook, Cumbria CA19 1TH. Tel Eskdale (09403) 219. A purpose-built modern hostel with 56 beds, close to The Woolpack Inn. Evening meal 19.00. Store. Car parking only. Closed 6 weeks before or after Xmas (alternates each year).

Borrowdale   H6

Longthwaite Youth Hostel
Longthwaite, Keswick, Cumbria CA12 5XE. Tel Borrowdale (059684) 257. Attractive, superior grade modern hostel, built of wood, in the centre of Borrowdale on the west bank of the River Derwent. 94 beds, evening meal 19.00. Small store. Car parking. Closed 6 weeks before or after Xmas (alternates each year).

Buttermere   G5

King George VI Memorial Hostel
Buttermere, Cockermouth, Cumbria CA13 9XA. Tel Buttermere (059685) 254. ¼m S of Buttermere village on the B5289 road to Honister Pass, overlooking Buttermere. 63 beds. Evening meal 19.00. Small store. Nearest shops and post office at Lorton. Parking available. Closed 6 weeks before or after Xmas (alternates each year).

Cockermouth   E2

Cockermouth Youth Hostel
Double Mills, Cockermouth, Cumbria CA13 ODS. Tel Cockermouth (0900) 822561. An attractive standard grade hostel in a 17thC watermill on the southern edge of the town. 28 beds. Evening meal 19.00, plus bar snacks and packed lunches. Small store. Parking for cars. Closed Wed & 6 weeks before or after Xmas (alternates each year). Open Thur–Tue.

Derwent Water   I4

Derwent Water Youth Hostel
Barrow House, Borrowdale, Keswick, Cumbria CA12 5UR. Tel Borrowdale (059684) 246. Superior grade hostel in converted mansion, overlooking Derwent Water, south of Keswick. 95 beds. Grounds have a waterfall and contain red squirrels. Evening meal 19.00. Store. Car and coach parking. Closed 6 weeks before or after Xmas (alternates each year).

Elterwater   J9

Elterwater Youth Hostel
Elterwater, Ambleside, Cumbria LA22 9HX. Tel Langdale (09667) 245. Standard grade hostel in a farmhouse situated in Great Langdale Valley. 42 beds. Evening meal 19.00. Store. Shops and post office in Chapel Stile. Parking in village. Closed Dec–end first week in Feb.

Ennerdale Water   E6

Black Sail Youth Hostel
Black Sail Hut, Ennerdale, Cleator, Cumbria CA23 3AY. Postal bookings only, sent well in advance – no telephone available. This is the most isolated youth hostel in England, set in an old bothy with 19 beds, simple accommodation. Evening meal 19.00. No access for cars. Nearest shop at Wasdale Head three miles away. Closed beginning Nov–end Feb.

Ennerdale Youth Hostel
Cat Crag, Ennerdale, Cleator, Cumbria CA23 3AX. Tel Lamplugh (0946) 861237. Standard hostel in two converted cottages, just to the east of Ennerdale Water. 24 beds. Evening meal 19.00. Small store. Closed beginning Nov–end Feb.

Glenridding   L5

Helvellyn Youth Hostel
Greenside, Glenridding, Penrith, Cumbria CA11 0QR. Tel Glenridding (08532) 269. 1½m W of Glenridding. Set 1000ft above sea level, a standard grade modern hostel in old Lakeland dwelling. Offers plenty of courses in outdoor activities. 74 beds. Evening meal 19.00. Small store. Parking available. Closed second week Nov–28 December.

Grasmere   J8

Grasmere Youth Hostel
Butharlyp How, Grasmere, Ambleside, Cumbria LA22 9QG. Tel Grasmere (09665) 316. Superior grade hostel in Victorian mansion with 89 beds. Set in beautiful grounds to the north of Grasmere village. Evening meal 19.00. Small store. Car parking only. Closed 6 weeks before or after Xmas (alternates each year).

Thorney How Hostel
Grasmere, Ambleside, Cumbria LA22
9QW. Tel Grasmere (09665) 591. ½m
NW of Grasmere. Standard grade hostel
in old farmhouse, first opened in 1932. 46
beds. Evening meal *19.00*. Small store. No
parking. *Closed 6 weeks before or after Xmas
(alternates each year)*.

Keswick   **I4**

Keswick Youth Hostel
Station Rd, Keswick, Cumbria CA12
5LH. Tel Keswick (0596) 72484.
Standard grade hostel in town centre on
banks of River Greta near Fitz Park; 91
beds, members kitchen. Breakfast *08.15*,
evening meal *19.00*. Packed lunches
available. Store. Shops in town. Parking
in town. *Closed 6 weeks before or after
Xmas (alternates each year)*.

Loughrigg   **K8**

High Close Youth Hostel
High Close, Loughrigg, Ambleside,
Cumbria LA22 9HJ. Tel Langdale
(09667) 313. Large, 96-bed hostel in
National Trust property, near Red Bank,
with great views to Grasmere. Breakfast
07.45–08.30, evening meal *18.30–19.15*.
Packed lunches. Store. Games Room. Car
parking only. *Closed 6 weeks before or after
Xmas (alternates each year)*.

Patterdale   **L6**

Goldrill House Youth Hostel
Patterdale, Penrith, Cumbria CA11 ONW
Tel Glenridding (08532) 394. Another
purpose-built hostel, set to the south of
Ullswater, just off A592 road to
Kirkstone. 78 beds, evening meal *19.00*.
Car parking only. *Closed 6 weeks before or
after Xmas (alternates each year)*.

Seatoller   **H6**

Honister Hause Youth Hostel
Seatoller, Keswick, Cumbria CA12 5XN.
Tel Borrowdale (059684) 267. Purpose-
built hostel at summit of Honister
Pass, west of village. 30 beds, breakfast
08.00, evening meal *19.00*. Small store.
Car parking. *Closed beginning Nov–
end Feb*.

Waterhead   **L9**

Ambleside Youth Hostel
Waterhead, Ambleside, Cumbria LA22
OEU. Tel Ambleside (0966) 32304. Large
hostel on Lake Windermere with 240 beds.
Full cafeteria service available daily for
breakfast and from *17.30* for evening meal.
Parking for cars only. Store. Shops and
post office in Ambleside. *Closed Wed & 6
weeks before or after Xmas (alternates each
year)*.

CARLISLE & THE SOLWAY COAST

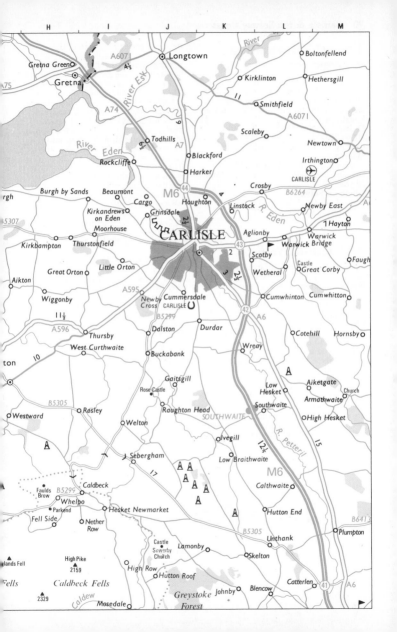

Tourist information centres

Carlisle   **K4**
Old Town Hall, Green Market. Tel (0228)
25517. Operates a local bed-booking
service. Access for disabled. *Open all year.*
Longtown   **J1**
21 Swan St. Near Carlisle. Tel Carlisle
(0228) 791201. Operates local bed-
booking service. *Open all year.*
Maryport   **A9**
1 Senhouse St. Tel (090081) 3738.
Operates local bed-booking service. *Open
all year.*
Silloth-on-Solway   **C5**
Council Offices, Eden St. Tel (0965)
31944. Access for disabled. *Open
Easter–Oct.*

The Countryside

North of Cumbria's small industrial belt
on the coastline between Whitehaven and
Workington, the landscape changes yet
again to present another varied side of the
countryside of Cumbria. This gazetteer
section embraces the northern limit of the
fells and historic Caldbeck, the river-
threaded rolling plain that runs west to
the coast and east to the great city of
Carlisle, and finally the Border country,
bisected these two thousand years by that
famous landmark, the Roman Wall, built
by the Emperor Hadrian.
The views in this part of Cumbria are
placid rather than dramatic. But if the
landscape lacks that scenic majesty which
the traveller can find around every corner
in the central fells, it makes up for it with
a great sense of space, sky and texture;
the cloud-tipped backcloth of the
mountains to the south and east, the sea
rippling away to the west and across the
Solway Firth, the green hills of Galloway
which seem close enough to touch.
The change from high fell to coastal plain
is fairly gradual, and indeed few parts of
the Lake District can match the Uldale
Fells or Caldbeck Fells for space and
beauty, though these are much gentler and
more even hills than the steep-sided
mountains just to the south, but well
supplied with views even so.
The plain, which is traversed north-east to
south-west by the great A595 road from
Carlisle to Cockermouth and Whitehaven,
is farming country, sprinkled with small
villages and hamlets. The pleasant valley
of the River Eden, one of the beauty spots
of Cumbria, makes its entrance to this
section south of Carlisle, before flowing
into the Solway Firth near Rockcliffe
Marsh.
North and east of the Eden, the Border
Country begins. This is the western part
of the so-called 'Debatable Land', fought
over by the Anglo-Scots raiders, known
as the Steel Bonnets, for hundreds of years
until the two kingdoms were united, at
least politically, in the 17thC with the
accession of James I to the English
throne. It was due to these numerous
Border Wars and endless forays that this
part of Cumbria, and notably the Eden
Valley, became endowed with so many
pele towers and castles. Some have fallen
into ruin, others have been absorbed to
form part of the fabric in newer buildings
which date from more peaceful times.
Enough remain, however, to provide a
unique feature of the landscape, perching

on the crest of a hill, or standing beside a bridge or ford.

All in all, this north-west corner of Cumbria is a restful place. Even in summer, it is quite possible to find an empty road, a deserted beach or a quiet path across the fells. There are some very agreeable towns and villages, and with the added attraction of the historic city of Carlisle, the visitor will find enough here to satisfy any desire, in fell or coast, in town or country.

Nature trail

Glasson Moss Nature Reserve   F3
Kynanc Farm, Bowness Common, Bowness-on-Solway. This is an open area of bogland, with unrestricted access, just south of Bowness-on-Solway, noted for rare mosses. Prolific birdlife in spring and early summer.

Lakes

Over Water   G10
Uldale. A small lake, less than a quarter of a mile long, which with Little Tarn, just to the south, feeds the River Ellen.

Mountains & fells

In this part of Cumbria, the hills lie to the south of the region, around John Peel's town of Caldbeck. The most notable are:

Caldbeck Fells   H10
S of Caldbeck village. Rising in long ridgebacks to High Pike, 2159ft.

Faulds Brow   H8
Set on the most northern tip of the National Park, this last outcrop of the fells, north-west of Caldbeck, rises to 1030ft, and offers great views to the north and west.

Uldale Fells   G10
These fells centre on Knolt, to the south-east of Longlands village. They are north facing hills on the north-western limit of the National Park, rising to 1690ft at Great Cockup, east of Bassenthwaite, and 1580ft at Longlands Fell, offering great, breezy walks. Ideal for when the central fells are crowded.

Viewpoints

Bowness-on-Solway   F3
This little village, set on a promontory and occupying the site of a fort built to hold the western end of the Roman Wall, offers fine views across the Firth to Galloway, and along the flat, windswept

coastline to Burgh-by-Sands. The road to the south is a picturesque route.

Longlands Fell   G10
Rising to 1580ft, this round-topped fell offers superb views north across the plain to the Solway Firth, and is reached by an easy path beside the beck, which runs down the valley to the east.

Parkend   H9
Parkend lies 2m W of Caldbeck on the road to Uldale, where a bridge spans the Park Beck. There are great views of the fells from any point north of the cattle grid.

The Coast

The coastline here begins by the little harbour at Maryport, and runs north, while sweeping east into the great bay of the Solway Firth. The coastline is flat and open, marked by great curving shallow bays, as at Allonby and Beckfoot, and deeper indentations, the result of river outfalls, as at Moricambe Bay, fed by the rivers Wampool and Waver. The most northern bay by Rockcliffe is an area of marsh and sand dune, fed by the Eden and the Esk. The tides and currents can be fierce along this coast so any seabathing should be carried out with care; the spring tides rise high enough to cut off the minor coast road close to Bowness-on-Solway, which can cause road diversions. But all in all, this coastline is most attractive, and a notable haunt of birdlife, especially in the late spring.

Beaches

Allonby   B8
This six-mile beach of sand, mud and rock has been used for seabathing for well over 100 years.

Beckfoot   C6
A long beach between Allonby and Silloth, of shingle and sand. Beware of strong currents and the ebb tide.

Silloth   C5
The beach here is sandy, but bathing is only advisable when the warning notices are complied with, and *never* during the ebb tide.

Towns & villages

Abbey Town   E6
5m E of Silloth. Abbey Town takes its name from the fact that in 1150, when this part of Cumbria belonged to the Scots,

the Cistercians built Holm Cultram
Abbey here. It now serves as the parish
church although only the nave and
doorway of the original Abbey remain.
The porch bears the Plantagenet arms,
and the sight is still impressive.

Allonby   **B8**
6m N of Maryport. Allonby is just a little
place, which was once a fishing village
before becoming a popular bathing resort
of the Victorians, who found the beach,
the breeze and the chill waters of Allonby
suitably bracing. There are good views
across the Solway, and the Victoria Sea
Water Baths are architecturally
interesting.

Aspatria   **D8**
8m NE of Maryport. *EC Thur. MD Fri.*
Aspatria lies on the north bank of the
attractive River Ellen, and is chiefly noted
for its beautiful church, which is basically
Victorian but incorporates many of the
features of the previous medieval church;
St Kentigern was only built in 1848, but
the arch is 14thC. In the churchyard is
the grave of Sir Wilfrid Lawson, the local
squire, and a staunch tee-totaller, who
died in 1906. On the local nine-hole golf
course visitors will find the 'Whisky
Pond' where Sir Wilfrid poured out the
contents of his cellar when he signed the
pledge. Aspatria is attractively situated
close to both the fells and the north-
western coast.

Bowness-on-Solway   **F3**
14m W of Carlisle. Bowness is a small
village set on the low-lying Solway coast
and built on the site of the Roman fort of
Maia, at the western end of Hadrian's
Wall. A plan of the old fort is attached to
the wall of the King's Arms. The small
church of St Michael dates from the early
11thC and has Norman doors and a
Norman font. From the ground to the
east, there are great views across the water
to Galloway.

Burgh-by-Sands   **I3**
5m NW of Carlisle. Another little village,
standing directly on Hadrian's Wall,
although since the stones of the wall were
used to build the village, no signs of the
Roman wall remain. St Michael's Church
is Norman, and one mile north of the
village, along a footpath, a monument
inside a metal railing marks the spot where
Edward I, the Hammer of the Scots, died
in 1306.

Caldbeck   **I9**
9m S of Thursby. Caldbeck has one great
and enduring claim to fame, and one that
attracts visitors to the village from all over

the world, for this is the birth and burial
place of the famous huntsman, John Peel,
he of the 'coat so gay'. Peel was born at
Parkend, two miles south-west of
Caldbeck, in 1776, and after a hunting
accident at Ruthwaite, was buried in St
Kentigern's churchyard here in
November 1854. His gravestone is
decorated with hunting horns. The song
which made his name 'D'ye ken John Peel'
was written by Peel's close friend, John
Graves of Caldbeck, after they had been
out hunting in 1832, and was first sung
in the Rising Sun Inn, which is now the
Oddfellows Arms in Caldbeck. Graves'
house in Caldbeck bears a plaque to his
memory. Caldbeck today is a rather small,
straggling village, at the northern foot of
the fells, a good departure point for
Uldale or the road to Mungrisdale and
Blencathra.

Carlisle   **K4**
16m N of Penrith. *Pop 105,000. EC Thur.
MD Wed & Sat.* Carlisle is a very old and
rather splendid Border town, the western
bastion of the Scots march during the long
centuries of the Border Wars. Today it is
rather quieter, and less traffic-ridden
than it used to be, now that the M6
motorway carries most of the heavy traffic
clear of the town. The Romans built the
first settlement here, behind Hadrian's
Wall which spans the county to the north
and runs to the sea at Bowness-on-
Solway, 12 miles to the west. William
Rufus began Carlisle Castle in 1092, but
it was not finished until well into the next
century, and has been in constant use as
a fortress, prison and barracks, ever since.
Mary Queen of Scots was imprisoned here
in 1568, and Jacobite prisoners from
Bonnie Prince Charles' retreating army,
languished in the dungeons in 1746. The
keep is Norman, the main gate dates from
1300, and the whole castle, which contains
the museum of The Border Regiment, is
well worth inspecting.
The Norman cathedral, which dates from
1124 and was built originally as a priory
for the Augustinians, is one of the smallest
in the country, but one of the oldest in
the North. Other attractions include the
late-medieval half-timbered Guildhall,
which now contains a local history
museum, and the Tullie House Museum
in Castle Street, which has a good
collection of prehistoric artifacts.
As a popular stop on the road to Scotland,
Carlisle has theatres, pubs, plenty of
hotels and restaurants, and is a good
touring base for the Borders and the Lake

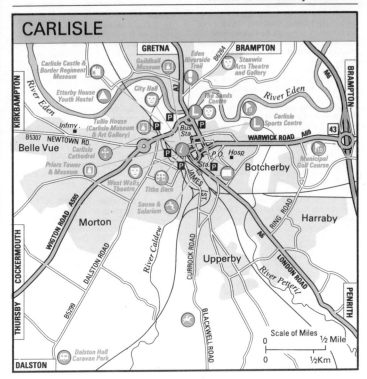

CARLISLE

District directly to the south. The town has two new and attractive developments; one the Sands Centre by the ring-road, which will present everything from concerts to exhibitions, and the vast new under-cover shopping area, The Lanes, between Lowther St and Scotch St.

Dalston   J6
5m SW of Carlisle. The road from Carlisle to Dalston gives fine views of the Northern Fells, while Dalston Hall, a former pele tower, guards the entrance to the village, which has an attractive 13thC church in the local red sandstone, and many 18thC houses.

Great Corby   L5
4m SE of Carlisle. This attractive village, the home of the Howards of Corby Castle for over 400 years, is now a conservation area. The castle is now essentially a country house but built around a 14thC

pele tower with many later additions, and has attractive grounds.

Hesket Newmarket   I9
½m E of Caldbeck. Hesket Newmarket is just a little place, almost a suburb of Caldbeck, but it has a charter for a market and was rebuilt for that purpose in the

Dalston Hall

18thC. The houses in the market square all look in towards the cross. Hesket Hall, built during the reign of Charles I, is an unusual, square-built house with pointed roof and a central chimney stack.

Ireby   F9
6m W of Caldbeck. Like Hesket Newmarket, Ireby, although just a little place, has a charter for a market which dates back to 1237. The village still retains the old market square, and the Moot Hall where traders disputes were settled. Today it is just a quiet residential village, but John Keats visited the Sun Inn in 1818 and this pub remains popular with the locals.

Longtown   J1
6m N of Carlisle. *EC Wed. MD Thur.* On the River Esk, Longtown is an old, rather featureless town. It was once a coaching stop on the road to Scotland, but is now a centre for the local farmers. The Graham Arms, and the old 18thC terraced houses are attractive.

Maryport   A9
7m N of Workington. *Pop 12,000. EC Wed. MD Fri.* Maryport is a fishing town on the estuary of the River Ellen, which became prosperous in the late 18thC as a shipping centre for the local coal and iron ore. A local industrialist expanded the old fishing village and changed its name from Ellenfoot to Maryport, after his wife. Today Maryport has lapsed into its former quiet state, but it is a popular touring base, with a pleasant harbour, good pubs, and an interesting Maritime Museum.

Mosedale   I10
6m S of Caldbeck. A quiet village on the River Caldew, close to the prehistoric hill fort on Carrock Fell. It was once a centre for the Quakers, who built a meeting house here in 1702, and it later became a mining village.

Newton Arlosh   F5
4m N of Abbey Town. Now well inland, Newton Arlosh was once a port, used by Edward I during his Scottish campaigns. The church of St James dates from 1303, and is built round a former pele tower, for times of defence, when even cattle would have been driven into the nave.

Silloth   C5
14m N of Maryport. *Pop 3000. EC Tue. MD Fri.* Silloth is a small but agreeable resort town on the Solway Firth. During the last century it had busy docks and was a ferry port for Ireland, and this period has left the town with wide streets and promenades, lots of lawns and gardens, and a small interesting harbour.

Uldale   G9
4m SW of Caldbeck. Set on the River Ellen, on the slopes of the Uldale Fells, near the little lake at Over Water, most of the buildings in this little village date from the 18th and early 19thC. John Peel's wife, Mary White, was born here in 1769, and it was from here that they eloped to Gretna Green in 1797.

Wetheral   L5
4m E of Carlisle. A prosperous village grouped around a large green on the banks of the Eden, overlooked from across the river by Corby Castle, a home of the Howards since the 16thC. Many of the family are buried in the church of the Holy Trinity, which also contains the effigy of Sir Richard Salkeld, who died in 1500.

Wigton   G6
11m SW of Carlisle. *EC Thur. MD Tue.* Set in the farming country between Carlisle and Maryport, Wigton is a busy little community, with a market charter dating back to 1262. There are some fine 19thC buildings in the main street, and some good country-style shops selling fresh farm produce. The Wigton horse sales bring dealers from all over the country.

Wreay   K6
5m SE of Carlisle. The great attraction in Wreay is the early Victorian church built in 1843 by the Losh family. The whole church is a memorial to Katherine Losh, and is covered with remarkable carvings of animals, insects, fruit and flowers.

Places of interest

Abbey Town   E6
Holm Cultram Abbey
The nave of the abbey church, which now serves as the parish church of St Mary is all that remains of the great Cistercian Abbey of Holm Cultram, built by the Cistercians in 1150. Edward I used the Abbey as his base during the Scots Wars of the early 14thC, and the church still carries a shield of the Plantagenet arms. The Norman door, and the 16thC porch are very fine examples of their period.

Bowness-on-Solway   F3
St Michael's Church
Village centre. This 12thC church is overlooking the Solway Firth, and has fine Norman doorways and a rare example of an early 11thC Norman font.

Burgh-by-Sands   I3

Edward I Monument
Set 1m N of the village, overlooking
Galloway across the Firth. This marks the
spot where Edward I died in 1306.

Lamonby Farm
Tel Burgh-by-Sands (022876) 580. Set by
the Solway Firth, this well-restored 17thC
cruck-framed farmhouse has clay walls and
a thatched roof; a rare surviving example
of a once common type of Solway
farmhouse. *Open daily 'at all reasonable
hours'.* **Charge.**

St Michael's Church
St Michael's is a fortified Border church,
the centre being a pele tower. Note the
narrow door, for ease of defence, and the
heavy iron gate.

Caldbeck   I9

John Peel's Grave
St Kentigern's Church. This church has
Norman elements but stands on a much
earlier Saxon or Danish site. John Peel's
grave, the tombstone carved with hounds
and horns, stands to the left of the path.

Carlisle   K4

Border Regiment Museum
Queen Mary's Tower, Carlisle Castle. Tel
Carlisle (0228) 32774. This fine museum
displays the 200-year-old history of this
famous regiment, now amalgamated to
form the King's Own Royal Border
Regiment, with weapons, uniforms,
trophies, displays of regimental silver, an
audio-visual and video film show and
books. The cost of the visit to this museum
is included in the charge for the Castle.
*Open 15 Mar–15 Oct Mon–Sun
09.30–18.30. 16 Oct–14 Mar Mon–Sat
09.30–16.00; Sun 14.00–16.00.* **Charge.**

Carlisle Castle
Town centre. Tel Carlisle (0228) 31777. A
very fine and well-preserved example of a
medieval Border fortress dating from the
reign of William Rufus, with many later
additions, including a tower built by

*View of Carlisle
Castle*

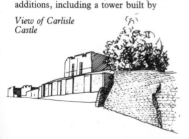

Richard III and a 14thC gatehouse. There
are fine views from the ramparts. Contains
the Museum of the Border Regiment and
an exhibition of memorabilia in the keep
from the castle's long and turbulent
history, notably the Roundhead siege
during the Civil War. Scots prisoners
captured in the 1745 rebellion were
imprisoned in the dungeons and carved
their initials on the walls, while Mary,
Queen of Scots, was confined here for two
months in 1568 and has left several
mementos. *Open 15 Mar–15 Oct Mon–Sat
09.30–18.30, Sun 14.00–18.30. 16 Oct–14
Mar Mon–Sat 09.30–16.00, Sun
14.00–16.00. Closed Xmas eve, Xmas day,
Boxing day, New Yr's day.* **Charge.**

Carlisle Cathedral

Carlisle Cathedral
Tel Carlisle (0228) 34781. Carlisle
Cathedral is basically Norman, dating
from 1124, and built in sandstone. It began
life as a church for Augustinian canons,
and was elevated to a cathedral when
Henry I appointed a bishop to the see in
1133. Much has been changed or altered
over the centuries but the overall effect is
very impressive. The choir was rebuilt in
the Decorated Gothic style after a fire in
1292, although the work was not
completed for 70 years. Yet another fire
followed and destroyed much of the
transept and central tower, which were
rebuilt by the orders of Henry IV, between
1400 and 1419. The stained glass in the
choir is very fine and the carving on the
choir stalls is early 15thC and shows the
lives of the saints. A small museum has
now been opened in the Priors Tower.
Among the buildings in the precincts are
the 16thC gatehouse and tower, and the
Chapter Library, in a building dating from

about 1500. Visitor amenities include a bookshop and a Buttery. The Cathedral is *open daily from 09.30–18.30 in winter; from 09.30–21.30 in summer.*

Carlisle Museum & Art Gallery
Castle St. Tel Carlisle (0228) 34781. Also known as the Tullie House Museum, and set in a Jacobean house near the city centre in its own grounds, this excellent museum contains an impressive collection of Roman artifacts, excavated on or near the Roman Wall. Viking finds include swords and brooches, and there are also displays of pottery and porcelain, costumes and paintings. The natural history section illustrates the wildlife of Cumbria, and other exhibits cover the area's social history and the decorative arts. *Open Apr–Sep Mon–Fri 09.00–19.00, Sat 09.00–17.00; Jun–end Aug Sun 14.30–17.00 also. Oct–Mar Mon–Sat only 09.00–17.00.*

Carlisle Museum & Art Gallery

The Guildhall Museum
Greenmarket. Tel Carlisle (0228) 34781. One of the few remaining examples of a medieval Guildhall left in England. Once the meeting place for the city's eight Trade and Craft Guilds, this 15thC half-timbered hall contains displays of the Town Guilds and local history exhibits include silver, the Guild bell, and their iron-bound muniment chest, as well as the town pillory and stocks. *Open May–Aug Mon–Fri 10.00–18.00, Sat 10.00–17.00; Sep–Apr by appointment only.*

Priors Tower & Museum
The Cathedral. Tel Carlisle (0228) 21834. This well-preserved 13thC pele tower now contains a museum covering the history of the Cathedral, and offering occasional temporary exhibitions. The painted 16thC ceiling has been restored to its original condition. *Open all year 09.30–18.30.*

Stanwix Gallery
Cumbria College of Art & Design, Brampton Rd. Tel Carlisle (0228) 25333.

Exhibits by college staff and students, local artists and firms. *Open during college hours.*

Tithe Barn
West Walls. Tel Carlisle (0228) 32515. An interesting example of a medieval tithe barn, used for storing the food rents due to the Cathedral Chapter. Coffee available *Fri & Sat 10.00–12.00. Open Mon–Sat & Nat hols 10.00–16.00.*

Town Centre Trail
A Town Trail, fully described in an illustrated leaflet, will take the visitor round all the historic parts of Carlisle, starting by the Townhall. This leaflet can be obtained in hotels and from the tourist information centre.

Great Corby   L4

Corby Castle
2m E of Carlisle off the A69 road, beside the River Eden. Only the gardens of this castle, the home of the Howards, are open to the public, but they offer pleasant walks by the riverside. *Open 1 Apr–30 Sep daily 14.00–17.00.* **Charge.**

Maryport   A9

Maryport Maritime Museum
1 Senhouse St. Tel Maryport (0900) 813738. A fascinating local museum in an old building just by the harbour, showing the town's maritime past, and other items of local and maritime interest. The tourist information centre is housed in the same building. *Open Oct–end Apr Mon, Tue, Thur, Fri & Sat 10.00–12.00 & 14.00–16.00. May–end Sep Mon, Wed & Fri 10.00–17.00; Tue, Thur & Sat 10.00–13.00 & 14.00–17.00; Sun 14.00–17.00.* **Free.**

Mealsgate   F8

Whitehall
By A595 road. This 14thC pele tower, with 16thC additions, can be viewed *by appointment only.* Apply to Mrs S. Parkin-Moore, 5 Eton Villas, London NW3.

Rockcliffe   I3

Castletown House
Tel Rockcliffe (022874) 205. This fine early 18thC house, still in private hands, contains a fine collection of furniture and marine paintings. *Open 1 Apr–30 Sep 14.00–17.00 Wed & Nat hol Mons only.* **Charge.**

Unthank   L10

Hutton-in-the-Forest
Tel Skelton (08534) 500. 1m E of Skelton.

This fine country house is built round a medieval pele tower dating from the early 14thC and is the home of Lord Inglewood. There are many later additions and much of the present house dates from the 1600s. Still in private hands, it now contains fine displays of armour, tapestry, furniture, china and paintings. The formal gardens contain a dovecote and a lake, and are *open daily. The house is open Nat hol Suns & Mons, also Thur from 24 May–25 Oct and Fri during Jul & Aug 13.00–16.00.* **Charge.**

Warwick Bridge   M4
Warwick Bridge Corn Mill
5m E of Carlisle off the A69 road. Tel Carlisle (0228) 60218. This is a good and as yet unrestored example of an early 19thC watermill. *Open by appointment only.* **Charge.**

Wreay   K6
St Mary's Church
This church was built in the 1840s as a memorial to a local lady, Katherine Losh, by her sister Sara. The church was designed by Sara and is decorated with carvings of animals, flowers, plants and insects – most unusual.

Local events & attractions

Craft centres

Carlisle   K4
Carlisle Pottery
Close Hse, Linstock. Tel Carlisle (0228) 26833. A working pottery, producing a wide range of articles for sale in the shop. *Open all year Mon–Sat 10.00–16.00.*
Crafts o' the Border
17 Fisher St. Tel Carlisle (0228) 30122. Close to the Townhall and the Cathedral, this shop offers craft goods from all over Cumbria, Galloway and the Borders, including pottery, basketware, kitchen goods. *Open Mon–Sat 09.00–17.30.*
Fiona Habbick & Hazel Campbell
2nd Floor, 54 Lowther St. Crafts in gold and silver, commissions accepted.

West Curthwaite   I6
Ian Laval
Meadowbank Farm. Tel Carlisle (0228) 710404. A cabinet-maker in native hardwoods, felled locally by the craftsman and fashioned in the carpenter's shop.

Commissions welcome. *Open all year Mon–Fri 09.00–18.00.*

Maryport   A9
The Harbour Pottery
South Quay Studio. See craftsmen and women at work in this hand-thrown pottery. *Open Mon–Sun Easter–Sep 11.00–18.00.*

Fairs & shows

Carlisle Great Fair   K4
Tel Carlisle (0228) 2341. Opens by proclamation at the Market Cross and centred on an open-air market in the city centre. An eight-day fair, with a wide range of events and activities for residents and visitors. Stall holders dress in period costume. Non-stop entertainment on a stage in front of the Townhall, plus displays, exhibitions, dances and a grand parade on the final Saturday. Details of daily events from the Townhall or all TICs. *Starts on the Sat nearest to 26 Aug.*
The Cumberland Agricultural Show K4
Bitts Park. Tel Carlisle (0228) 710687. The county's major agricultural show, with produce and livestock competitions and events, horse shows, fell running and Cumberland wrestling. Full details from TICs. *Held in Carlisle on the Sat next to the last Thur in Jul.*
Maryport Carnival Week   A9
Tel Maryport (0900) 814062. Said to be the largest and longest carnival in the North of England, with a week-long series of events, music and competitions. Procession through the streets of the town on the final Saturday. Details from local TICs. *Held annually during the second week of July.*
The Skelton Show   K10
Tel Penrith (0768) 62953. This is basically an agricultural show, with a wide variety of public events, a fancy dress competition, a beauty contest to choose the 'County Princess', bands, show jumping, parades of draught horses and vehicles. Details from local TICs. *Held on the third Sat in Aug.*
Wigton Horse Sales   G6
Tel Wigton (0965) 2202. These annual horse sales were started in the 1880s and once lasted several days, although they are now compressed into one frantic 12-hour event. Said to be the largest of its kind in the country, usually involving the sale of over 700 horses. Details from local press and TICs. *Held on the last Wed in Oct.*

Leisure & entertainment

Car tours

1. South from Carlisle

Leave Carlisle on the A595 road, turning off while still in the city onto the B5299, for Dalston. This road soon leads in to some very attractive country, with the fells peeping up ahead at Welton, and so into John Peel's village of Caldbeck, where everyone will want to stop and visit his grave in the churchyard. After half-an-hour here, follow the B5299 road again, up to Parkend, and so to Uldale and John Peel's birthplace at Ruthwaite, before turning north, out of the National Park, to Ireby and Aspatria, and heading north again on the A596 to Carlisle through Wigton. *Total distance: 50m.*

2. The Eden Valley

The Eden Valley is one of the beauty spots of Cumbria, and the river itself provides an attractive route as it runs south from the Yorkshire Dales right across Cumbria from north to south, and cursing into the sea north-west of Carlisle. The valley itself is unlike any other part of Cumbria, and although most of it lies outside this particular region, there are still some pretty places in the valley close to Carlisle, which no visitor should miss.

Eden & Wetheral Viaduct

Leave Carlisle for the east, on the main A69 road for Brampton, and then turn off at Warwick Bridge for the village of Faugh, which has a very popular inn, the String of Horses. This whole area along the River Eden is a network of little places, Scotby, and Wetheral, which has a fine church, and on the far bank, Great Corby, the ancestral home of the Howards. Follow the river south to Armathwaite, before turning west to pick up the A6 road for a while to the south for Plumpton,

turning west here for Hutton-in-the-Forest and Skelton, before returning to Carlisle, on minor roads through Ivegill and Durdar, back again into the city. *Total distance: 50m.*

3. Maryport to Carlisle

This is a pleasant, undemanding coastal tour which begins in the town of Maryport by the harbour, and if it is open, with a visit to the Maritime Museum. Leave Maryport for the north on the A596 road, turning off left after half a mile onto the B5300, which is signposted to Allonby, past the nine-hole golf course on the shore, and into the great curving sweep of Allonby Bay. Allonby is just a little place, so press on through Salta, and if the tide is low, on the road past the great expanse of beach, sand and shingle at Beckfoot, and so into Silloth which is a fairly large and pleasant resort. Bright and breezy, Silloth is a good stopping place for coffee or tea, and for enjoying a leisurely walk along the promenade.

A minor road leads up to Skinburness, where the reaches of Morecambe Bay force the road back, so join the B5302 road and follow it to the south-east into Abbey Town. Only the parish church remains of the once mighty Holm Cultram Abbey, but it stands just beside the road and is worth visiting. From here go north to Angerton on the B5307 before cutting across Bowness Common to Bowness-on-Solway. It is also possible to follow the coast road here, but this lies just outside the shore and is cut by high tides, so be sure it is passable before you set out. Bowness-on-Solway has a very pleasant pub, The King's Arms, and marks the western end of Hadrian's Wall, although the Roman remains are hardly noticeable. From here go east along the shore of the Solway Firth, with views north to Galloway, through Port Carlisle, Drumburgh and so to Burgh-by-Sands, where you can leave the car for a short walk to the Edward I memorial stone overlooking the river, where the warlike King died in 1306. Go north from here to Rockcliffe, and then follow the River Eden south into the busy city of Carlisle. *Total distance: 46m.*

Cinemas

Carlisle   K4

Lonsdale Cinema
Warwick Rd. Tel Carlisle (0228) 25586.
Studios 1 & 2
Botchergate. Tel Carlisle (0228) 21144.

Coach tours

Carlisle   **K4**

Blair & Palmer
East Tower St Coach Station, Drover's La.
Tel Carlisle (0228) 22470. Organises an
eight-lake tour of the Lake District taking
in Bassenthwaite, Derwent Water,
Thirlmere, Grasmere, Rydal Water,
Windermere, Brothers Water and
Ullswater. *On May Day Nat hol Mon only.*

Cycle hire

Crosby   **B9**

Bikeline (Carlisle) Ltd
Unit 2, Holme End Farm

Wigton   **G6**

Wigton Cycle & Sports Shop
23 West St. Tel Wigton (09654) 42824.

Discos

Carlisle   **K4**

Topper's Nightspot
Swallow Hill Top Hotel, London Rd.
Tel Carlisle (0228) 29255. A disco with
cocktails and food available. *Every Tue
21.30–02.00. Also Thur during Dec.* **££.**

Fishing

Fishing is available in many parts of the
area and along the coast, but licences and
good advice on local waters can be
obtained from the following places.

Aspatria   **D8**

The Colour Shop
Outgoing Rd. Tel Aspatria (0965) 20514.

Carlisle   **K4**

Carlisle Angling Centre
105 Lowther St. Tel Carlisle (0228) 24035.
McHardys
South Henry St. Tel Carlisle (0228) 23988.
North-West Water Authority
Cumberland River Unit, Chertsey Hill,
256 London Rd. Tel Carlisle (0228)
25151.
R. Raine & Co
21 Warwick Rd. Tel Carlisle (0228) 23009.
Geoff Wilson
Gunsmith & Fishing Tackle, 36 Portland
Pl. Tel Carlisle (0228) 31542.

Maryport   **A9**

R. Thompson
127/129 Crosby St. Tel Maryport (090081)
2310.

Plumbland   **D9**

D. Hodgson
Inglenook, Plumbland. 2m S of Aspatria.
Tel Aspatria (0965) 20672.

Silloth   **C5**

Stanwix Park Holiday Centre
Tel Silloth (0965) 31671.

Thurstonfield   **H4**

The Lough Trout Fishery
Tel Burgh-by-Sands (022876) 552.

Wetheral   **L5**

The Killoran Hotel
The Green. Tel Carlisle (0228) 60200.

Wigton   **G6**

Saundersons Ltd
11/13 King St. Tel Wigton (09654) 2611.

Flying

Kirkbride   **F4**

Border Aviation Ltd
Microlight Flying Centre, Kirkbride
Airfield. Tel (day) Kirkbride (09655)
51620, (eve) Carlisle (0228) 25820. Trial
lessons and training in flying microlight
aircraft up to PP1 (Group D) microlight
standard. **Charge.**

Golf

Aglionby   **L4**

Carlisle Golf Club
2m E of Carlisle. Tel Scotby (022872) 303.
18 holes, visitors welcome. Trolleys and
clubs for hire. Pro shop, lunches and teas
available if ordered in advance. **Charge.**

Carlisle   **K4**

Carlisle Municipal Golf Course
Stoney Holme Golf Course. Tel Carlisle
(0228) 34856. 9 holes, visitors welcome.
Trolleys and clubs for hire. Bar. Meals
available by arrangement. **Charge.**

Maryport   A9

Maryport Golf Club
Bank End. Tel Maryport (090081) 2605.
1m N of Maryport. 11 holes, visitors
accepted. Booking advisable. Bar. **Charge.**

Silloth   C5

Silloth-on-Solway Golf Club
Tel Silloth (0965) 31179 or 31796. 1m S of
Silloth. 18 holes, visitors welcome.
Trolleys and clubs for hire. Pro shop. Bar.
Meals available by arrangement with the
steward. **Charge.**

Horse racing

Carlisle Racecourse   K4
Carlisle Racecourse Co Ltd, Blackwell Ho.
Tel Carlisle (0228) 22504 (the manager).
This race course, to the south of the city,
holds regular flat and National Hunt
events throughout the year. Details from
local TICs.

Riding & pony trekking

Allonby   B8

Allonby Riding School
The Hill. Tel Allonby (090084) 273.
Instruction, trekking and hacking. Age 6
plus. No experience required. Hats
provided. *Open all year.* **Charge.**

Blackford   J3

Blackdyke Farm
2m N of Carlisle. Tel Rockcliffe (022874)
633. This centre is for instruction and
hacking. Age 7 plus. No experience
required except for hacking. Hats
provided. *Open all year.* **Charge.**

Cargo   J3

Cargo Riding Centre
3m NW of Carlisle. Tel Rockcliffe
(022874) 300. Instruction, hacking and
jumping. All ages welcome, no experience
required except for hacking. Hats
provided. *Open all year.* **Charge.**

Great Orton   I5

Stonerigg Riding Centre
The Bow. Tel Burgh-by-Sands (022876)
253. Instruction and hacking. Age 6 plus.
No experience required. Hats provided.
Open all year. **Charge.**

Silloth   C5

Greena's Corral Trekking Centre
Stanwix Park Holiday Centre. Tel Silloth
(0965) 31671. Trekking and hacking.

Ages 10 plus. No experience required.
Open Easter–end Sep. **Charge.**
The Pony Trekking Centre
Solway Lido. Tel Silloth (0965) 31575.
Trekking and children's camp rides. All
ages, no experience required. Hats
provided. *Open Apr–end Sep.* **Charge.**

Wigton   G6

Wigton Riding Centre
Kirkland House Stables. Tel Wigton
(09654) 44155. Centre with all-weather
arena. Ages 8 plus, no experience
required. Hats provided. *Open all year.*
Charge.

Sports centres

Carlisle   K4

The Sands Centre
Ring Rd. Tel Carlisle (0228) 25222. This
newly built centre offers a full range of
sports, games and exercise facilities.
Restaurant and two bars. *Open
10.00–22.30 Mon–Fri; Sat & Sun
09.00–22.30.*
The Sports Centre
Strand Rd. Tel Carlisle (0228) 29218. Full
facilities, sports hall, squash court, judo
room, cafe. Facilities for disabled people.
*Open 09.00–23.00 Mon–Fri; 09.00–16.00
Sat; 10.00–17.15 Sun.*

Swimming

Carlisle   K4

Indoor Pool
James St. Tel Carlisle (0228) 22105. Three
pools, including learner pool. Turkish
bath, sauna, solarium, cafe. *Open
09.00–21.00 Mon, Wed, Fri; 09.00–19.00
Tue; 09.00–17.00 Sat & Sun.* **Charge.**

Longtown   J1

Lochinvar Centre
Tel Longtown (0228) 791488. A school
pool, open to the public when not in use
by the pupils. **Charge.**

Maryport   A9

Netherhall School
Tel Maryport (0900) 812161. A school
pool, open to the public when not in use
by the pupils. **Charge.**

Wigton   G6

Wigton Baths
Town Centre. Tel Wigton (0965) 42412.
One indoor pool open to the public when
not in use by the schools. *During term time*

*open 15.30–20.00 Mon–Fri & Sat morn;
during school hols 09.00–11.30,
13.00–20.00 Mon–Fri & Sat morn.*
Charge.

Theatres

Carlisle   K4

The Sands Centre
Ring Rd. Tel Carlisle (0228) 25222. The
Sands Centre is a complete leisure
complex, offering everything from sports
to pop concerts, plays and orchestral
recitals.

Stanwix Arts Theatre
Cumbria College of Art & Design,
Brampton Rd. Tel Carlisle (0228) 25333.

West Walls Theatre
West Walls. Tel Carlisle (0228) 33233.

Walks

In this part of Cumbria, the best walks
will be found in the gentle but still
striking fells around Caldbeck and Uldale.
There are good tracks and footpaths,
offering walking which is every bit as
interesting as that found to the south, but
which is usually less testing. A compass
and the appropriate 1:25 000 OS map will
still be very useful.

1. Low Pike from Calebreck   I10
This is a more testing walk, which gives
good views from the fells to the north,
and begins in the little hamlet of
Calebreck, about two miles south of
Hesket Newmarket. A track leads out to
the west of the village, but the footpath

ignores this and veers directly south and
west to another old track, now disused,
which runs up the south of West Fell to
an old mine. Follow this track,
contouring the fell, keeping to the north
when the footpath cuts south over
Carrock Beck, and carry on to meet the
foothpath which runs between Low and
High Pike. When this path is reached, turn
north and follow it downhill to the north
to meet yet another track to yet another
mine. Turn east here and follow this track
back to Calebreck. *Approximate time: 3hrs.*

2. From Parkend   G9
Parkend is a little hamlet about two miles
west of Caldbeck on the B5299 road to
Aspatria. Park in the village and take the
track that leads south, with a wall on the
left, into open fields where it veers west,
before turning south for a mile into the
hamlet of Fellside. From Fellside,
continue south for a mile and a half into
the narrow, steep-sided valley of Dale
Beck, proceeding as far as the point by
Hay Knott where you cross the beck and
turn back, first to Fellside, then along the
minor road west for half a mile into
Branthwaite. Fork right and follow the
track north again to Clay Gap, crossing
another beck on the way and then take
the footpath which leads back east, into
Parkend. *Total distance: 6m.*

3. Uldale to Chapelhouse Reservoir G9
Uldale is an attractive village, close to John
Peel's birthplace at Ruthwaite. Take the
road that runs out to the south-west for
three hundred yards, to the first bend,
where a footpath runs off along the bottom

of Green How Fell, following the hillside, with good views into the valley of the River Ellen. After a mile and a half, this leads into the little hilltop hamlet of Longlands. Turn south through the village across the spur that runs to the north-west and once across the beck, take the path running west, down the little valley to Chapel House Farm at the north end of Chapel House reservoir. From here the path leads back to the bridge across the Ellen and down the road into Uldale. *Approximate time: 2hrs.*

Eating & drinking

Bowness-on-Solway　　　　　　　F3

King's Arms
Village Centre. Tel Kirkbridge (0965) 51426. A simple village pub but one serving good snacks and bar meals; fresh salmon in season, home-made pies. Decorated with photographs of old village scenes. Real ale. *Open all year during normal licensing hours. Bar meals Tue–Sun.* **£.**

Carlisle　　　　　　　　　　　K4

Chaplin's Wine Bar & Restaurant
26 Lowther St. Tel Carlisle (0228) 43447. An agreeable wine bar in the town centre, serving charcoal-grilled steaks from the barbecue and good salads. *Open all year LD Mon–Sat 11.30–14.30 & 18.00–22.00. Closed Sun.* **££.**

Crown & Mitre Hotel
English St. Tel Carlisle (0228) 25491. The largest hotel in town, with a fast-food coffee shop attached. Only bar meals available at lunchtime, but the elegant Eden Restaurant offers a wide choice of meals, including regional dishes and some interesting low-calorie specialities, at reasonable cost. *Restaurant open all year Mon–Sun D only 18.30–21.45.* A.Ax.Dc.V. **££.**

Cumbrian Hotel
Court Sq. Tel Carlisle (0228) 31951. Classy Victorian Hotel in the town centre with a pleasant restaurant serving roast beef, steaks and casseroles. Cocktail bar. Children's portions available. Also provides bar lunches *Mon–Sat. Open all year LD Mon–Sun 12.30–14.30 & 19.30–21.30.* A.Ax.Dc.V. **££.**

Dundas Coffee House
18 Fisher St. Tel Carlisle (0228) 37341. Close to the Bitts Park showground, this restaurant serves good salads, sandwiches and a range of semi-vegetarian dishes. No licence. *Open all year Mon–Sat 10.00–18.00.* **£.**

Hudsons
Treasury Ct, Fisher St. Tel Carlisle (0228) 47733. A simple, attractive coffee shop in a flower-draped courtyard, serving snacks, salads, teas etc. *Open all year Mon–Sat 09.30–17.00. Closed Sun & Nat hols.* **£.**

Crosby　　　　　　　　　　　L3

Crosby Lodge Hotel Restaurant
Crosby-on-Eden. Tel Crosby-on-Eden (022873) 618. A beautiful restaurant with excellent food, terrines, Stilton croquettes, grilled sole, steaks, pheasant. Good wine list. *Open all year LD Mon–Sun 12.00–13.45 & 19.15–20.45. Closed D Sun. & 24 Dec–end Jan.* A.Ax.Dc.V. **££–£££.**

Dalston　　　　　　　　　　　J6

Dalston Hall Restaurant
Tel Carlisle (0228) 710271. The area's most elegant restaurant – just the place for an evening out – in a hotel on the outskirts of the town, standing in seven acres of landscaped gardens. Wide choice of wines, French and English cuisine. *Open LD 12.00–14.30 & 19.00–21.00. Closed L Sat.* A.Ax.Dc.V. **£££.**

Faugh　　　　　　　　　　　M5

The String of Horses
Heads Nook. Tel Hayton (022870) 297/ 509/425. Appealing pub and restaurant in a much-restored 17thC inn. Lavish cold buffet at lunchtime in the bar lounge, while in the restaurant proper, there's a wide choice of dishes including various curries, excellent steaks and appetising desserts. It's all *très* 17thC – the interior features a large collection of settles, prints and cartoons. Five open fires in winter. Outdoor eating in summer. Cocktail bar, too. Limited accommodation with good amenities is also available. *Open all year LD Mon–Sun 11.00–14.00 & 19.30–22.30.* A.Ax.Dc.V. **££.**

Ireby   F9

The Sun Inn
Tel Low Ireby (09657) 346. John Keats
recommended this roadside inn, so it
must be good. A hopefully typical
Cumbrian pub with good bar food and
hot snacks. Children welcome. *Open all
year during normal licensing hours. Bar
meals Tue–Sun.* **£**.

Maryport   A9

The Golden Lion Hotel
Senhouse St. Tel Maryport (0900) 812663/
812323. The Golden Lion is the grand old
inn of Maryport, overlooking the harbour.
Fletcher Christian and William
Wordsworth have dined here. The menu
offers seafood cocktail, mackerel salad,
steak & kidney pie, hamburgers and
steaks. *Open all year LD Mon–Sun
10.00–14.30 & 19.00–21.30.* **££**.

The Old Ship Chandlers
South Quay. Tel Maryport (0900) 815270.
An attractive restaurant by the harbour,
serving salads, grills, steaks and afternoon
teas. *Open Mar-Oct LD 10.00–17.00 &
19.00–21.00. Closed L Fri & Sat.* **£**.

Parkend   G9

Parkend Restaurant
Tel Caldbeck (06998) 422. This restaurant
lies 2m outside Caldbeck on the road to
Uldale. Inside is an old-world restaurant,
a rather welcome and unexpected find in

such a remote spot. Good lunches, high
teas and excellent dinners with French
and English cooking. *Open all year LD
Tue–Sun 12.00–13.45 & 19.00–20.45.
Closed Mon.* **££**.

Silloth   C5

Queen's Hotel
Park Ter. Tel Silloth (0965) 31373. A
Victorian hotel, fully modernised inside,
with superb views over Silloth Green,
across the sea to the Scottish mountains.
The dining room offers an essentially
English menu of roasts, stews, soups,
steaks and sweet trolley, although there is
always one continental speciality of the
day. Comprehensive wine list. Children
welcome. Bar lunches all week, full lunch
on Sun. *Open all year LD Mon–Sun
12.00–14.30 & 19.00–21.00. Closed Xmas
day. A.V.* **££**.

Susanna's Pantry
14–16 Eden St. Tel Silloth (0965) 32244.
A pretty cafe-restaurant with a fine
collection of stone jars and shoe-horns,
serving home-baked scones, snacks,
lunches and teas. *Open all year Wed–Mon
09.30–17.00 or 13.30–17.00 Sun. Closed
Tue.* **£**.

Wetheral   L5

Fantails
The Green. Tel Wetheral (0228) 60239.
Good restaurant in a 17thC barn, with

plenty of beams and oak floors. Fine food, a mixture of French, English and local cooking, pleasantly served. *Open LD Mon–Sat 12.00–14.00 & 18.00–21.30, Sun 12.00–14.00 & 19.00–21.30. Closed Feb.* A.Ax.Dc.V. **££.**

Whelpo G9

Swaledale Watch Tearoom
Whelpo, Caldbeck, Wigtown.
Tel Caldbeck (06998) 404. ¾m W of Caldbeck on B5299. This famous teashop lies on the Uldale road between Caldbeck and Parkend, and serves local home-made specialities like cider cake, scones and fruit pies. Teas only. *Open May–end Sep Mon–Sun 14.30–18.00.* **£.**

Camping & caravanning

Camping and caravan sites become scarcer outside the Lake District National Park, so it will pay to book ahead by telephone and letter. The largest concentration of camping sites is on the coast at Silloth.

Allonby C8

Manor House Caravan Park
Edderside Rd. Allonby, Maryport, Cumbria. Tel Allonby (090084) 238/236.
A large touring site just to the north of Allonby village, with children's swings, showers, a shop, a golf course nearby, and hook-up points for touring caravans. Space for 50 touring caravans and 10 tent pitches. *Open Mar–Oct.* **££.**

Beckfoot C6

Abbey Holme Caravan Site
Beckfoot, Silloth. Tel Silloth (0965) 31653. 3m S of Silloth. A small tourist site, close

to the beach, with a shop, washing and ironing facilities and power points. Space for 20 caravans and 5 tents. *Open Apr–Oct.* **£.**

Blitterlees C5

Moordale Caravan Park
Blitterlees, Silloth, Cumbria. Tel Silloth (0965) 313754. 1m S of Silloth. A very small site but one with good facilities – a shop, swings, electricity and showers – all for a maximum of 12 touring caravans. No tents. *Open Mar–Oct.* **£.**

Blackford J3

Dandy Dimont Caravan & Camping Site
Blackford, Carlisle, Cumbria. Tel Rockcliffe (022874) 611. 4m N of Carlisle. A touring site with showers, electricity and drying rooms available. Space for 27 touring vans and 20 tents. *Open Mar–Oct.* **£.**

Carlisle K4

Dalston Hall Caravan Park
Dalston Rd. Carlisle, Cumbria. Tel Carlisle (0228) 25014/710165. A well-equipped site on the southern outskirts of the city with a shop, swings and sandpit, showers and all modern facilities. Touring campers only, with 60 tent or caravan pitches available. *Open Apr-Oct.* **££.**

Longtown J1

Rangiora Caravan Park
Sandysikes, Longtown, Carlisle, Cumbria. Tel Carlisle (0228) 791248. A small site with adequate facilities including a children's play area. Open to tourists only, with 20 caravan and 5 tent pitches. *Open Apr–Oct.* **£.**

Mealgate   F8

The Larches Caravan Park
Mealsgate, Carlisle, Cumbria CA5 1LQ.
Tel (09657) 379. A country caravan and
tent park, with good facilities, hot
showers, heated open-air pool and
facilities for the disabled. 73 pitches. *Open
Mar–Oct.* **££.**

Newby Cross   J5

Orton Grange Caravan Park
Wigton Rd, Carlisle, Cumbria CA5 6LA.
Tel Carlisle (0228) 710252. 4m SW of
Carlisle. A small attractive site with good
facilities, on the road to Thursby.
Facilities include licensed bar, heated
outdoor pool, children's playground.
Pitches available for up to 30 caravans and
20 tents. Bus service to Carlisle. *Open all
year.* **££.**

Silloth   C5

Hylton Park Holiday Centre
Central Silloth, Silloth, Cumbria. Tel
Silloth (0965) 31707. A large caravan and
camping site in the town centre, with full
facilities, and good shopping in the resort;
95 pitches available for tents or caravans.
Open Apr–Oct. **££.**

Solway Lido Holiday Centre
Silloth, Cumbria. Tel Silloth (0965) 31236.
This is a vast site, and actually a holiday
camp, with bars, restaurants, music and
dancing, pubs, a golf course, riding – the
lot. It does get very crowded in peak
months so booking is essential. 600
touring pitches for tents or caravans, plus
100 static caravans and chalets for hire.
Open Mar–Oct. **£££.**

Stanwix Park Holiday Centre
Rose Award Pk, West Silloth, Cumbria.
Tel Silloth (0965) 31671. A very well-
appointed site, with the highest standard
of facilities and everything available from
sandpits to restaurants, bars, electricity,

showers and shops. 57 touring caravan
pitches, 50 tent pitches, plus static
caravans and chalets. *Open Apr–Oct.* **£££.**

Wigton   G6

Clea Hall Holiday Park
Westward, Wigton, Cumbria. Tel Wigton
(0965) 42880. Fairly large country site,
with a pool, bar, shop and good facilities
for children. *Open Mar–Nov.* **££.**

Youth hostels

This northern area of the fells and the
country running up to the Border is more
blessed with bed and breakfast
accommodation than youth hostels, so
booking ahead is essential.

Carlisle   K4

Carlisle Youth Hostel
Etterby House, Etterby, Carlisle, Cumbria
CA3 9QS. Tel Carlisle (0228) 23934. This
standard grade hostel lies on the banks of
the River Eden, half a mile from Carlisle
City Centre. Small store, shops nearby. 73
beds. Evening meal by arrangement at
*19.00. Closed 6 weeks before or after Xmas
(alternates each year). Also closed Mons in
some months.*

High Row   I10

Carrock Fell Youth Hostel
High Row Cottage, Haltcliffe, Hesket
Newmarket, Wigton, Cumbria. Tel
Caldbeck (06998) 325. 1¼m NW of
Hutton Roof. A small standard grade
hostel lying north-east of Canock Fell,
above the Canock Beck. There is a small
store at the hostel but the nearest shops lie
at Hesket Newmarket which, in spite of
the address, is nearly three miles away. 16
beds. Evening meal *19.00. Closed
beginning Nov–end Feb.*

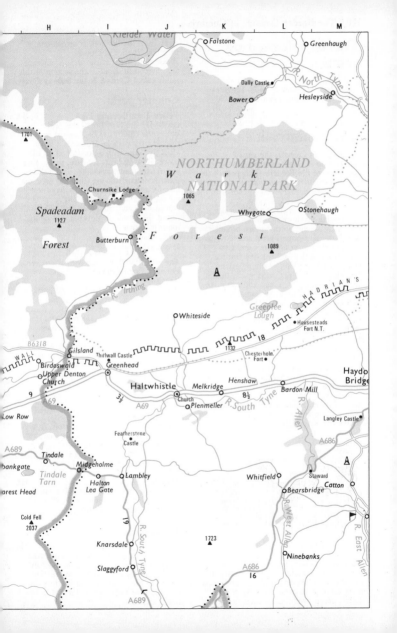

Tourist information centres

Brampton
Moot Hall. Tel (06977) 3433. Provides accommodation list. *Open 1st May–30 Sep.*

The Countryside

North-east of Carlisle, the varied countryside of Cumbria gives way to the open hills of the Borders. This part of the county actually lies somewhat to the north of Scotland's border, flanked as it is to the west by the hills of Galloway.
The countryside is rolling, with many areas being given over to forestry, especially on the north-eastern boundary where the Kershope Forest and Spadeadam Forest are the Cumbrian extensions of the well-wooded Border Forest Park and the Northumberland National Park. Woodlands apart, this is farming country for sheep and cattle, an area of small villages and hamlets. There is only one town of any size, Brampton, and the chief feature of the landscape is man-made rather than natural; the Roman Wall of Emperor Hadrian, rightly said to be the most impressive Roman monument north of the Alps. It runs along the northern edge of the hills, cresting every escarpment, and is most noticeable and best seen, (at least in Cumbria), from the minor road east of Brampton, by Lanercost Priory, running alongside the road between Banks and Birdoswald, where there are the ruins of a Roman fort above the River Irthing.

Lanercost Priory

This section owes rather more to the surrounding counties than the central pull of Cumbrian lakeland. But that said, it has attractions of its own, not least in vast views, green, well-tended countryside and,

away from the few tourist attractions, a merciful absence of crowds.
Please note that Carlisle and its environs are covered in detail in the section of this guide called **Carlisle & the Solway Coast.**

Country parks

Talkin Tarn Country Park   **F8**
On B6413 2m S of Brampton. Tel Brampton (06977) 3129. Created in 1972, this country park incorporates a large, attractive lake with a good hotel on the shore. Rowing boats for hire, picnic sites and refreshments available. The Talkin Tarn Amateur Rowing Club has used the lake for over 125 years and today there are facilities for dinghy sailing, windsurfing and fishing as well. The walk round the shore is enjoyable. **No charge** for admission.

Forests

The area is well wooded with a number of Forestry Commission plantations.
Kershope Forest   **F2**
This occupies a large area in the northern tip of Cumbria, jutting up into the Borders, west of Bewcastle Fells. The forest is cut by the B6138 road and there are a number of footpaths and rides.
Spadeadam Forest   **H4**
Much of Spadeadam, which lies north-east of Brampton, is a military training area, not open to the public. Beware of wandering across this area when red firing range flags are flying.

Tarns

Talkin Tarn   **F8**
Off the B6413 2m S of Brampton. A large, attractive lake which is now part of a country park. Talkin Tarn was once believed to be bottomless, but the actual maximum depth is around 12 metres (40ft).
Tindale Tarn   **H8**
This lies to the north of the Tindale Fells, and can be reached by a minor road off the A689 road at Hallbankgate.

Viewpoints

Turrets   **H6**
½m W of Gilsland. The best-preserved and easiest seen sections of the Roman Wall lie to the east, in Northumberland, but from the minor road at Turrets the Cumbrian sections can be viewed to the north and east.

Birdoswald H6
6m NE of Brampton. A hamlet
magnificently sited above the River
Irthing, at the end of a long stretch of the
Roman Wall and well worth a visit.

Towns & villages

Banks G7
4m E of Brampton. At Banks the first
sections of the Roman Wall come into
view, and run east from here to
Birdoswald. There is also the remains of
a Roman fort or mile-castle.

Bewcastle G4
10m N of Brampton. Bewcastle is a small
village set under Bewcastle Fell, between
the forests of Kershope and Spadeadam,
and is built on the site of a Roman fort.
The chief attraction here is a well-
preserved 7thC cross in the graveyard of
St Cuthbert's. The church is Norman, but
was restored by the Victorians.

Brampton F8
9m E of Carlisle. *Pop 4000. EC Thur. MD
Wed*. Brampton is on the A69 road, a small
but busy market town, full of interesting
buildings. The Market Place contains the
early 19thC Georgian Moot House, and
other Georgian buildings run from here
down the main street to St Martin's
Church. Brampton has plenty of cafes and
restaurants, a number of hotels, and is a
favourite touring centre for exploring the
Border, and the western sections of
Hadrian's Wall.

Castle Carrock F9
5m S of Brampton. Castle Carrock is
another hamlet, at the foot of the fells that
run on here from the distant Pennines. It
lies close to good walking country along
the River Gelt, and has a large reservoir
just to the south.

Gilsland H6
8m E of Brampton. A small village on the
River Irthing, surrounded by relics of
Imperial Rome, in the Wall and the
remains of mile-castles.

Greenhead I7
1m S of Gilsland. A small village on the
A69, tucked in the valley, with a station,
a youth hostel, and some Roman ruins,
including a bridge.

Irthington E8
2m NW of Brampton. Set close to Carlisle
airport, this red-stone village dates back
to the 12thC, and still preserves a motte,
or hill, which once carried a small castle.
The church dates from the 19thC,
although the interior contains Norman

features from a previous building.

Upper Denton H7
1m W of Gilsland. A hamlet near the Wall,
Upper Denton is chiefly noted for the
church, built of stone filched from the
Wall and rebuilt in 1881.

Talkin Village F9
3m S of Brampton. Talkin lies to the
south of Talkin Tarn, at the foot of Talkin
Fell. A small but picturesque little place,
with a good pub, the Blacksmith's Arms.

Places of interest

Bewcastle G4

Bewcastle Castle
This castle was built by Edward I about
1300, but is now completely in ruins with
only one remaining wall.

Bewcastle Cross
St Cuthbert's Graveyard. Although the
head is missing, this 7thC cross is of great
interest as it is richly carved and one of
only two 7thC crosses remaining in the
United Kingdom.

7thC Bewcastle Cross

Birdoswald H6

Birdoswald Fort
Gilsland, Carlisle. Tel Gilsland (06972)
260. These remains of a Roman cavalry
fort are magnificently sited on a plateau
overlooking the twisting gorge of the
River Irthing. It was built to guard the
Roman bridge carrying Hadrian's Wall
over the river at Willowford. The fort is
located on a particularly well-preserved
section of the Wall and while the internal
buildings have not been excavated, a
bronze arm-purse was found here in 1948.
It contained 28 Roman coins (now in

Carlisle Museum) which date the fort to the time of the Emperor Hadrian. *Open Mon–Sun 10.00–17.00.* **Charge.**

Brampton   **F8**

High Cross Street
This is one of the oldest streets in the town, with many fine buildings. Bonnie Prince Charlie lodged here during the siege of Carlisle in 1745.
St Martin's Church
This church was built to the design of Philip Webb between 1874 and 1878, and contains stained glass by William Morris and Burne-Jones.
Moot Hall
Town Sq. The present octagonal building with a clock tower dates only from 1817, but stands on the site of the medieval Moot Hall, surrounded by Georgian buildings. The town stocks stand outside, and the building contains the local tourist information centre.
Brampton Old Church
1m SW of town. A little chapel, now disused, with a vast graveyard on a hill outside the village.

Hadrian's Wall   **G6**
Hadrian's Wall, or the Roman Wall, was built to mark the northern boundary of the Roman Empire in Britain and as a bulwark against the Picts. It was built between AD122 and AD128, following a visit to Britain by the Emperor Hadrian, and runs from Wall near Newcastle to Bowness on Solway, a total distance of 73 miles. Originally, the defenses consisted of a ditch, the wall itself, and various forts or mile-castles as well as marching camps a little to the south where reinforcements were garrisoned in case of incursions from the north. The wall was originally 40ft thick and 15ft high. It was over-run frequently during the remaining years of the Empire and abandoned in the late 4thC, when the legions were withdrawn from Britain.
However, the Wall continued to mark the frontier with Scotland and served as a defensive work in this much-disputed area, although the stones were gradually whittled away to provide dressed material for other buildings. The present excellent state of preservation owes much to the work of antiquarians in the 19th and 20thC.
Much of the Wall lies to the east, in Northumberland, but visitors to Cumbria can still see long sections of it between Banks and Birdoswald, north-east of

Brampton, and the remains of Roman forts, roads and camps at Gilsland and along the heights above the River Irthing.

Hadrian's Wall

Lanercost   **F7**

Lanercost Priory
2m NE of Brampton. Tel Brampton (06977) 3030. This was built about 1166 with stones from the Roman Wall to the order of Robert de Vaux for the Augustinian friars. A good deal of the priory remains, and the nave still serves the parish and holds services every Sunday. Parking available. *Open Apr–Sep Mon–Sat 09.30–18.30, Sun 14.00–16.00.* **Charge.**

Naworth Castle   **G7**
2m NE of Brampton. Naworth Castle is a splendid pile, a stronghold of the Dacres, which then became the seat of the Earls of Carlisle. It is now a country house, built around the old pele tower and not normally open to visitors, but it can be easily seen from the minor road off the A69 near Lanercost Priory.

Leisure & entertainment

It cannot truthfully be claimed that this tiny north-eastern corner of Cumbria has a great deal to offer by way of entertainment. For any kind of nightlife, people slip into Carlisle, or even travel east to Newcastle-on-Tyne, which is no great distance away on the A69. Even the main Roman sites lie beyond the Cumbrian boundary, so the main leisure activities available are touring about on foot, car or bicycle.

Car tours

1. A car tour from Brampton.
Leave Brampton on the A69 and then fork
left, north to Lanercost Bridge on the
River Irthing, crossing the river for a visit
to the Priory and then continuing up to
Banks. Turn east here for the road follows
the line of the Roman Wall, which pops
up on either hand for three miles or so to
Birdoswald. Birdoswald has Roman
remains on every side, and good views
down into Irthing Gorge. Turn north
here, onto the B6318 and follow this north-
west, over the rolling country along the
Mill beck to the minor road signposted to
Bewcastle on the right. Turn north here,
and follow this road to Bewcastle, for a
look at the famous cross, before turning
west to the B6318 again, and then south
back to Brampton. This route runs across
some very deserted countryside, but the
views are excellent, and the countryside
very beautiful. *Total distance: 40m.*

Fishing

There is good fishing hereabouts in the
rivers and tarns, notably in Talkin Tarn.
Licences and information can be obtained
either from TICs or from the following
outlets.

Brampton   F8
G. Graham
7 Moat Side. Tel Brampton (06977) 2386.
B. Warwick (Sporting Goods)
Market Pl. Tel Brampton (06977) 2361.

Gilsland   H6
Mrs Robson
7 Rose Hill. Tel Gilsland (06972) 337.

Golf

Brampton   F8
Brampton Golf Club
Talkin Tarn. Tel Brampton (06977) 2000.
18-hole course close to the Tarn. Trolleys

and clubs available, pro-shop, bar and
restaurant. Meals by arrangement with
stewardess. **Charge.**

Riding & pony trekking

Walton   F7
Thorney Moor Stables
Tel Brampton (06977) 3019. Instruction,
trekking and hacking. No experience
required, all ages catered for, hats
provided. *Open all year.* **Charge.**

Swimming

Brampton   F8
William Howard School
Tel Brampton (06977) 2212. An outdoor
pool. *Open to the public Sat & Sun and
during school holidays.* **Charge.**

Walks

1. Circular walk to Low Row taking in the Pennine Way
The Pennine Way, Britain's longest
footpath, slices through this corner of
Cumbria, and can be sampled for a short
distance from Gap Shield Farm on the
A69, south of Gilsland, on a fairly long
circular walk from Gap Shield to Low
Row, which lies four miles further to the
west.
Leave Gap Shield Farm on a track heading
due south which leads to a footpath which
runs up an undulating slope to the trig
point on Wain Rigg, at 950ft (289
metres). The path is boggy but quite
distinct and leads down to a minor
metalled road near Batey Shield. Turn left
here, to the east and follow this road for
a mile to where a track junction juts right
and leads to a footpath heading west
below Denton Fell Woods, and cuts along
the south edge of Stoop Rigg after a mile
and a half. Where this path forms a farm
track, another footpath heads north
towards the wood. Follow this through the
wood, across a minor road, and up to the
A69 by Denton House. The starting point
at Gap Shield lies to the east. *Total
distance: approximately 12m.*

Eating & drinking

Brampton   F8
Farlam Hall Restaurant
2½m SE of Brampton on A689 (*not in
Farlam village*). Tel Hallbankgate (06976)

234. Literally in the middle of nowhere, a large mainly Victorian house, which conveniently offers accommodation for prospective diners. In the restaurant, a four-course fixed price menu, usually with a choice of three dishes every night – from seafood, to roasts and game. Small, but diverse wine list with a good selection of half bottles. Recommended purely English cheeseboard. *Open Mar–Oct D Mon–Sun at 20.00, L Sun only; last two weeks Nov–end Jan open D Wed–Sun & L Sun. Closed first two weeks Nov, Xmas week & all Feb.* A.Ax.V. **£££**.

Howard Arms Hotel
Front St. Tel Brampton (06977) 2357. This hotel in the main street of the town provides both bar snacks and restaurant meals. Five-course table d'hôte menu and an à la carte menu which specialises in steak dishes (10–12 different ones) and game. Children's portions available. *Open LD Mon–Sun.* A.Ax.V.**££**.

Joan's Pantry
23–25 Market Pl. Tel Brampton (06977) 3481. A small, friendly restaurant-cum-bar, popular with the walking and cycling community, serving such staples as gammon steak with pineapple, beefsteak pie, chicken and chips, grills and soups. *Open Mon–Sun 07.30–21.00. Closed Boxing day & 2 Jan.* **£**.

Lanercost   **F7**

New Bridge Hotel
Tel Brampton (06977) 2224. A small, cosy hotel offering good bar snacks at lunchtime. In the evening, a splendid restaurant serves such specialities as guinea fowl in Calvados and boeuf chasseur. Excellent cheeses and sweets, and a comprehensive wine list. Log fires when the weather is chilly complete the scene, and don't miss the display of model cars by the door. *Open all year LD Mon–Sun.* **££**.

Talkin Village   **F9**

The Blacksmith's Arms
Talkin Village. Tel Brampton (06977) 3452. Pleasant pub with beer garden and restaurant. Good range of pub grub from sandwiches, soups and pies to grills. The grill menu is offered both at the bar and in the restaurant proper. *Open all year LD Mon–Sun during normal licensing hours.* **£**.

Talkin Tarn   **F8**

Tarn End Hotel
Tel Brampton (06977) 2340. Seafood is the great speciality here – oysters, salmon, sea trout and scampi provençale. At the bar, also such regulars as chicken curry and

steak and kidney pie. In addition to the fish, the Lakeside restaurant offers an extensive selection of dishes on both the à la carte and table d'hôte menus. Cooking to a high standard and a renowned sweet trolley. Afternoon tea is also available with scones and home-made cakes. *Open LD Mon–Sun. Tea 15.00–17.00. Closed Oct & Xmas day.* A.Ax.Dc. **£££**.

Camping & caravanning

Brampton   **F8**

Irthing Vale Caravan Park
Old Church La, Brampton, Cumbria. Tel Brampton (06977) 3600. A site for touring caravans only, with no tent pitches, and moderate facilities; hot water, showers, a shop, laundry room. *Open Mar–Oct.* **£**.

Youth hostels

Opening times may vary from year to year, so it is always advisable to check in advance of arrival.

Greenhead   **I7**

Greenhead Youth Hostel
Greenhead, Carlisle, Cumbria CA6 7HG. Tel Gilsland (06972) 401. A standard grade hostel on the Pennine Way, set in what was a Methodist chapel. 40 beds. Shop and PO nearby. Small store in hostel. Evening meal available 19.00. *Open Fri & Sat only Nov–Feb. Closed Tue Mar–May, Sep & Oct; closed Wed Mar & Oct.*

EASTERN LAKELAND & WESTERN PENNINES

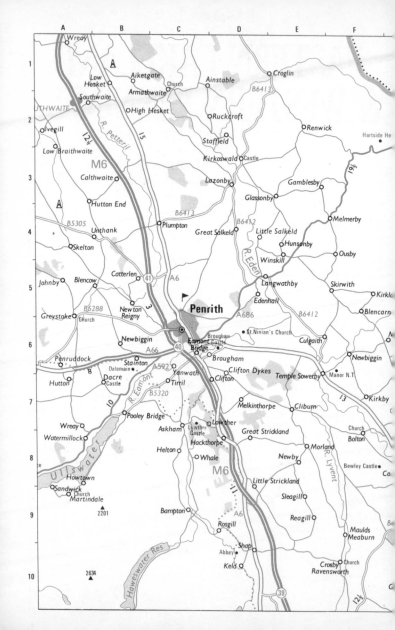

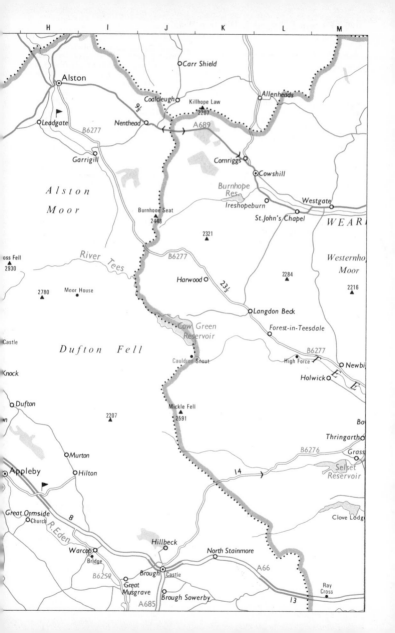

Tourist information centres

Alston H1
The Railway Station. Tel (0498) 81696.
Operates local bed-booking service. *Open all year.*

Appleby-in-Westmorland G8
The Moot Hall, Boroughgate. Tel (0930) 51177. Operates local bed-booking service and 'Book-a-bed-ahead' accommodation service. *Open all year.*

Brough J10
The 'One Stop' Shop, Main St. Tel (09304) 260. Operates local bed-booking service and 'Book-a-bed-ahead' accommodation service. Access for disabled. *Open all year.*

Penrith C6
Robinson's School, Middlegate. Tel (0768) 67466. Operates local bed-booking service. Access for disabled. *Open Easter–Oct.*

Pooley Bridge B7
Eusemere Car Park. Tel (08536) 530. Operates local bed-booking service. *Open Easter–Oct.*

The Countryside

This central part of Cumbria runs from the northern tip of Ullswater in the east, to the steep western slopes of the Pennines, leaping across the beautiful Eden Valley on the way. No other part of Cumbria can offer such a glorious diversity of landscape, or provide such a variety of attractions in such a small area.
In the west, south of Penrith, that central gateway to the Lakes, the countryside is typically Lakeland, rising to the fells around Shap, and provided with lakes, in

the shape of a part of Ullswater, or the vast expanse of Haweswater Reservoir.
East of Penrith lies the Eden Valley, held by many to be Cumbria's best-kept secret. The Eden rises in the north of Yorkshire, a mere trickle that grows rapidly, fed by countless becks and moorland streams, and reaches full strength by Kirkby Stephen, where it curves north and west to cross this region neatly from south to north. It is a route well worth following by car, through a host of little-known villages.
Beyond the Eden Valley, roughly east of a line between Alston, Appleby and Brough, the Pennines begin, and if this is Cumbria, it is a far cry from that Lakeland which the modern tourist knows so well. Here are great green, sweeping fells, well indented with valleys, and good walking country, spanned by the Pennine Way, Britain's oldest and longest long-distance footpath.
These western slopes of the Pennines are deserted, given over to sheep and the hooded crow. Most of the population lives astride the Eden Valley in the flatter country, now crossed by the M6 motorway and the main A6 and A66 roads, which do at least offer easy access to this varied and attractive part of Cumbria.

Nature trails

Appleby G8

Appleby Castle Nature Trail
A short one-and-a-half-mile trail which begins at the castle gateway – leaflet available on the rare breeds of farm animals on view. **Charge.**

Woodland Nature Trail
A tree-lined trail which begins along the River Eden. Leaflet available from local TIC in Moot Hall.

Pooley Bridge   B7
Guided Nature Walk
Begins from TIC by Eusmere Lodge car park. Details from TICs.

Lakes

Haweswater Reservoir   B10
Haweswater lies just to the south of Penrith and is one of the largest lakes, four miles long and half a mile wide at the broadest part. It is really a reservoir, but offers good bank fishing for char and brown trout.

Mountains, fells & valleys

Cross Fell   G5
Cross Fell, the highest spot in the Pennines, is one of a long series of fells which run along the Pennine chain and overlook the Eden Valley to the west. These include such splendid heights as High Cup Nick, Great Dun Fell, Little Dun Fell, and Murton Pike above Appleby. But, at 2930ft (893 metres) Cross Fell is the highest and most impressive, and crossed by the Pennine Way, which turns off east at this high point and makes for Alston.
Shap Fell (see map of South East Cumbria)
Lying beside the A6, just south of the village of Shap, the pass over this mountain is a notorious snow trap, blocking traffic on the main road during most winters. From the top of the fell, at 1483ft, (452 metres) there are fine views north to Penrith, west to the central fells of Lakeland and east to the Pennines.
The Eden Valley   G8–I10
The River Eden is one of the great rivers of Cumbria and can be seen at its best in this part of the country, especially in the region just to the north of Appleby, or where it winds gently around Warcop.

Viewpoints

Hartside Cross   F2
5m W of Alston. This famous viewpoint lies on the A686, and usually has a car-crammed car park where people sit and look out across the void below to the great sweep of the fells of Lakeland. The A686 drops away steeply at this point and winds away down to Penrith.

Pennine Viewpoints
The high western crest of the Pennines is full of good viewpoints, all the way north from Brough, but few if any of these, Murton Pike, High Cup Nick, Knock Fell, or Long Fell, to name but a few, are accessible without effort, and all lie far from any road. Those who are well shod, will find plenty of good views on every hand, at all high points on the Pennine Way.
Penrith Beacon   C5
Lying just a short walk to the north from the centre of Penrith, this high point set in parkland offers views to Ullswater, the Pennines and, on a clear day, to the hills of Galloway across the Solway.

Towns & villages

Alston   H1
20m E of Penrith. *Pop 2300. EC Tue.* A small, jumbled little town with steep streets and plenty of cobbles. Alston is said to be the highest market town in England. It lies at 920ft on the slopes of Cross Fell and has a busy independent air about it.

Sights worth seeing include the 18thC Quaker Meeting House in the main street, and a walk round the streets and alleys will soon reveal buildings of great character and considerable antiquity, if of no great architectural merit. A town which well deserves a visit and a good touring centre for the Pennines.
Appleby-in-Westmorland   G8
12m E of Penrith. *Pop 2100. EC Thur. MD Sat.* Appleby was once the county town of the now sadly defunct county of Westmorland, and it still retains that certain central county town air. It lies on the Settle to Carlisle railway line and is the site of a famous annual horse fair, held

on the first Wednesday in June. Chief sight in the town for the rest of the year is Appleby Castle which dates from the 11thC but was considerably restored in the 17thC by Lady Anne Clifford. It is open to the public and the grounds contain a rare breeds conservation centre, concentrating on farm animals. From the castle the high street falls away past the Moot Hall and the High Cross to St Lawrence's Church, which suffered periodic destruction during the Border Wars. This fine building contains the tombs of the Cliffords and has another monument dedicated to Lady Anne which illustrates the Clifford family tree. St Michael's Church in Bongate is less interesting, although equally old. Appleby is a pleasant little town, a good centre for touring the Eden Valley.

Askham C7
4m S of Penrith. A most attractive village with an extremely large number of listed buildings including Askham Hall, which dates from the 14thC, and the much restored 13thC church of St Peter. Most of the village houses date from the early 18thC and they are lined to great effect along the street which leads from the River Lowther.

Bampton C9
6m S of Penrith. Bampton lies within the National Park, close to Haweswater, and is best known for the Children's Sports Day held here in September, and the Shepherds' Meet which gathers near the Well Inn on the Saturday nearest 20 November.

Brough J10
8m S of Appleby. *Pop 500. EC Thur.* Little more than a large village, overtopped by the rather splendid ruins of a medieval castle – built like so many of these Eden Valley castles, to guard against the regular incursions of the Scots. It dates from the 11thC, but was burned down in the 16thC, and yet again in the 17thC. It now belongs to The Heritage Commission. The little church of St Michael nearby, is worth a brief visit.

Clifton C7
2m S of Penrith. Clifton, on the A6 road, is an undistinguished place today, but the last battle ever fought on English soil took place here in December 1745 (the Battle of Clifton Moor), when the English Army caught up with Bonnie Prince Charlie's returning Highlanders. A plaque on the Rebel Oak at the southern side of the village records the deaths of five Scots and five of the eleven English soldiers killed

in the battle, who are buried in the same grave.

Crosby Ravensworth F10
8m SE of Appleby. A small, rather neglected village, with one worthwhile sight, St Lawrence's Church, which stands surrounded by a thick belt of trees in the village centre. It has a six-pier nave dating from the mid 13thC, and various interesting side chapels. A recently excavated Roman settlement stands close by at Ewe Close.

Dacre B7
4m SW of Penrith. A beautiful village and one of the most historic spots in Lakeland. Dacre Castle began life as a pele tower defence against the Scots (as did most of the Cumbrian castles), but it was extended in the 14thC, and is still in very fine condition, with well-preserved walls and battlements.
Dalemain, an Elizabethan mansion, set in a deer park one mile to the east, is a private house but open to the public. It contains period furniture and the regimental Museum of the local Westmorland and Cumberland Yeomanry.
The final attraction of the village is Dacre Church, which is basically Norman and contains in the churchyard curious carvings of four stone bears, one set in each corner; they may have originally come from the castle. The lock on the south door of the church dates from the 17thC and bears the initials of Lady Anne Clifford, Countess of Pembroke, the church's patron.

Eamont Bridge C6
1m S of Penrith. Eamont is notable for a prehistoric henge monument.

Great Musgrave I10
2m W of Brough. A small, quiet village by the River Eden, set in lush countryside, and the centre for the annual Musgrave rushbearing held on the first Saturday in July.

Kirkoswald D3
10m N of Penrith. *EC Wed.* Kirkoswald lies by the River Eden and is therefore endowed with yet another of those castles built to bar this valley to the Scots. Kirkoswald Castle is now in ruins but retains the moat, and the church of St Oswald is very interesting, built on the site of a pagan wishing well, which still flows out by the west wall. The bell tower stands apart from the church and dates from the 18thC. Kirkoswald today is a quiet, attractive little place, with good gardens open to visitors at the Nunnery Walks.

Kirkoswald

Little Salkeld **D4**
5m NE of Penrith. There is not a lot to see in Little Salkeld, but two interesting visits locally are to the prehistoric stone circle called Long Meg and her

Daughters, and the working flour mill on the banks of the Eden.

Lowther **D7**
4m S of Penrith, by the A6 road. Lowther New Town was new in the 17thC, built by the Lowther family, the Earls of Lonsdale, to house their estate workers. The church contains many memorials to the family, and the old castle park now contains the Lowther Wildlife Park, a fascinating place, full of rare breeds.

Newton Reigny **B5**
3m NW of Penrith. This small, pleasing village by the River Petteril has a fine 18thC church, and in Catterlen Hall by the river, a fine example of a medieval manor house, complete with pele tower.

Penrith **C6**
17m S of Carlisle. *Pop 12,000. EC Wed. MD Tue.* Penrith lies a good way south of the present border, but it is for all that

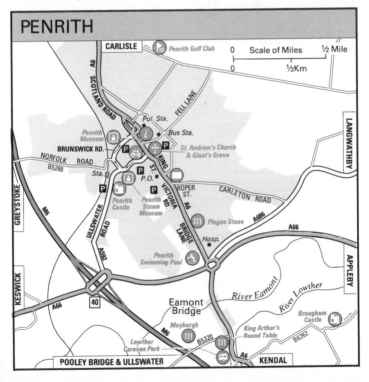

a Border town, with narrow streets, stoutly built sandstone houses and the remains of a great castle built as a defence against the Scots at the end of the 14thC, and owned for centuries by two great northern families, the Nevilles and the Cliffords. Two of the most famous residents were Warwick the Kingmaker and Richard, Duke of Gloucester, husband of Anne Neville, later Richard III.
The castle fell into ruins in the 16thC but parts of the walls and two towers remain. St Andrew's Church has a defensive central tower and dates from the 12thC, although it stands on an earlier Saxon site. The churchyard contains a so-called 'Giant's Grave', actually a group of 10thC crosses and gravestones. In the Bishop's Yard nearby stands the building which once housed Dame Birkett's school, attended by the Wordsworths.
The Market Square has several good pubs and coaching inns, as well as the 15thC Gloucester Arms, said to have been lived in by Richard III. Castlegate contains the fascinating Penrith Steam Museum, a fine collection of traction engines and rollers. The favourite walk from Penrith is the short, uphill ramble to Penrith Beacon, a little to the north of the town, which offers fine views of the surrounding countryside. Penrith today is a busy town, crammed with traffic, but well worth a short visit.

Pooley Bridge   **B7**
4m S of Penrith. Set most effectively at the northern end of Ullswater, Pooley Bridge is an attractive lakeside village, a centre for walks around the shore and the northern terminus for the Ullswater Navigation Company's lake launches. Barton Church, half a mile from Pooley Bridge, is more interesting than the village church, with a fine Norman tower.

Shap   **D10**
8m S of Penrith. *EC Thur, Sat. MD Mon.* Shap is a straggling village on the A6, under the loom of Shap Fell which lies a little to the south. It stands some 800ft (200 metres) above sea level, and is a centre for quarrying granite. Shap Abbey, by a farm in a valley just to the west, is now in ruins and dates from the 12thC.

Temple Sowerby   **E7**
7m E of Penrith. Beside the A66 on the road to Appleby, Temple Sowerby is a pleasant little village chiefly noted for the Acorn Bank gardens, set in National Trust property, and now rented to a charity for the disabled. The herb garden is fascinating, and the spring flowers glorious in late April and May.

Warcop   **I10**
3m N of Brough. Warcop is a small village with a nice green and a celebrated rushbearing ceremony held on St Peter's Day (29 June), unless this falls on a Sunday. The rushbearing is accompanied by children's village sports.

Warcop Bridge

Yanwath   **C6**
2m S of Penrith. Too small to appear on many maps, but it lies on the B5320 close to Eamont Bridge and contains in Yanwath Hall what is said to be the best example of a memorial hall in all England. The hall, dating in part from 1322, is now a private farmhouse but easily seen from the lane nearby.

Places of interest

Appleby-in-Westmorland   **G8**
Appleby Castle & Conservation Centre
Town centre. Tel Appleby (0930) 51402. A fine example of a medieval castle with extensive grounds. Norman keep and Great Hall are open to visitors and house excellent furniture, as well as the Clifford family triptych. The Conservation Centre concentrates on rare breeds of farm animals, and also contains an extensive collection of waterfowl, owls and game birds. *Open Easter week Mon–Sun 10.30–17.00; 4 May–30 Sep Mon–Sun 10.30–17.00.* **Charge.**

Askham   **C7**
Lakeland Country Base & Museum
Robin Cottage. Tel Hackthorpe (09312) 418. This Interpretive Centre, owned by the Lonsdale Estates, contains displays on Lake District life, and arranges farm visits. *Open by appointment only, and to groups.* **Charge.**

Brough J10

Brough Castle
Situated on a commanding site, much of
this once formidable 12thC castle is in
ruins and what remains is now in the care
of the English Heritage Society, which
guards ancient monuments on behalf of
the DOE. *Open 15 Mar–15 Oct Mon–Sat
09.30–18.30. Sun 14.00–16.00. 16 Oct–
14 Mar Mon–Sat 09.30–16.00, Sun
14.00–16.00.* **Charge.**

Brougham D6

Brougham Castle
Overlooking the River Eamont, 1m E of
Penrith. This 12thC castle stands on the
site of a Roman fort, Brocavum, and was
once restored by Lady Anne Clifford. It is
now in the care of the English Heritage
Society. *Open 15 Mar–15 Oct Mon–Sat
09.30–18.30, Sun 14.00–16.00. 16 Oct–
14 Mar Mon–Sat 09.30–16.00, Sun
14.00–16.00.* **Charge.**

Dacre B7

Dacre Castle
Tel Pooley Bridge (08536) 375. An
impressive 14thC pele tower, restored in
the 17thC by the Earl of Sussex. Little
altered over the centuries and still lived
in. *Open to visitors by written appointment
only.* Apply to Dacre Castle, Penrith,
Cumbria CA11 0HL.

Dalemain House & Garden
1m E of Dacre, 2m W of Penrith. On the
A592 road. Tel Pooley Bridge (08536)
450. This historic house, with medieval,
Tudor and Georgian features, contains
the regimental museum of The
Westmorland & Cumberland Yeomanry, a
collection of furniture and agricultural
bygones. In the grounds – an adventure
playground, a picnic area, and deer. Teas
available. *Open 6 Apr–10 Oct Sun–Thur &
Nat hols 12.00–18.00.* **Charge.**

Hackthorpe D8

Lowther Adventure Park
Tel Hackthorpe (09312) 523. A family
adventure park, set in the Lowther
Estate, which offers boating, games, circus
entertainment and train rides, as well as
a children's play area. No dogs allowed.
*Open 1 Apr–31 Oct Mon–Sun
10.00–17.00.* **Charge.**

Little Salkeld D4

Watermill
Off A686 road. Tel Langwathby (076881)
523. Situated in the Eden Valley, this is
one of Britain's few remaining water-
powered flour mills still producing
traditional stone-ground flour.
Refreshments available. *Open by prior
arrangement only.* **Charge.**

Long Meg and her Daughters
½m N of Little Salkeld. A late Neolithic
stone circle dominated by Long Meg, a
block of red sandstone, set in farmland.

Penrith C6

Penrith Castle
Castlegate. What remains of this medieval
fortress, a wall and two towers, is now in
the care of the English Heritage Society.
Open all year Mon–Sun. **Free.**

Penrith Steam Museum
Castlegate Foundry. A fine display of
traction engines, farm machinery, steam
models, steam rollers, a working
blacksmith's shop and a Victorian
cottage. *Open 5 Apr–30 Sep Mon–Fri
10.00–17.00, Sun 12.00–17.00. Also open
Sats of Nat hols 12.00–17.00.* **Charge.**

Shap D10

Keld Chapel
Village centre. This pre-Reformation
chapel is now a National Trust property.
Open 'all reasonable hours'. See notice on
church door for location of key.

Keld Chapel

Shap Abbey
½m W of the village. This ruined 12thC abbey is set in a deep valley and is now surrounded by a farm. The ruins are in the care of the English Heritage Society. *Open all year Mon–Sun.* **Free.**

Staffield   **D2**
Nunnery Walks
2m NW of Kirkoswald. Tel Lazonby (076883) 537. These gardens are set beside the River Eden and viewed from walks by the river to the Croglin Gorge. Refreshments available. *Open all year Mon–Sun 09.00–18.00 or dusk.* **Charge.**

Temple Sowerby   **E6**
Acorn Bank Garden
This garden is set beside a National Trust property, now leased to the Sue Ryder Foundation, which was once a 16thC manor house. The garden contains an outstanding variety of herbs, a wild plant garden and a fine display of bulbs. The house itself is not open to the public. *Garden open 1 Mar–31 Oct Mon–Sun 10.00–17.30.* **Charge.**

Warcop   **I10**
Dykes Nook Farm Museum
Barn End, Dyke Nook. Tel Brough (09304) 207. On A66 1m outside Warcop. A fine collection of farm implements and machinery with, as a special treat, working teams of Clydesdale horses, Highland cattle and Jacob sheep. *Open Easter weekend & end May–end Sep Mon–Sun 13.00–17.00.* **Charge.**

Local events & attractions

Competitions

Lowther Horse Driving Trials   **D7**
Lowther Pk. Tel Hackthorpe (09312) 392. These trials attract carriage-driving enthusiasts from all parts of Britain and abroad. Information also available from TICs. *Early Aug.*

Craft centres

Brough   **J10**
A. J. Designs
Clifford House, Main St. Tel Brough (09304) 296. In a converted barn, a gold and silver workshop, with items for sale and illustrated lectures by arrangement.

There's also a craft shop selling quality British crafts – pottery, hand-blown glass, jewellery, individual mohair jumpers, wood-turned objects and toiletries. Coffee shop providing home-baked snacks as well. *Open end Mar–end Nov Mon–Sun 09.00–18.00; end Nov–end Mar Mon–Sat 09.00–18.00*

Clifton Dykes   **D7**
Wetheriggs Country Pottery
3m S of Penrith. Tel Penrith (0768) 62946. Workshop for both weaving and pottery, with articles for sale and commissions accepted. Traditional slipware; cushions, floor rugs and wall hangings made from natural fleeces. A small museum on pottery and a tea shop also. *Open all year Mon–Sun 10.00–17.00.* **Charge** (for museum).

Wetheriggs Country Pottery

Rushbearing

Musgrave Rushbearing   **I10**
Great Musgrave, Nr Brough. Tel Brough (09304) 260. This is one of the finest of the rushbearing ceremonies. The children's procession is led by a band and the service includes a rushbearing hymn. After the service, tea is served in the village hall and there are children's sports. *First Sat in Jul.*

Warcop Rushbearing   **I10**
Tel Brough (09304) 379. An attractive ceremony, where the children walk in procession through the village. The girls are crowned with flowers, the boys with rush crosses, which can be seen throughout the year over the inside of the church door. *Held on St Peter's day (29 Jun), except when this falls on a Sun, when the ceremony takes place on the previous Sat.*

Fairs

Appleby Horse Fair   **G8**
Tel Appleby (0930) 51177. Appleby Horse Fair dates back to a charter granted by James II in 1685, and has been held

annually ever since. Gypsies and horse-traders gather from all over the country to trade and enjoy themselves – a rare sight. *Second Tue & Wed in Jun.*

Brough Hill Fair J10
Tel Brough (09304) 260. 1½m W of Brough on A66. This annual fair is much smaller than the Appleby event but still features gypsies and their horses. *Held on 30 Sep.*

Leisure & entertainment

Car tours

In this part of Cumbria, the worthwhile car tours lie on a north-south axis, for access to the east is restricted to only two roads, the one to Alston and the one from Brough, which quickly runs out into Durham. The tours which follow can be linked into one, or make two long, full-day excursions.

1. Alston to Brough
Alston is well worth half a day of anyone's time, but then leave on the A686, which runs west over the moors up to the great view of Hartside Height. Stop here to have a cup of tea or coffee in the cafe by the car park, and enjoy the great sweep of Cumbria to the west, before descending down in wide sweeps to Melmerby. From here take the minor roads that run across the foot of the Pennine valleys through the little hamlets of Skirwith, Milburn, Knock and Dufton. This route offers great views of the Pennine tops to the east, and leads at last into Appleby-in-Westmorland.

Village of Dufton

Appleby really merits a whole day, but those on a tour can content themselves with a visit to the castle and a walk down the main street past the Moot Hall to the church. From Appleby turn out onto the main A66 road, and head south past the golf course for Brough, where the castle is worth inspection. *Total distance: 48m.*

2. The Eden Valley: Brough to Penrith
This tour can be made in either direction, but from Brough, which is only a little place, take the minor road west to Great Musgrave and Warcop, which hold two of the finest Cumbrian rushbearing ceremonies. The B6259 road links these attractive villages along the banks of the River Eden. Minor roads follow the river to Appleby, Colby and Bolton, where the wise traveller rejoins the A66 and turns north for Temple Sowerby and a visit to the National Trust herb garden at Acorn Bank. From here follow the A66 road, past the castle at Brougham, and so into Penrith. *Total distance: 35m.*

3. A circular tour to the north of Penrith
This route also follows the Eden Valley, but heads east to join it, following the A686 road to Langwathby, where a minor road leads to Little Salkeld and the prehistoric stone circle, Long Meg and her Daughters. Then press on to the north through Lazonby to Kirkoswald, where the church is worth a stop. Continue on the B6413 road towards Croglin, turning off to climb up through Renwick to Hartside Height and into Alston. Return on the A686 through Melmerby to Penrith; a delightful full-day tour through moor and valley. *Total distance: 55m.*

Cinemas

Penrith C6

Alhambra Cinema
Middle Gate. Tel Penrith (0768) 62039.

Coach tours

Coaches ply across the area from other parts of Cumbria but local companies include the following.

Appleby-in-Westmorland G8

Robinson's Coaches
The Sands. Tel Appleby (0930) 51424.

Great Strickland D8

Taylor's Coaches
Yew Tree House. Tel Hackthorpe (09312) 235.

Langwathby D5

Langwathby Minibus
Pennine Lodge, Culgaith Rd.
Tel Langwathby (076881) 615.

Penrith C6

Martindale Post Bus
Crown Sq. Tel Penrith (0768) 62212.

Cycle hire

Appleby-in-Westmorland   G8

Appleby Cycle Centre
Station Yd. Tel Appleby (0930) 51664.

Penrith   C6

Harpers Cycles
1–2 Middlegate and 48 Castlegate.
Tel Penrith (0768) 64475.

Pooley Bridge   B7

Treetops
Tel Pooley Bridge (08536) 267.

Fishing

Fishing is widely available along the River
Eden and in the Western Pennines.
Licences and information can be obtained
from TICs or the following licence
distributors.

Appleby-in-Westmorland   G8

J. Pape
Market Pl. Tel Appleby (0930) 52148.
Licences, permits, rods, tackle, fishing
tuition.
Tufton Arms Hotel
Market Sq. Tel Appleby (0930) 51593.

Brough   J10

The One Stop Shop
Tel Brough (09304) 260.

Kirkoswald   D3

West View Stores
Tel Lazonby (076883) 280.

Langwathby   D5

Post Office Stores
Tel Langwathby (076881) 342.

Lazonby   D3

Midland Hotel
Tel Lazonby (076883) 8107

Penrith   C6

John Norris Tackle
21 Victoria Rd. Tel Penrith (0768)
64211.

Pooley Bridge   B7

Lake Leisure Sport & Marine
Chestnut House. Tel Pooley Bridge
(08536) 401.
Treetops
Tel Pooley Bridge (08536) 267. Permits
and rod hire.

Golf

Alston   H1

Alston Moor Golf Club
The Hermitage. Tel Alston (0498) 81625.
9-hole course, open to visitors with
honesty box for green fees by the first tee.
Parties accepted by arrangement. Bar and
snacks available. **Charge.**

Appleby-in-Westmorland   G8

Appleby Golf Club
Brakenber Moor. Tel Appleby (0930)
51432. 18 holes. Visitors welcome and
parties by arrangement with stewardess.
Bar meals available. **Charge.**

Penrith   C6

Penrith Golf Club
Salkeld Rd. Tel Penrith (0768) 62217. 18
holes. Visitors must have a handicap and
be members of a golf club. No beginners.
Parties by prior arrangement only.
Trolley and clubs for hire. Bar, shop,
meals available. **Charge.**

Riding & pony trekking

Appleby-in-Westmorland   G8

Stoneriggs Stables
Hilton. Tel Appleby (0930) 51354.
Trekking. All ages welcome, no
experience required, hats provided. *Open
spring Nat hol–Oct.* **Charge.**

Brough   J10

Grey Horse Riding Stables
Tel Brough (09304) 651. Trekking,
hacking and instruction. All ages
welcome, no experience required, hats
provided. *Open all year.* **Charge.**

Clifton   C7

White Horse Stables
Tel Penrith (0768) 64486. 1½m S of
Penrith. Set beside the A6. Trekking and
hacking. Minimum age 8. Hats provided.
Open Easter–Oct. **Charge.**

Penrith   C6

Round Thorn Riding Centre
Beacon Edge. Tel Penrith (0768) 64811.
All ages welcome, no experience required.
Hats provided. Instruction, trekking and
hacking. *Open all year.* **Charge.**

Pooley Bridge   B7

Ellerslea Trekking Centre
Roe Head Lane. Tel Pooley Bridge (08536)
405. Trekking. Minimum age 5, no

experience required; special treks by arrangement. Some hats available. *Open Apr–Oct.* **Charge.**

Tirril   **C7**

Sockbridge Riding Centre
The Cottage, Sockbridge. Tel Penrith (0768) 63488. 1½m SW of Penrith. This centre is for trekking only. All ages welcome. Hats provided. *Open Apr–Oct.* **Charge.**

Swimming

Appleby-in-Westmorland   **G8**

Appleby War Memorial Swimming Pool
Chapel St. Tel Appleby (0930) 51212. An outdoor heated pool, with car park and picnic area. *Open mid May–mid Sep.* **Charge.**

Askham   **C7**

Askham Pool & Baths
Tel Hackthorpe (09312) 570. A heated outdoor pool with a heated learner pool, picnic area and refreshment bar. *Open Mon–Sun mid May–mid Sep.* **Charge.**

Penrith   **C6**

Penrith Swimming Pool
Southend Rd. Tel Penrith (0768) 63450. Average size 25-metre indoor pool. *During school term open to public afternoons, evenings, Sat & Sun only. During school hols open to public all week.* **Charge.**

Train trips

The Settle to Carlisle Railway Line
Cumbria has a number of short steam train rides, notably the 'Ratty', but this one, the Settle to Carlisle, is not a tourist train but a genuine service operated by British Rail, although now in grave danger of closure. It is still billed as 'England's Greatest Historic Scenic Rail Route', and much of it runs through this part of Cumbria from the Crosby Garrett viaduct to Lazonby. The full journey, from Settle, north of Skipton in Yorkshire, to Carlisle, takes the traveller across some beautiful country, and is one excursion that no visitor to Eastern Cumbria should miss. There are up to four trains a day and full details are available from TICs or any British Rail information office or railway station.

Walks

The best walking in this part of Cumbria lies either around Haweswater Reservoir and Shap, or in the Pennines close to Appleby, although there are plenty of good walks all along the Eden Valley.
1. Brough to Great Musgrave   **J10**
This is a gentle walk beside the River Eden, but one easy to follow and full of interest. Pass through the centre of Brough to see the castle ruins and church before taking the road to the south of the church and following it down towards the river.

After the road peters out, the footpath leads to the river bank, then turns to follow the flow down to the bridge, where the walker crosses over and into Great Musgrave for a look at the church. Return by taking the minor road north towards Langrigg for half a mile, then the footpath east across Lowgill Farm back to Brough. A pleasant morning's excursion. *Total distance: 5m.*

2. Dufton to High Cup Nick   **G7**
This walk was recommended by the proprietor of the Appleby Manor Hotel, and what a good suggestion it is! The route follows the Pennine Way from Dufton and the views at the top are marvellous. Besides, it is a fairly short walk and requires only a morning. By car, follow the minor road north-east out of Dufton, past the first Pennine Way sign and park.

View of High Cup Nick

Then walk up the road, which is now rising gently as the houses are left behind, and turn sharp right at Peeping Hill. Just past the turn the Pennine Way footpath begins and follows the northern edge of High Cup Gill, a great slash of a valley slicing into the Pennines. After a mile this leads onto the edge of the rocky escarpment, and up to the tip of High Cup Nick. From here, the views to another valley, Middle Tongue, or east to the wild expanses of Dufton Fell, are quite outstanding. Return by the same route and allow a full morning for the trip. *Approximate time: 3hrs.*

3. Around the Rolfland Forest   **D10**
Take the minor road west on the south side of Shap, and head for Ullsmoor and Steps Hall, which stands on the boundary of the National Park. The path runs directly ahead, south-west, and rises to the 1000ft mark to contour around the northern edge of Wet Sleddale Reservoir – a clear landmark. At the western edge of the reservoir, turn north, following the path that leads past the Great Ladstones,

through jumbled country and down to the beck opposite Truss Gap. This beck can be crossed easily a little further up, but stay on the right bank and follow this around Swindale Foot on to a farm track that leads up to Tailbert. Keep left at the track and path junction down to another main crossing, where turn left, over the open fell and down to Shap Abbey. From here a metalled road leads back to Shap village. This is a fairly long but varied walk, which can be muddy. Light boots and gaiters advisable. *Total distance: 10m. Approximate time: 4hrs.*

Eating & drinking

Alston   H1

Brownside Coach House
On A686 towards Penrith. Tel Alston (0498) 81263. This converted coach house, situated beside the main road, offers a wide range of attractive dishes. Specialities include banana and toffee flan, bacon and egg pie, quiches, home-cured trout, cheesecake, home-made icecream. Morning coffee, lunch, afternoon tea and high tea. *Open Easter-beginning Oct Wed–Mon 10.00–18.00. Closed Tue. £.*

Appleby-in-Westmorland   G8

Appleby Manor Hotel
Roman Rd. Tel Appleby (0930) 51571. The elegant Appleby Manor Hotel stands just outside the town and overlooks the castle. Delightful Victorian house, with hand-painted fireplaces, and superb views to the Lake District on clear days. The cocktail bar offers a vast range of malt

Appleby Manor Hotel

whiskies and the restaurant offers such specialities as honey roast ham with asparagus, Eden salmon, Manor House beef steak and oyster pudding, Orchard hare and the Thornby Moor fillet—fillet steak, stuffed with locally hand-made cream, goat's cheese and chives, wrapped in bacon and grilled. There's also a table d'hôte menu which changes daily and an extensive wine list. Well worth visiting for that special occasion. *Open all year D Mon–Sun. (L only if parties of four or more reserve in advance.)* A.Ax.Dc.V. **££–£££**.

The Copper Kettle
Boroughgate. Tel Appleby (0930) 51605. A clean, cheerful café in the town centre, opposite the Moot House. The walls gleam with warming pans and copper kettles. Breakfast, morning coffee, teas, scones, good sandwiches, hot and cold snacks. Set lunch available. *Open Mon–Sat 09.00–17.30, Sun 13.00–18.00. From end Oct–Easter closed Sun & Thur afternoons.* **£**.

Tufton Arms Hotel
Market Sq. Tel Appleby (0930) 51593. A welcoming coaching inn with an archway leading to a cobbled yard. There's been an inn on this site since the early 17thC, but the present building is now completely modernised. A good range of bar snacks served at every session, and in the restaurant you can choose from a full à la carte or multi-choice table d'hôte menu. Essentially English cooking – the owner's wife is well-known for her pies. Other specialities include Appleby sausages, roasts and casseroles. *Open all year LD Mon–Sun. Restaurant closed D Sun.* A.Dc.V. **££**.

White Hart Hotel

The White Hart
Boroughgate. Tel Appleby (0930) 51598. This small, owner-managed hotel stands in the main street, just below the castle. An extensive choice of bar snacks available and an excellent à la carte menu in the restaurant. Everything is home-made; fish, grills, roasts and steaks are among the specialities. Traditional roast

beef lunch from the bar on Sundays. *Open all year LD Mon–Sun.* A.V. **££**.

Askham   **C7**

The Queen's Head Inn
Tel Hackthorpe (09312) 225. A charming 17thC inn, with a model railway in the back garden. Mrs Askew's cordon bleu cuisine comes in the form of hot and cold snacks, bar lunches and steak suppers (no chips). Full meals in the dining room, which is open for dinner only and it is advisable to reserve. Local game features strongly on the main menu and there's an exceptional selection of steak dishes served from the bar. *Open all year LD Mon–Sun during normal licensing hours.* **£–£££**.

Edenhall   **D5**

Edenhall Hotel
Tel Langwathby (076881) 454. Small, pleasant country hotel offering good, English cooking. Wholesome bar lunches and traditional English roast on Sundays. One speciality is the highly recommended poached salmon from the River Eden. Fine wines also. *Open all year LD Mon–Sun.* A.Ax.Dc.V. **££**.

Haweswater Reservoir   **B10**

Haweswater Hotel
Tel Bampton (09313) 235. Situated about 4m S of Bampton, this quiet hotel is right by the great lake and has marvellous views over the fells. Ideal base for a walking holiday. Specialises in English dishes – hot-pots, casseroles, roasts, good salads and a wide variety of sweets. Lunchtime bar snacks are served in the lounge bar and include basket meals, ploughman's, soups and desserts. Restaurant open for dinner only; booking essential. *Open all year LD Mon–Sun. (In winter the restaurant is sometimes closed.)* A.Dc.V. **££**.

Melmerby   **F4**

Shepherd's Inn
Tel Langwathby (076881) 217. A very attractive, roadside pub in the centre of the village. Recently expanded to incorporate the next-door 18thC barn. Serves a notable Sunday lunch, good bar meals and Marston's real ale. Some of the specialities are: barbecued spare ribs of pork, spiced lamb with prunes and raisins, Cumberland sausage hot-pot, syllabub and home-made apple pie. It is said that the steak and kidney is well worth the journey! Semi-access for the disabled.

Open all year LD Mon–Sun during normal licensing hours. Closed Xmas day. £–££.

Village Bakery

Tel Langwathby (076881) 515. Teashop and licensed restaurant serving light meals, snacks and full à la carte lunches. The bakery only uses flour from the local watermill and all the baking is done in a wood-fired brick oven. Unpretentious, good home-cooking utilising organically grown fruit and veg and free range eggs. Pies, pasties, pizzas, soups, freshly baked cakes and biscuits, lamb kebabs, Borrowdale teabread and barbecued trout (in season) are typical fare. Especially recommended: the Cumberland rum Nicky for pudding, and the set cream tea, with its savoury selection. Also has a take-away counter. *Open Easter–Xmas Tue & Thur–Sun 08.30–17.00; open Wed Jun–Sep only. Restaurant closed Xmas-weekend before Easter & Mon all year.* £.

Penrith   C6

Bluebell Tearoom

Three Crowns Yard. Tel Penrith (0768) 66660. Situated next to a bookshop, this little cafe serves a range of teas and coffees and specialises in home-baked teabreads and cakes. Try the date and orange cake, Portree plum cake or the walnut teacake. *Open all year Mon–Sat 09.30–16.45. Closed Sun, Nat hols, Xmas & New Yr.* £.

The George Hotel

Devonshire St. Tel Penrith (0768) 62696. Bonnie Prince Charlie is numbered among those who have stayed in this traditional old inn, with its open fires and oak panelling, in the heart of Penrith. A good cold buffet with ham, chicken and a joint is available in the large lounge bar at every session Mon–Sat. The restaurant offers reliable English dishes from an à la carte menu at lunch and a table d'hôte in the evening. Children welcome. *Open all year LD Mon–Sun.* A. ££.

Glen Cottage Hotel

Town centre. Tel Penrith (0768) 62221. Three-hundred-year-old, black-and-white painted building made pretty with hanging flower baskets. Reasonable range of bar snacks served at every session and more extensive meals available in the panelled dining room. English cooking – plaice, scampi, mixed grills, fresh vegetables and a selection of tempting sweets, with some old-fashioned specialities; jam sponge and apple sponge with custard. *Open all year LD Mon–Sun. Closed Xmas day, Boxing day & New Yr's day.* A.Ax.Dc.V. £.

In Clover Restaurant

Poets Walk. Tel Penrith (0768) 67474. A wholefood restaurant and teashop in a Georgian-style pedestrian precinct. Offers dishes such as broccoli and almond crêpe, casseroles, quiches, chicken and mushroom pie and good desserts. *Open Mon, Tue, Thur–Sun 09.00–17.00. Closed Sun, Wed & Nat hols.* £.

Passepartout

51 Castlegate. Tel Penrith (0768) 65852. In the town centre, this attractive and unusual restaurant defies categorisation. A very varied menu which features such items as pickled herring, blinis and grav lax, as well as a fair share of Italian dishes – fresh pastas, fegato, various veal main courses and a wide range of sweets. All the herbs used are absolutely fresh from the restaurant's own herb garden. A further attraction is provided by the proprietor-chef, whom you can watch at his craft while you eat. A truly international wine list including Lebanese, Chilean, Bulgarian, Australian, New Zealand and Californian bottles among the more regular French, German, Italian and Austrian vintages. Even the taped music selection is interesting – ranging from Vivaldi to the Grateful Dead. *Open Jul–Aug D only Mon–Sun; Sep–31 Dec D only Mon–Sat; mid Feb–Jul D only Mon–Sat. Closed 1 Jan–mid Feb, Xmas day & Boxing day.* A.V. £££.

Pooley Bridge   B7

Crown Hotel

Village centre on A592. Tel Pooley Bridge (08536) 217. Small, friendly hotel close to the northern tip of Ullswater. Very much a typical village pub which offers bar meals ranging from fish fingers to steak and local trout. The same menu is available in the 'grillette' which is *open in the summer Mon–Sun 11.30–22.00*. In the dining room, it is also possible to partake of soups, grills and roasts but only when advance bookings are made. There's a lovely garden which stretches down to the River Eamont. *Open all year LD Mon–Sun during normal licensing hours.* £.

Shap   D10

Greyhound Hotel

Main St. Tel Shap (09316) 474. Set beside the A6 road, this old inn has welcomed travellers for over 300 years, but was extensively refurbished in 1980. The inn is reputed for its big range of bar snacks including home-made steak and kidney pie, chicken and mushroom pie, pork, ham or beef platters and salads. Set meals or special roast luncheons can be provided in the dining room to advance orders only. Children welcome. Facilities for horse-driving, trekking and pony-riding. *Open all year LD Mon–Sun during normal licensing hours.* **£.**

King's Arms Hotel
On A66 at edge of village. Tel Kirkby Thore (0930) 61211. This hotel was built in 1630 as a coaching inn and the old English tradition is maintained with a full range of English dishes served from the bar; roasts, casseroles, shepherd's pie, steak and kidney pie, grills, soups and various sweets. Traditional roast beef lunch on Sunday in the dining room. Private fishing available too. *Open all year LD Mon–Sun.* **£.**

Camping & caravanning

Wild Rose Caravan & Camping Site
Appleby-in-Westmorland, Cumbria. Tel Appleby (0930) 51077. A very attractive site in the Eden Valley, south of Appleby with 114 caravan and 80 tent pitches (touring vans only). Facilities include swimming and paddling pool, play areas, shop, TV lounge and excellent laundry. *Open all year.* **££.**

Low Moor Caravan Site
Kirkby Thore, Penrith. Tel Kirkby Thore (0930) 61231. 4m N of Appleby. This small site has 12 touring or tent pitches available. Good facilities include a shop, electric points, showers and a children's play area. *Open Apr–Oct.* **££.**

Fox Inn Caravan Park
Ousby, Penrith, Cumbria. Tel Langwathby (076881) 374. 7m N of Penrith. Situated in a small village, this is a small 9-pitch site for touring vans only; no tents. Surprisingly good facilities for such a small site with a shop, electricity, hot showers, all mod cons. *Open Apr–Oct.* **££.**

Lowther Caravan Park
Eamont Bridge, Penrith, Cumbria. Tel Penrith (0768) 63631. ½m from junction 40 on M6. A good-sized site by the river with 146 caravan pitches and 50 tent pitches. All the best, clean, modern facilities, including a shop, children's room and laundry. Over 300 static caravans as well. Fishing available. No cats. Very convenient for Lowther Wildlife Park. *Open Mar–Oct.* **££.**

Greenacres Caravan Park
Plumpton, Penrith, Cumbria. Tel Plumpton (076884) 206. Another small site with 10 van pitches and 2 tent pitches. Good facilities though – shop, showers, bar. *Open Mar–Oct.* **££.**

Hill Croft Caravan Park
Roe Head Lane, Pooley Bridge, Penrith, Cumbria. Tel Pooley Bridge (08536) 363. A small site for touring caravans only, close to Ullswater and very attractive. Shop, sailing and horse-riding available. *Open Mar–Oct.* **££.**

Parkfoot Caravan & Camp Site
Howtown Rd, Pooley Bridge, Penrith, Cumbria. Tel Pooley Bridge (08536) 309. A good-sized site mostly for tents, with 90 tent pitches and 15 van pitches. Many facilities—shop, bar, music, fishing, riding, TV room. Also excellent walks and lake tours round about. *Open Mar–Oct.* **££.**

THE SOUTH EAST OF CUMBRIA

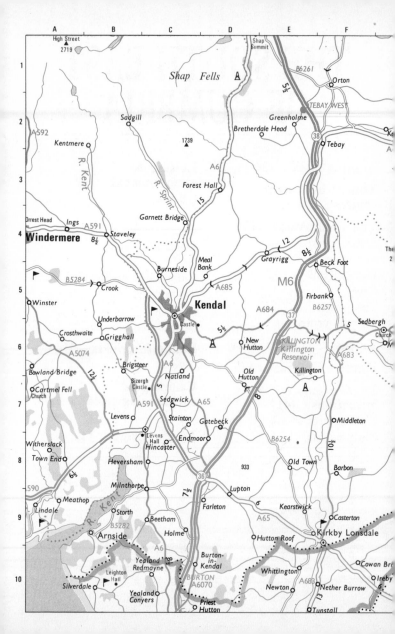

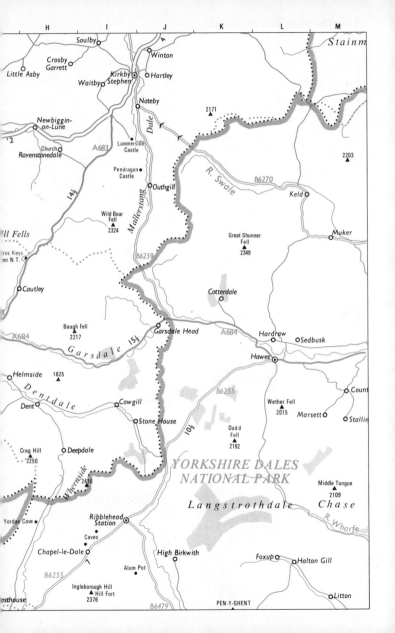

Tourist information centres

Kirkby Lonsdale **F9**
18 Main St. Tel (0468) 71603. Operates
local bed-booking service and 'Book-a-
bed-ahead' accommodation service. Access
for disabled. *Open all year.*

Kirkby Stephen **I1**
Bank House, 22 Market St. Tel (0930)
71804. Access for disabled. *Open all year.*

Sedbergh **G6**
72 Main St. Tel (0587) 20125. Operates
local bed-booking service. Access for
disabled. *Open Easter–Oct.*

The Countryside

Although this part of Cumbria lies just a
little to the east of the Lake District, and
only a few miles from such popular tourist
centres as Kendal and Grange-over-
Sands, the difference between this south-
eastern corner and the central Lakeland
area just to the west is almost startling.
Here the crowds fall away, the roads are
empty of traffic and, but for the
administrative embrace of Cumbria, the
traveller might well consider this a
separate, very different county.
Indeed, this is truly the case; for this part
of Cumbria once belonged to Lancashire,
and still considers itself Pennine, rather
than Lakeland, a point which is made
even more strongly as the traveller
wanders east and north. That said, it
remains a marvellous part of England and

makes a unique contribution to the glories
of modern Cumbria.
From the west, the countryside in this
section begins in the valley of the River
Lune, where the vast expanse of Killington
Reservoir, east of Kendal, is a notable
landmark. The River Lune, a beautiful
stream fed by such tributaries as the
Roeburn and the Wenning, finally flows
out into Morecambe Bay, south of
Lancaster, but it acts as a foreground to
some spectacular Pennine countryside,
much of it in what is now the Yorkshire
Dales National Park. These dales sweep
down from the high, bare tops of the
Pennines, and although many of them lie
outside the grasp of Cumbria, and the
scope of this book, a few beautiful
examples remain – in Garsdale and
Dentdale – a region of steep hillsides and
deep valleys, rushing brooks and the
constant tugging of the wind.
There are few roads, a scattering of
villages, very few towns of any size, but
great natural beauty and even in high
summer, a merciful absence of crowds. In
the east, the hills fall away into the valley
of the infant River Eden, which rises in
the Pennines by Wild Boar Fell, to
complete an area where the scenery is
often dramatic and never less than
beautiful.
Though small, this region is not usually
teeming with tourists, so when the crowds
become too much, consider a visit to this
corner of Cumbria, where the beautiful
high country of the smooth, rounded
Howgill Fells is sure to be empty of
people.

Lakes & tarns

Killington Reservoir   **E6**
3m W of Sedbergh. This reservoir by the
M6 motorway is a paradise for
birdwatchers in the spring.
Lily Mere   **E6**
A small lake, or mere, just to the east of
Killington Reservoir.
Wyndhammere   **E8**
Just off the B6254 road, 6m NW of Kirkby
Lonsdale. An attractive lake.

Mountains & fells

The east of this region is very
mountainous, although most of the high
tops lie outside Cumbria. But, the few
which lie inside the county are dramatic.
Baugh Fell   **H6**
(2217ft). Baugh Fell rises to the north of
Garsdale, a vast hump of a hill, the top
dotted with small tarns, the slopes
threaded with rushing gills or becks.
The Calf   **G4**
(2217ft). Situated to the north-west of
Baugh Fell, and by some coincidence the
same height, The Calf stands on the edge
of the Yorkshire Dales National Park
between Howgill Fells and Brant Fell, and
offers great views in all directions.
Crag Hill   **H8**
(2250ft). Crag Hill overlooks the deep cleft
of Dentdale, on the northern edge of
Barton High Fell, an area dotted with
small tarns, and plenty of rushing gills.
Shap Fell   **D1**
Lying beside the A6, just south of the
village of Shap, the pass over this
mountain was a notorious snow trap,
blocking traffic on the main road during
most winters. From the top of the fell, at
1483ft, (452 metres) there are fine views
north to Penrith, west to the central fells
of Lakeland and east to the Pennines.
Wild Boar Fell   **I4**
(2322ft). Wild Boar Fell is best seen when
coming from the north on the B6259 road
or railway that runs beside the River Eden.
It is a high steep-sided hill dominating the
surrounding countryside.

Dales & valleys

Although often claimed by the Yorkshire
Dales National Park, this region of
Cumbria can take the credit for some
beautiful valleys.
Dentdale   **H7**
Dentdale lies to the east of Sedbergh, a
long, winding valley traversed by the

River Dee, overlooked to the north by Aye
Gill Pike and to the south by Crag Hill
and Whernside. The road which runs
through the dale offers some of the finest
scenery in Cumbria.
Garsdale   **I6**
Runs parallel with Dentdale but to the
north, no less beautiful, and the route for
the River Clough. There is no real centre
to the dale, just a long litter of attractive
cottages and scattered hamlets. The dale
ends in the west at Sedbergh, and runs
out to the north-east at Garsdale Head.
The Lune Valley
The Lune, like the Eden, is one of those
calmer rivers in Cumbria, flowing gently
along for much of the time, with Kirkby
Lonsdale as the central point for visitors.

Along the river lie a host of picnic places,
rocky viewpoints, and deep trout-filled
pools.
Mallerstang Dale   **J3**
Unlike Dentdale and Garsdale,
Mallerstang runs north to south, along
the western edge of the Pennines. It is a
spectacular route to Garsdale Head from
Kirkby Stephen, and one well worth
following, past Pendragon Castle,
through Outhgill.

Caves

The limestone country of the Cumbrian
section of the Yorkshire Dales National
Park has over 300 caves open to exploring
potholers. Caving is not an activity to
undertake without guidance or experience,
and would-be cavers should apply for
further information to Whernside Manor
Cave & Fell Centre, Dent, Sedbergh,
Cumbria LA10 5RE. Tel Dent (05875)
213.

Viewpoints

River Lune at Kirkby Lonsdale   **F9**
One of the most famous views in this

corner of Cumbria lies on a bend of the
Lune on the northern outskirts of Kirkby
Lonsdale, reached by a footpath from the
centre and looking across the river towards
Casterton. Ruskin pronounced this view
'. . . one of the loveliest in England and
therefore in the world'. Don't miss it.

Visitors' centre

Yorkshire Dales National Park   **G6**
Information Centre
Main St, Sedbergh. Tel Sedbergh (0587)
20125. In the town centre, this
information office has helpful staff and a
fine display of the surrounding
attractions. Also books and leaflets on self-
guided walks. Can advise on
accommodation locally. *Open 1st Apr or
Easter–mid Sep Mon–Sun 10.00–17.00;
mid Sep–end Oct open six days only
10.00–17.00.* **Free.**

Towns & villages

This small inland corner of Cumbria is
sparsely inhabited, but the few places of
any size are well worth visiting.

Dent   **H7**
4m S of Sedbergh. Dent is a tiny village,
attractively situated in the centre of
Dentdale. A popular centre for cavers and
hill walkers.

Devil's Bridge

Kirkby Lonsdale   **F9**
12m S of Kendal. *Pop 1500. EC Wed. MD
Thur.* A large village on the River Lune,
most noted for the views over the river
which were praised by Ruskin and
painted by Turner. Both stayed here in
their time. The church of St Mary in the
centre is Norman, with attractive later
additions. The main street runs down to
the narrow, medieval Devil's Bridge, built
for packhorse traffic, over the sparkling
waters of the Lune.

Kirkby Stephen   **I1**
4m S of Brough. *Pop 1600. EC Thur. MD
Mon.* Kirkby Stephen is just a little place
but an excellent touring centre for the
Western Pennines or for those who wish
to travel east into the National Park. The
church of St Stephen, also known as the
'Cathedral of the Dale', dates from the
13thC, but contains a number of relics
from some earlier building. In one of the
chapels is the effigy of Lord Wharton,
who played a major role in the 16thC
Border Wars, and nearby, another of Sir
Richard Musgrove, who is said to have
killed the last wild boar in England. A
popular excursion from Kirkby Stephen is
out to the south for four miles to the ruins
of Pendragon Castle, which lie just beside
the road and are said to mark the home
of Uther Pendragon, the father of King
Arthur. The parts that remain today owe
much to Lady Anne Clifford, who restored
this old pele tower in the 1660s.

Outhgill   **J3**
4m S of Kirkby Stephen. This hamlet in
Mallerstang has a post office, the church
of St Mary's, and a chapel, but very little
else except good walks towards the
Pennines or in the surrounding fells.

Ravenstonedale   **H3**
4m SW of Kirkby Stephen. Another small
hamlet with a notable church, parts of
which date back to the 13thC. The tower
once contained a sanctuary bell, giving
freedom to anyone who could ring it. The
village claims to be one of the prettiest
and most unspoilt in Cumbria. Well worth
a visit.

Sedbergh   **G6**
9m E of Kendal. *EC Thur. MD Wed.*
Sedbergh is another little town which is
barely more than a sprawling village. It is
the capital for that tongue of Yorkshire
which pokes into Cumbria and was bitten
off in the 1974 reorganisation of county
boundaries, although it still lies within the
Yorkshire Dales National Park. The
town's main claim to fame is Sedbergh
School, which occupies many old
buildings in the town centre, St Andrew's
Church, a basically Norman building, and
the Brigflatts Quaker Meeting House, a
whitewashed house where George Fox
preached to the early Quakers.

Tebay   **F2**
12m W of Kirkby Stephen. *Pop 700.* A
small village built to serve the Settle to
Carlisle railway. The church of St James
was built by the navvies. The big local
attractions are the gorges of the River
Lune nearby.

Places of interest

Kirkby Lonsdale   F9
Church of St Mary
Town Centre. This basically Norman
church contains a number of interesting
objects, notably a stone coffin unearthed
from under the Middleton Chapel, and a
14thC carving of the Virgin.
The Devil's Bridge
River Lune. This elegant three-arched
packhorse bridge over the river dates
from the 13thC, and is very photogenic.

Kirkby Stephen   I1
St Stephen's Parish Church
Known locally as 'The Cathedral of the
Dale', St Stephen's stands on the site of
a former Saxon church and dates in part
from the early 13thC. The interior
contains many Saxon relics, including a
carving of the devil in chains, while in the
churchyard lies a flat stone used until 1836
for the collection of church rents and
tithes. Well worth a visit.

The Cloisters, Kirkby Stephen

Town Centre
Much of the town centre of Kirkby
Stephen is now listed as a Conservation
Area, and buildings worth seeing include
the so-called Cloisters, once the butter
market, the Grammar School founded in
1566, and the Parsonage buildings, which
date from 1677.

Pendragon Castle   J3
4m S of Kirkby Stephen, beside B6259
road. Pendragon Castle, which stands on
a small mound beside the road, is now in
ruins amid a clump of trees. Although
supposedly the site of the home of Uther

Pendragon, the father of King Arthur, the
present ruins are all that remain of a
medieval pele tower dating from the
12thC, and once restored by Lady Anne
Clifford about 1660. Closed to the public,
but easily seen from the road.

Ravenstonedale   H3
Parish Church
This attractive building, rebuilt in the
1740s, has a 'three-decker' pulpit and the
pews are arranged so that the congregation
face each other.

Local events & attractions

Craft centres

Dent   H7
John Cooke
The Hill Studio. Tel Dent (05875) 354. A
painter of local landscapes in a variety of
media. Exhibition *open to the public
Mon–Sat 10.00–17.30.*

Helmside   G7
Dent Craft Centre
On the road between Dent and Sedbergh,
2m NW of Dent. Tel Dent (05875) 400.
An incredibly full range of craft goods
from pottery to knitwear, silver to
miniature dolls, pottery to wood carving.
*Open Easter–Xmas Tue–Sun 10.00–18.00.
Closed Jan & Feb and Mon all year.*

Kirkby Stephen   I1
Heredities
Crossfield Mill, Kirkby Stephen. Tel
Kirkby Stephen (0930) 71543. This
foundry is now the world's largest creator
of cold-cast bronze statues. Showroom
open, visitors welcome, parties by
arrangement. *Open all year Mon–Fri
08.30–17.00.*

Little Asby   H1
Burtree Woodcrafts
Burtree House. Tel Newbiggin-on-Lune
(05873) 342. 2m W of Crosby Garrett just
off tarmac road across from Little Asby.
Pyrography centre where you can watch
items in sycamore, beech, hornbeam and
lime being worked. Commissions
accepted. The craft shop sells all manner
of locally made goods and the tearoom
(with crafts on display) offers a full range
of teas, freshly ground coffee, home-made
scones and cakes.
This is also where East of Eden Body

Preparations are produced. Eight different types of soap from vegetable oils are made on site, plus a range of cosmetics. The company blend their own talcum powder and their own pot-pourri. It is also the only firm in the UK to make old Elizabethan perfume balls. The finishing of the cosmetics can be watched in progress. There are swings to amuse the kids while the adults ponder their purchases. *Open 1 Mar–31 Dec Mon–Sun 10.00–20.00. Closed Jan & Feb.*

Sedbergh   G6

Brackensghyll Pottery
Black Lane. Tel Sedbergh (0587) 20233. This pottery produces a wide variety of work; jugs, bowls, pots for plants and commissioned articles. Showroom *open all year Mon–Wed, Fri & Sat 10.00–17.00. Closed Thur & Sun.*

Winton   J1

Langrigg Pottery
Winton. Tel Kirkby Stephen (0930) 71542. This attractive working pottery lies beside the A685 road and is set in an old hay barn. Tableware, plant pots and some decorative items. *Open Mon–Sun Easter to mid Oct and Tue–Sat mid Oct–Easter 09.00–17.00.*

Costume fair

Kirkby Lonsdale   F9

Victorian Weekend
Kirkby Lonsdale town centre. An annual event when the townsfolk dress up in Victorian costume. Morris dancing, a fair, stalls and entertainment. Details from Kirkby Lonsdale TIC (0468) 71603. *Weekend early in Sep.*

Leisure & entertainment

Car tours

In this little corner of Cumbria there are very few roads, but the region does offer one superb drive through the spectacular scenery of the Cumbrian Pennines and the western edge of the Yorkshire Dales from Kirkby Stephen to Kirkby Lonsdale.
1. Circular tour from Kirkby Stephen to Kirkby Lonsdale & back
Leave Kirkby Stephen on the B6259 road, forking right at Nateby on the road for

Outhgill. The road rises steadily, past the ruins of Pendragon Castle on the right, overhung by the steep green sides of the fells on either side. Stop at Garsdale Head for a snack at the Moorcock Inn before following the road west, under the Settle to Carlisle railway line, and down Garsdale to Sedbergh. Pause here for a stroll to stretch the legs before turning up Dentdale, another beautiful valley, for a look at the little village of Dent. From here a very minor road leads south-west over the hills and down to Kirkby Lonsdale in the Lune Valley. To complete the circuit, the traveller can run north on the A683 road, through Sedbergh again, then up to the A685 road, and so back again to Kirkby Stephen. This route offers no major centres but some very fine scenery, and the most marvellous airy views across the hills and dales. *Total distance: 60m.*

Caving

National Caving Training Centre   H7
Whernside Cave & Fell Centre, Dent, Sedbergh, Cumbria LA10 5RE. Tel Dent (05875) 213. This is the National Centre for caving and offers a wide variety of residential courses for field studies and caving. **Charge.**

Coach tours

Fellrunner Minibus Tours
The Fellrunner is a 15-seat minibus which offers guided tours around the Eden Valley and the Cumbrian Pennines. Bookings and information through the TIC in Kirkby Stephen and other main centres. **Charge.**

Fishing

Fishing is widely available on the Western Pennine streams, but it is as well to obtain information from local TICs. Licences are issued at the following outlets.

Kirkby Stephen   I1
C. J. & J. R. Mounsey
46/48 Market St. Tel Kirkby Stephen
(0930) 71203.

Sedbergh   G6
Lowis's (Sedbergh) Ltd
23/25 Main St. Tel Sedbergh (0587) 20446.

Tebay   F2
Cross Keys Inn
Tel Orton (05874) 240. Contact Mr J. S.
Marsden.

Golf

Sedbergh   G6
Sedbergh Golf Club
The Riggs, Millthrop. Tel Sedbergh
(0587) 20993. 9-hole course, visiting
parties accepted by arrangement. **Charge.**

Riding & pony trekking

Crosby Garrett   H1
Blackthorne Cottage Stables
Crosby Garrett, Kirkby Stephen.
Tel Kirkby Stephen (0930) 71917.
Instruction, trekking and hacking. Age
5 plus, riding holidays available, hats
provided. *Open all year.* **Charge.**

Town trails

Kirkby Lonsdale   F9
Kirkby Lonsdale Town Trail
This one-mile trail starts at the parish
church and takes in the Devil's Bridge,
Ruskin's View and the town centre.
Leaflet available.

Sedbergh   G6
Sedbergh Town Trail
A circular walk of less than a mile, through
the school grounds and the old 'yards'.
Leaflet available.

Walks

All this area is splendid walking country,
bearing such fine trails as the Pennine
Way and the Dales Way. These require a
certain tenacity, but there are plenty of
shorter walks which give a good feel of the
countryside.
1. Around Kirkby Stephen: J1
Hartley to Nine Standards
Leave Hartley to the east of Kirkby
Stephen and take the quarry road, past

Fell House, turn right where the metalled
road ends. From here the route is
waymarked and the footpath leads south-
east beside Faraday Gill and up to the
Nine Standards at 2172ft (662 metres).
The Standards is a row of beacons which
have stood here for centuries offering good
views over the surrounding fells. Return
on the same path to Hartley. *Total distance:
7m. Approximate time: 4hrs.*

Village of Hartley

2. Sedbergh to The Calf & back   G6
Leave Sedbergh centre on the minor road
for Howgill, turning off after 400 metres
(¼m) onto the footpath from Lockbank
Farm. This leads round the southern
slopes of the Winder and on the eastern
side, where another footpath joins in, the
path climbs steeply to Arant Haw 1988ft
(606 metres) and then heads north along
a ridge onto Brant Fell. On the top turn
sharp left at the track junction and follow
this open path up the ridge past Bram Rigg
Top 2204ft (672 metres) and finally up to
The Calf 2219ft (676 metres) from which
there are great views over the Howgill
Fells to the north. Allow at least half a day
for the return trip, and keep an eye on
the weather. Weather information can be
obtained by ringing Windermere (09662)
5151. *Total distance: 10m. Approximate
time: 4hrs.*
3. On the Howgill Fells: H4
The Temperance Inn to Adamthwaite
The Howgill Fells make great walking
country, but are best suited to serious,
well-equipped travellers rather than the
casual stroller. The following walk is,
however, within anyone's grasp.
This walk begins at the former
Temperance Inn beside the A683 road,
north of Cautley. Cross the river and turn
right, following the footpath to
Narthwaite, from where a broad track
leads up to Mountain View and so round
the contours of Wandale Hill to

Adamthwaite. A track from here leads back around the eastern side of the hill, above the Wandale beck to Handley's Bridge, Narthwaite and the Temperance Inn. A pleasant walk for any adequately shod walker. *Total distance: 5m. Approximate time: 4hrs.*

Eating & drinking

Barbon   F8
Barbon Inn
Tel Barbon (046836) 233. A very traditional 17thC coaching inn, with all the traditional trimmings – open fires and a four-poster bed in the room where Cromwell is said to have slept. Bar food available at every session. In the candlelit dining room, good soups, roasts, grills and sweets from a table d'hôte menu. *Open all year D Mon–Sun, L Sun only. A.V. ££.*

Cautley   G5
Cross Keys Temperance Hotel
4m N of Sedbergh on A683. Tel Sedbergh (0587) 20284. Ideally situated for walkers in the Howgill Fells, this old inn claims to have put the craft back into catering and offers a warm welcome to hikers. Provides morning coffee, home-made snack lunches (soups, quiches, pies, sandwiches), afternoon tea, ham and eggs for high tea, and a four-course dinner menu. Bed and breakfast, too. Although the premises are unlicensed, you can bring your own bottle. Essential to reserve for dinner in advance. *Open Tue–Sun. Closed Mon & mid Jan–mid Mar. £–£££.*

Helmside   G7
Dent Craft Centre Tearooms
2m NW of Dent on road to Sedbergh. Tel Dent (05875) 400. Small, attractive teashop with stone-flagged floor and attached to an interesting craft centre. Home-made quiches, cakes, pastries, salads, sandwiches. *Open Tue–Sun 10.00–18.00. Closed Mon & Xmas–Easter. £.*

Garsdale Head   J6
Moorcock Inn
By A684 road. Tel Hawes (09697) 488. This good walker's pub is set in some marvellous scenery and lies just 50 yards outside Cumbria by the Settle to Carlisle railway. Soups, grills, steaks and fish at the bar or in the small restaurant. *Open all year LD Mon–Sun during normal licensing hours. £.*

Kirkby Lonsdale   F9
The Copper Kettle
3–5 Market St. Tel Kirkby Lonsdale (0468) 71714. Exceptionally good value restaurant run by a husband and wife team. Olde-worlde ambience in a 1610 building. Good choice of home-cooked lunches, grills, salads and fish for high tea and an extensive à la carte menu for proper evening meals. *Open LD Wed–Mon 12.00–21.00. Tue D only. High tea 15.00–18.30. Closed one week Nov & two weeks Jan. A.V. ££.*

Mews Coffee House ·
Main St. Tel Kirkby Lonsdale (0468) 71007. Relax in a pleasant tearoom serving a wide variety of filling snacks, salads, soups, casseroles and quiches. In the summer, the proprietor specialises in home-made, original fruit pies, meringues and cakes. *Open Thur–Tue 10.00–17.00, Sun 13.00–17.00. Closed Wed, also Tue Nov–Mar, Xmas day & Boxing day. £.*

Snooty Fox Tavern
Main St. Tel Kirkby Lonsdale (0468) 71308. A listed 17thC inn, very friendly and atmospheric. You can choose from a fairly extensive menu and eat either at the bar or in the dining room. Special dishes vary from day to day, but featured regularly are duck, lamb, venison, pies and Cumberland sausage. Terrace for summer drinking and open fires for less clement weather. *Open all year LD Mon–Sun during normal licensing hours. ££.*

Whoop Hall Inn
On outskirts of town beside A65. Tel Kirkby Lonsdale (0468) 71284. An old, oak-beamed pub dating from the 1730s, made cosy with settles and open fires. Good reputation for lunchtime bar snacks – especially the home-made steak and kidney pie, cured gammon, toasties and local fish dishes. Garden, and swings for children who are always welcome. No food in the evening. *Open all year Mon–Sun during normal licensing hours. V. £.*

Kirkby Stephen   I1

King's Arms
Market St. Tel Kirkby Stephen (0930)
71378. Warm, welcome and comfortable
surroundings. Bar meals include home-
made soups, pies, salads, kedgeree and
casseroles. Separate restaurant which
offers set dinner and menu changes daily.
Also full, traditional Sunday lunch. *Open
all year LD Mon–Sun 10.30–15.00 &
18.00–22.30. Closed Xmas day.* A.V. **£–££**.

Kirkby Stephen

Tophers Restaurant
39 North Rd. Tel Kirkby Stephen (0930)
71832. Small, attractive restaurant in a
converted smithy. Specialises in local and
Scottish produce—lamb, pork fillets,
grills, and what the menu describes as 'a
bit of this and a bit of that', including
'freshly shot haggis'! Fully licensed. *Open
all year LD Mon–Sun.* A.V. **££**.

Orton   F1

Tebay Mountain Lodge
Service area N of junction 38 on M6. Tel
Orton (05874) 351. Modern hotel with
comfortable lounge bar for lunchtime
snacks. In the restaurant proper, full
meals from an à la carte menu, as well as
simpler dishes – fried chicken, fish and
chips, roasts. *Open all year D Mon–Sun.*
A.Ax.Dc.V. **££**.

Ravenstonedale   H3

The Fat Lamb Inn
2m S of Ravenstonedale on junction with
A683. Fell End. Tel Newbiggin-on-Lune
(05873) 242. Set in marvellous
countryside, this pleasant country inn
offers good, filling home-cooked food and
an unusual sight – a llama in the garden.
Bar snacks at every session include cold
platters, and the speciality, 'Cheesie
Murphy'. Magnificent views from the

restaurant which offers an à la carte menu
– Scotch poached salmon, baked ham in
Cumberland sauce and a dish of the day
called 'Pot Luck'. Children welcome. *Open
for bar snacks LD Mon–Sun. Restaurant
open L most days, D Mon–Sun. Closed Jan.*
££.

Sedbergh   G6

Oakdene Country Hotel
Garsdale Rd, 1m E of Sedbergh. Tel
Sedbergh (0587) 20280. Country hotel in
an old Victorian house which retains many
original features – marble fireplaces,
gaslight fittings and authentic Victorian
bathroom. The one-acre garden has a
pond with appealing, ornamental water
fowl. Nourishing bar snacks (home-made
soups and main course), morning coffee,
afternoon tea and high tea (ham and eggs)
are served throughout the year. An
English à la carte menu in the restaurant
– fresh produce only. *Open LD Mon–Sun.
Closed mid Jan–end Feb.* A.Ax.Dc.V. **££**.

Ye Olde Copper Kettle
43 Main St. Tel Sedbergh (0587) 20995.
Very homely, olde-worlde tearoom
serving good snacks, toasted sandwiches,
vegetarian and fish dishes, grills and
home-made cakes. Also provides full
English breakfasts. *Open all year
Wed–Mon 09.00–18.00 in summer, to 17.00
winter. Closed Tue.* **£**.

Tebay   F2

Barnaby Rudge Tavern
Main St. Tel Orton (05874) 328. Situated
½m off M6, close to junction 38.
Completely renovated in Dickensian style,
with oak beams and tapestried walls, this
pub makes an ideal stop for lunch or
dinner. A full range of meals are served
in the cellar bar; all food is cooked to
order. In the Gallery restaurant, there's
also an à la carte menu of English and
French dishes, including a mixed grill
house special. Extensive choice of wines
and ales. *Open all year LD Mon–Sun
during normal licensing hours. No food Mon
in winter.* A.V. **£–££**.

Winton   J1

Bay Horse Inn
Facing village green. Tel Kirkby Stephen
(0930) 71451. This attractive pub offers a
warm welcome in its low-ceilinged bars, with
a display of local photographs on the
walls. Bar snacks during the week include
sausages, beefburgers, rolls, and pâté,
with steaks and gammon available at

weekends. In the dining area, a
straightforward set menu is on offer every
evening. Well-behaved children are
welcome. Also has a big beer garden. *Open
all year LD Mon–Sun during normal
licensing hours.* **£.**

Camping & caravanning

Cautley   G5
Cross Hall Caravan Site
Cautley, Sedbergh, Cumbria.
Tel Sedbergh (0587) 20668. 2m N of
Sedbergh. A small site, with only 20
pitches for tents and caravans. Simple
facilities. *Open Apr–Oct.* **££.**

Kirkby Lonsdale   F9
Woodclose Caravan Park
Chapel House Lane, Casterton, Kirkby
Lonsdale, Cumbria. Tel Kirkby Lonsdale
(0468) 71403. A touring site for caravans
only on the eastern outskirts of Kirkby

Lonsdale. Facilities include hot showers,
a children's play area, and electricity.
Open Mar–Oct. **£.**

Orton   F1
Tebay Caravan Park
Orton, Tebay, Penrith. Tel Orton (05874)
482. A fairly large site for touring
caravans only, with 70 pitches, each with
light and water points. Shop and snacks
available. *Open Apr–Oct.* **££.**

Sedbergh   G6
Pinfold Caravan Park
Sedbergh, Cumbria. Tel Sedbergh (0587)
20576. A good sized, well-equipped site
on the outskirts of Sedbergh, with 60
pitches for tents and caravans. Facilities
include a shop, laundry facilities and
availability of golf and fishing nearby.
Open Mar–Oct. **££.**

Youth hostels

Opening times may vary from year to year,
so it is always advisable to check in
advance of arrival.

Cowgill   I7
Dentdale Youth Hostel
Cowgill, Dent, Sedbergh, Cumbria LA10
5RN. Tel Dent (05875) 251. 3½m E of
Dent. A standard grade hostel set beside
the River Dee, and on the route of the
Dales Way. 40 beds. Evening meal 19.00.
Store at hostel. Car parking available.
*Open Fri & Sat only Nov–Feb, also open
Xmas. Closed Sun Mar–Oct except Nat hol
Suns. Closed Mon Mar & Oct.*

Index